# *The* NATURE OF POETRY

DONALD A. STAUFFER

# The NATURE
# OF POETRY

*New York*

W · W · NORTON & COMPANY · INC·

FOR

*E. D.* AND *W. B. C. W.*

# CONTENTS

PROLOGUE
*Page 11*

CHAPTER ONE
POETRY IS EXACT
*Page 26*

CHAPTER TWO
POETRY IS INTENSE
*Page 59*

CHAPTER THREE
POETRY IS SIGNIFICANT
*Page 91*

CHAPTER FOUR
POETRY IS CONCRETE
*Page 120*

CHAPTER FIVE
POETRY IS COMPLEX
*Page 154*

CHAPTER SIX
POETRY IS RHYTHMICAL
*Page 189*

CHAPTER SEVEN
POETRY IS FORMAL
*Page 228*

NOTES      BOOK LIST      INDEX
*Page 265*     *Page 283*     *Page 289*

# ACKNOWLEDGMENTS

FOR THEIR generosity and co-operation in granting permission to quote from copyrighted materials, the author thanks the following publishers:

Clarendon Press for quotations from the poems of Robert Bridges; Harcourt, Brace and Company, for T. S. Eliot; Henry Holt and Company, for A. E. Housman and Walter de la Mare; Houghton Mifflin Company, for Archibald MacLeish; Little, Brown and Company, for D. G. Rossetti; Macmillan Company, for Alfred Tennyson, John Masefield, and William Butler Yeats; Oxford University Press, for Gerard Manley Hopkins; Random House, for W. H. Auden; and Charles Scribner's Sons, for George Meredith.

Specific references will be found either in the text or in the Notes.

# PROLOGUE

FEW PEOPLE have ever been brave enough to define poetry. Not many among those few have felt happy with their definitions. Yet most of us have experienced poetry, and many of us believe that we can recognize it when we see it, just as we can recognize life when we see it, although we cannot satisfactorily define it. Like life, poetry exists in so many forms and on so many levels that it triumphantly defies description. Keats has written of poetry as the realms of gold, and has noted its many goodly states and kingdoms, its many islands held in fealty to Apollo. The metaphor is a good one, though it hardly goes far enough. There are more poems than there are islands in the Caribbean, or the Mediterranean; and they vary more in shape, size, color, contour, and human habitability.

Furthermore, any individual poem, as Keats wrote of Homer's *Iliad*, may in itself be a complete domain, illimitable as the Pacific, ruled by its own king and creator, a wide expanse arched over by a pure and serene air. Or—and here is the rub —it may not be like that at all. It may be as small and limited as an epigram by Martial, as precipitous and rocky as a lyric by Donne, as barely above sea level as a poem by Edgar Guest. And it might be quite different from any now known. Surely there is good reason to avoid a definition of poetry. The clearer and more concise the definition is, the more poems it leaves out.

If we are to understand the nature of poetry, we must view the realms of gold from many points of vantage. We must travel on various single quests across many islands. At the start we must take certain bearings and ask certain questions. Are we to consider the *medium* of words in which poetry is composed? Or the *subjects* which poetry treats? Or the *purposes* for which the subjects are being used? Or the *forms* created in that verbal medium in order to give expression to certain subjects and purposes? The first of these possibilities will occupy us in later paragraphs. The second need not detain us, for the answer, if we judge by actual practice, is that any subject matter may furnish raw materials for poets, from Chaucer, who used warts and running sores, to T. S. Eliot, who uses statistics. The last two possibilities present the further question: Are we to consider poetry or poems? Poetry, of course, may serve as a generic name for a group of poems or for all poems taken together. Often, however, the word is used to describe the spirit or mood which may find expression in a poem but may also find expression in, say, a painting or a piece of music. Many critical battles and misunderstandings have arisen because one man was viewing the qualities of the *poetic spirit* and his opponent was seeing only the qualities of a *poem*. We might at this point decide on a procedure: to consider first those elements which most usually combine in the poetic spirit; and then, more narrowly, the technical and formal elements which shape words into a poem.

Poetry labors under the further handicap of being the most misunderstood of all the arts. And yet of all the arts, poetry should afford to the greatest number of people the most delight. Actually it does nothing of the kind. Instead, the average adolescent or adult (for children know what poetry is) feels uncomfortable or irritated or bored when he confronts a poem. Partly this defect in sympathy may be attributed to the many easy substitutes that now satisfy everyone's natural craving for esthetic experience—the comic strips and the movies, the detective stories and the weekly magazines, the soap opera on the radio and the trip in the car. A debased currency will always drive out the genuine article, and there are plenty of ways to-day to get others to do our thinking and our feeling for us. Partly the misunderstanding springs from the amount of rapid reading we do, skimming newspapers and billboards and novels, so that we are impatient when anything demands close scrutiny. We have also had little practice in taking in through the ear esthetically ordered words. The eye has displaced the ear as the instrument for literary communication, although it is quite possible that the radio, some day in the future, may help to restore the enjoyment of poetry as a verbal pattern of meaningful *sounds*.

But the main cause of the popular uneasiness before poetry lies in the very medium which this art uses—the medium of words. We are accustomed to using words almost solely for the practical purposes of living. We cannot understand without an effort—or better still, without long experience—that in poetry words are used in a different way and serve different purposes. Poetry alone among the arts suffers this serious handicap. We understand that almost all the other arts are not aiming at the practical. No one supposes that ballet dancers are building up their muscles for military service or are running to the store to buy a loaf of bread. A painting and a symphony concert cannot readily be considered to be of immediate practical usefulness, and there is little likelihood of approaching them with dangerously wrong expectations. But let us imagine for a moment that from childhood we had constantly used square or rectangular surfaces solely as dining tables, writing tables, or checkerboards. A painting might then fill us with contempt because it would be so poorly designed to satisfy what we felt to be its natural functions. Or suppose from the cradle up we had sipped our milk and drunk our coffee from receptacles resembling saxophones. Would it not then seem to us ludicrous to see a man blowing into his cup in order to make it produce inedible and therefore unedifying saxophonic sounds?

We need not resort to such far-fetched parables when we turn to poetry. We are already in the midst of a comedy, or tragedy, of errors. Continually we use words to say: "Please pass the butter," or "I think free trade is obviously the solution," or "I hear Marjorie has given up Steve for Dick." And when the words of poetry fail to say similar things satisfying similar purposes, we are irked or bewildered. Or worse, we try to force them into our ordinary modes of practical or logical thought. We are constantly coming out with the wrong answers. We call poetry a means of escape—as if we actually lived all the time, or even most of the time, in the practical and active world, and never among dreams, aspirations, values, and the sheer sensations of being alive. Even when we know that there are other ways of life than the business of the world, we fail to look for them in poetry, for the barrier of words is still there, and words in our experience are used for immediate utilitarian purposes. And therefore we collect a small handful of commonplace notions and facts from the rich mines of poetry. We feel that we have settled Hardy's business when we label him pessimistic and fatalistic, we consider *Macbeth* simply as a tract to show that too much ambition is a bad thing, we read *Childe Harold's Pilgrimage* because it deals with travels through Europe and an actual battle of Waterloo, or we abstain from *Paradise Lost* because Milton was a Puritan who took the story of Adam and Eve literally. Poetry, we feel, contains some history and some facts, but the *World Almanac* organizes them more efficiently.

Another of our misapprehensions is that reason is the prime distinction of man and that poetry is inferior intellectually to mathematics or philosophy. One of America's most notable critics, John Crowe Ransom, finds the distinguishing mark of poetry to lie in the logical irrelevancy of its local details; to most readers this would immediately appear a flaw in poetry resulting from the ignorance or perversity of poets. That there are other modes of thought and of knowledge than the logical and the practical is not one of our habitual assumptions.

The first chapter of this book, therefore, is designed to present an approach to poetry as poetry. It tries to show how poets use words. The notion is difficult to express and to grasp, but it is also, I think inevitably, the basic assumption for any further profitable discussion. Stated in its simplest terms, this whole book rests on the assumption that a poem is like a person. We can classify persons as Vermonters or Italians, just as we can classify poems as elegies, ballads, and the rest; but perhaps such categories do little to help us understand either personality or poetry. The first safe generalization to make about persons is that each one of them is individual, unmistakable, unduplicable, and that if he were not—if there were any identical substitute for him—he would not be a person. The same is true of a poem, of any poem. The opening section of the book applies this general idea to the medium of poetry: words, language. I have tried to express this notion in the title of the first chapter: "Poetry is exact." The phrase is not good enough: its very failure proves the point I am attempting to establish. A poem, through its overtones, its suggestions, the relations between its words and motifs, and its other complexities, may express with complete adequacy a definite and unique experience. But the limited language of analysis, in such a phrase as "Poetry is exact," does not satisfactorily "cover" its subject. If it did, I would not have the chapter to write. Even in this first sketching of the idea, without amplification or illustration or qualification, I must at least point out that the exactness of poetic language is not the logical invariability of a mathematical proposition; rather, it is the unmistakability by which we recognize one person as different from another, depending upon a multiplicity of traits, features, and qualities, material and immaterial, which defy complete analysis. The mere fact that the words of a poem can *not* be analyzed and described exhaustively does not make it less exact: instead, it constitutes the peculiar "exactness," the particularity, the uniqueness, of that poem. Wherever we find poetry, we find also this pleasure in recognizing the unique.

The same voice is not speaking in

> The curfew tolls the knell of parting day

that speaks in

> For God's sake, hold your tongue and let me love,

and there is no good in trying to make them sound alike. Even when the same poet speaks, he may speak in various moods. We should not bring the temper of the "Elegy in a Country Churchyard" to a reading of

> Ruin seize thee, ruthless King!
> Confusion on thy banners wait!

All of this is only a way of saying that the first enjoyment we may get from poetry comes from accepting it for what it is and not for something else. We do not enjoy a friend by reducing him to a set of categories: age, 30; hair, dark brown; nationality, U.S.; religion, Methodist. And the better we know the friend, the less we are satisfied to ticket him as 30% justice; 30% cantankerousness; 20% amiability; 15% laziness; and 5% hot temper. Instead, we take pleasure in recognizing that

> I must confess it could not choose but be
> Profane to think thee anything but thee.

A poem, just as clearly, is a fusion of innumerable elements, large and small, in many fields of experience, obvious or subtle or even not consciously noticed or describable. Experienced fully as a poem, it is not made up of separable or interchangeable parts, and its exactness lies in this unique wholeness.

We may grasp completely the meaning of a scientific law such as "For every action there is an equal and opposite reaction" when that law is stated in other words. But we have lost something when we take the last line of Dante's *Divine Comedy*,

*L'amor che move il sole e l' altre stelle,*

and translate it literally as

The love which moves the sun and the other stars.

Furthermore, in the Italian, that line gains its full illumination, its precision of meaning, only in its relation to all the rest of the poem with its great weight and glory of details.

The poetic world is the world seen through the eyes of an individual and expressed in his words. Even when that world appears most abstracted and generalized, the poetic view is still unique, and cannot be changed or added to or translated into other terms, as can the propositions in the communal and rational world of science. A poem is an individual imaginative experience recorded as faithfully as possible by an individual poet.

Suppose we accept as the necessary first approach to poetry this recognition that poetic exactness consists in the unique individuality of each complete poetic expression. Does it follow, then, that any further observations on the nature of poetry are rendered impossible because each separate poem is a law unto itself? Does anarchy or multiplicity crowd out order? By no means. But the order cannot be mechanical, for a poem is comparable to a living organism. The succeeding chapters are therefore not written with any desire to set up shop as Procrustes and reduce all poems to a long or short bed. On the contrary they are written with continual awareness that the art of poetry is not the exclusive possession of any century or school or age or race or nation. The range of poetry is immense, and good poems are inexhaustible in number and in variety.

This book proposes to present, through a series of seven interlocking essays, a single argument regarding the nature of poetry—that a poem is like a person. Now a person does not lose his personality because he is subject to certain general laws: of gravity, of chemistry, of heredity, or of Nemesis. If one considers the laws governing poetry not as grim fiats, but as descriptions of what usually happens in a poem, as generalizations based on experience, they need not seem stern and inflexible and forbidding. The nature of poetry is fluid, so that the laws of poetry, like the laws of nature, may be deduced as great guiding principles within which individual entities move easily, in accordance with their own particular natures, and with no sense of let or hindrance. The biological laws of intussusception and of senescence apply equally to an Anopheles mosquito, an oak tree, and an elephant, but they do not compel the mosquito to be the elephant. Similarly, the qualities of poetry which succeeding chapters propose are found as constants in all poetry, yet are uniquely embodied in each particular poem. No one law of poetry reveals all its secrets; and only open, comprehensive, tolerant minds will save us from clamping poetry in too narrow a cage.

The second chapter maintains that poetry is intense. It rests on the premise that to create any work of art requires strenuous effort, and that only an experience of more than average intensity is strong enough to compel an artist to reproduce that experience as exactly as poetry requires. The more traditional way of stating the fact of poetic intensity would be to say that poetry is emotional or passionate. Calling poetry emotional, however, suggests to some people that poetry gushes and sentimentalizes. So it does, when it wishes, and still it remains poetry: far too many modern critics and readers assume that sentiment and even sentimentality are no fit parts of human experience. But romantic sentiment is not the only way of expressing feeling; restraint and understatement can produce equally powerful emotional effects. Profound thought, no less than smiles and tears, may stamp passion upon a poem; and following the convolutions of a controlled argument may produce an exhilaration and an awareness which cannot be distinguished from emotion. Nevertheless, to avoid the popular limitations set upon the word "emotion," I have chosen to speak of the *in-*

*tensity* of poetry. Even the idea of intensity must be considered closely to prevent misunderstanding. It might imply that the sensation of poetry is comparable to an electric shock or an exploding firecracker; and much of the chapter, in consequence, is devoted to showing how intensity may be secured through diffusion as well as through compression, through simple serious statement as well as through distortion and hyperbole, through repetition as well as through epigram. For again, though the goal of intensity is single for all poems, it may be reached by various individual paths.

A man does not write a poem in a typhoon or on the bier of his child. He must be at least detached enough from any intense experience to express satisfactorily its meaning for him. The third chapter states that poetry is significant. The care to put exact words in right places, the intensity evoked by the poet and felt by the reader—these could not exist if the poet did not believe that he was being exact and intense about *something*. In part, then, this chapter attacks the idea of art as an end in itself, an ivory tower walled off from and raised beyond the world of common sense. In part also, since poetry presents one man's consciousness as he regards his material, and since his material is usually human life, this chapter maintains that poetry almost inescapably contains judgments on human values. The discussion, therefore, again argues the venerable case, now somewhat unfashionable, that the end of art is to teach, and that the significance of poetry is primarily a moral significance. Poetry may even be considered as the most effective of moral agents, since it presents not bloodless propositions, but one man's answer to particular situations. In other words, it affords useful examples, for each of us must reach his own moral decisions under similar circumstances of particularity. Such a position demands that many warning signs be set up to show that moral beliefs need not be expressed directly; that poetry is not narrow, rigid, and crude in dogmatism; and that a poem, though it strives toward meaning as intently as a sermon, a legal brief, or a scientific journal, possesses a significance different in kind and different in expression.

In developing this argument, the fourth chapter naturally follows: "Poetry is concrete." Its significance is embodied in the symbols of all the senses; and moral statements, abstract speculations, convictions, hopes, and tenuous emotions, are all set forth to walk in images and actions. Like the ordinary man, the poet naturally grasps an idea in terms of an example. He "sees" his thought. His pictures and vivid instances convey his sense of the immediacy, the tangibility, the actuality, of the world and of his own existence. The gorgeous galleries of poetry afford ample illustrations that the typical poet thinks in images, and there is little further that this chapter must do except to point out that even philosophical or reflective or didactic poetry possesses, to a remarkable degree, this quality of concreteness.

The fifth chapter constitutes a pause in the argument, or better, it surveys the argument as it has developed and draws a conclusion that should surprise no one: "Poetry is complex." The earlier principles are, I think, applicable to all poetry; each is quite able to get along independently; each differs from the others; yet how are they to subsist simultaneously in the same poem? Words must be set down in a satisfying and inevitable order; figures and panoramas and symbols must be summoned up before the mind's eye; the dance of the words and figures must not be meaningless, but must rouse in the reader a sense of significance; and thought, words, images, must not clog each other, nor interfere with the sense of heightened experience, of intensity, which gives to art its life and joyousness. The various modes of living—in sensation, in intellect, in emotion, in desire, in conscience—must be allowed full and harmonious interplay. This is the miracle of poetry. This is the mystery of unity-achieved-through-variety which again makes inevitable the comparison: a poem is like a person. The four first chapters express merely a few of the great guiding general

principles in poetry; there are innumerable smaller laws and local
ordinances and temporary edicts and proclamations in time of
emergency. Fortunately the immense domains of poetry can
never be reduced to mathematical or legal order; and this fifth
chapter is not so much a law as a description, a recognition, of
the complexity of poetry. In art, and perhaps only in art, are
the full possibilities of man's existence imaginatively realized,
so that life may be apprehended, for a moment, at its highest
and its most complete.

Although the illustrations for the first five chapters have
been drawn almost solely from poems, and from poems in English, the principles themselves might well apply, with changes in
emphasis, to any of the arts. They represent the artist's way
of looking at the world; they try to catch the qualities in his
nature. The last two chapters narrow consideration to the specific artistic qualities of the poetic spirit when it uses words
as its medium of expression. This topic was also considered in
the first section, although there the focus was primarily on the
quality of poetic words rather than on their formal arrangement. Stated in other terms, the first five chapters consider
primarily the *qualities* of poetry, the last two chapters (and to
some extent the first) consider the qualities of *a poem*.

The sixth chapter holds that poetry is rhythmic. A poem
maintains its life by walking the knife-edge between rhythmical
formlessness on one side and mechanical meter on the other.
The chapter is largely devoted to the pleasant pastime of ex-
ploring the purposes of these verbal patterns in sound, and
to considering how sheer technical achievements may be devoted to clarifying and intensifying the substance of the
poem.

Finally, the seventh title states that "Poetry is formal." The
word is forbidding in its stiffness, and again much of this chapter, as of others, is busy in preventing wrong implications. But
here, as in the first and sixth chapters, we are dealing with the
most purely esthetic aspects of our subject, the most strictly

poetic. And we are finding that poetry is not only a way of looking at the world, but a way of speaking about it. Though the subject is limited in this chapter, then, it affords an apt climax and conclusion to the book, and an adequate balance to the first chapter, or return to that initial argument: for no one can enjoy a poem to the full who does not take it on its own incomparable terms, not only in its unique words and images and rhythms, but also in its form. The structures of poems are as beautiful in themselves as the structures of music or architecture. That poems may appeal to us on so many additional levels is no adequate reason for neglecting or minimizing the delight they afford through the sheer beauty of their forms. We may agree with Plato and with Spenser that

> Soule is forme, and doth the bodie make.

But conversely, we arrive at the highest and purest pleasures of poetry by observing the control, the shape, the harmony, which the artist's activity has brought into being; we may be

> Transported with celestiall desyre
> Of those faire formes.

This, then, is the progressive argument which this book develops. The nature of poetry is not mechanical. Its laws are not edicts, but observations; they are not forced upon poetry, but derived from it. In all fairness, I should offer here, in very brief compass, an illustration. Let us take a short poem by Housman:

> Into my heart an air that kills
>   From yon far country blows:
> What are those blue remembered hills,
>   What spires, what farms are those?
>
> That is the land of lost content,
>   I see it shining plain,
> The happy highways where I went
>   And cannot come again.

The voice is unmistakably Housman's: even a parody of it, though it might catch salient traits, would destroy some of the nuances that give it its *exactness*. No word can be changed without changing the effect of the whole. If we substitute "distant countries" for "yon far country," we not only destroy Housman's characteristic sense of the past underlying the present, which he manages to suggest through the use of the slightly archaic word "yon," but we also lose the almost concrete action of pointing which "yon" gives, and we weaken the unity of the stanza by canceling the echoing "far" and "farms." We might say also that literally the air is not "killing" anything; the image would be closer to possible sensations if we substituted "an air that chills." But "kills" is the more exact word, for it can suggest the emotional *intensity* of Housman's intuition, which he has made even more poignant by the statement, meaningless in the actual world of matter, that the killing air blows into his heart. This intensity he makes specific by speaking of the content, the shining happiness, which now is lost. Few of us would miss his *significance*—that youth is irrecoverable, or that ecstasy, once past, cannot be recaptured; many of us would feel that judgments of value are also implicit: that content and happiness are good, and that if we cannot have them, it is good at least to see clearly what we have lost, and to recognize time as evil, truth and self-control as good. Any such values are not stated in abstract propositions, but with *concreteness*, in controlled and harmonized images, so that we are made to feel the air, the country, the hills, the spires, the farms, the land, and the highways of Shropshire, perhaps even the plains. *Complexity* is evident enough in the working together of these disparate elements. "Far," for instance, conveys in the thought the years between past and present; in the emotion, regret; in the image, the distant panorama; in the sound, a link with "farms" and other words. Complexity arises from those ambiguities which, to a greater or less degree, all readers find in a poem. If they heard it read orally, many readers might sense as the prime meaning of the sixth line, "I see *its* shining *plain*"; and is this panoramic overtone lacking even when we see that it is not grammatically permissible in the printed version? "Spires," for me at least, is better than "towers" because it makes me think of "aspiring" and "suspiration." Such complexities are not controlled, but will vary from reader to reader; so long as they remain relevant to the whole, they enrich the poem.

We respond to the complex nature of poetry, our imaginations becoming eager and alert, because of the formal qualities of the poem itself. *Rhythm* has a powerful emotional effect, rousing and quieting at the same time, so that we take delight, usually an unconscious delight, in points in the pattern—the alternate rhymes, and the alternating line lengths which compel a pause after each even-numbered line to fill it up to the rhythmical length of its odd-numbered predecessor. Variations from the rhythmical pattern are here not only pleasing in themselves but aid in successful expression: the two inverted first feet—"Ínto my heart" and "Whát are those blue"—suggest spontaneous emotion, and the extra accented syllables—"yón fár cóuntry," "Whát spíres, whát fárms"—add power to the thought and emotion, extension to the landscape. And finally, the perfect *form* of the whole, the echoes, repetitions, and balances, the contrast between the question of the first stanza and the answer of the second, make all these materials into a poem. And the poem, as distinct from its poetic qualities and potentialities, consists precisely in *these* words, *this* rhythm, *this* form. Therein lies its esthetic delight, so that we would not trade the eight lines themselves for eight bushel baskets of such analyses as this. Nevertheless, developing one's power to analyze increases one's capacity to enjoy.

One word more. This prologue has briefly indicated the essence of the entire book, so that each section may be seen more clearly in its relation to the whole, and so that the qualifications and illustrations which such simple and rash chapter headings require might not seem needless delays and meanderings. This book seeks the unifying *principles* of poetry. Quotations are used to illustrate statements and not to furnish proportionate representation to all good poets. I have tried not to overlook completely any important period or movement in English poetry, and I have avoided drawing too many examples from very recent poetry in order to keep a better perspective. Needless to say, it is my belief that the *nature* of poetry is constant, though the emphasis on certain of its principles and the relative neglect of others shift with time and the individual poet. Since I wish to present the constant nature of poetry, I have devoted special attention in each chapter to those poets or periods where the general principle under discussion might seem least applicable. For the rich variety among the poets themselves should not make it impossible to see them all as blood brothers.

Every page of this book shows borrowings, varying from the minute to the impressive, from previous writers. I hope that this single general acknowledgment will express some small measure of my indebtedness and gratitude. The positive service which a book about poetry can render is to turn more readers, or better readers, directly back to actual poems. If criticism can accomplish this end, it needs no further excuse. I have found that books about poetry have not acted as substitutes for poetry itself, but they have frequently helped me to read or reread poems with more awareness, more sympathy, and more pleasure. This book is addressed to those who believe criticism may have such power.

# CHAPTER ONE

# POETRY
# IS EXACT

PRECISION is unattainable. Not completely realized in any human activity, precision is particularly difficult to achieve in language. Ordinary language is inexact. Anyone who has struggled with a paragraph, wilted under cross-examination in a courtroom, or attempted to describe a friend's face, knows well enough that words are intractable and inadequate. What else could they be? Only a creature cursed with the extraordinary imagination of the human animal would have dreamed of utilizing articulated sounds to convey things and thoughts to other creatures. For a rose is not like a sound, and grief is not like a sound, and God's grace is not like a sound. All three are soundless, they have little in common; yet man has dared to create sounds to symbolize whatever may happen to his senses and his heart and his spirit. That such sounds can be as efficient as they are is a further sign of the amazing power of his imagination.

He goes further and invents writing, so that a visual arrangement of letters may arbitrarily suggest a certain sound, and that in turn bring to mind the object or idea he is writing and talking about. The letters in the word ROSE cannot resemble the sound they conjure up, but the sound is there for most of us, and back of the sound, the ghost of the rose.

Furthermore, our imaginations pull us so strongly toward unity that we tend to confuse such conventional verbal symbols with the emotions and thoughts and sensations that brought them into being. In making practically effective my signature on a check, the growth of Roman law and social stability, the development of the capitalistic system, and my own sense of responsibility are basically more important than my bank balance, since I have no goods of real value in the bank. But when I sign the check I do not consider these matters: the signature, rather than the intention to pay or the social system, seems momentous in and for itself. And when after the marriage ceremony the question of loving, honoring, and obeying arises, does not the recalled speaking of the words "I do" weigh, in the years to come, along with domesticity and religion and emotion?

Our imaginations and our sense of tradition, then, have given erratic power to words, spoken or written, which logically they do not and cannot possess in themselves. The intellectual attack upon words has frequently been made, in an attempt to strip them of their unreasonable strength and give them in exchange a certain steadiness. For various technical purposes such endeavor is valid. Philosophy, law, the sciences, limited types of criticism and history, need a vocabulary which is unmistakable, unambiguous, unemotional, a vocabulary which will allow the writer to establish a solid position because it has excluded words that wobble or say several things at once. Yet this is not using language normally; it is creating symbolic logic. Pages of special definitions and strictures may show a philosopher's distress at the failure of words to be consistent and to hold an invariable content; these same pages, however, also show that he finds it necessary to depart from the world of common usage. Language is firmly rooted in common experience; well used, it is also personal. When, for perfectly valid reasons, a lawyer does away with Maximilian Flint, who is an individual, and substitutes "the party of the first part," he is writing a legal document. The more admirably incontestable a last will and testament is, the less it is common speech.

Language cannot be transformed into a completely efficient instrument for practical or theoretical reasoning. Unpredictable associations will bob up. "The party of the first part" may make the lawyer think of his stenographer, or of a classroom in the law school, or of an old joke. Even when algebra has drained the blood from words and replaced them with pure signs, the formula $a + b = c$ gives a certain "greaterness" to $c$, and an air of precedence to $a$, like a plump young lady before her angular escort. Is it possible for all of us to think of $\pi$ merely as the mathematical relation between diameter and circumference? And in higher mathematics, are all associations and emotions and images absent when we encounter $\infty$, the symbol for infinity, or $\Sigma$ for summation?

All words veer with the wind. This first observation on the nature of poetry, for instance, runs: "Poetry is exact." What do I mean by *exact?* In this chapter I should define it as: capable of reproducing (or of creating the illusion of reproducing) in another man's mind, fully and faithfully, what is in the creator's consciousness when he is thinking primarily as an individual, as a person.

Yet this definition is no fit substitute for every use of the word *exact* in this chapter. We would never be able to think if we always had to think of the definition of each word as we used it. The meaning of the word shifts, so that only the contexts will show that at one time I am thinking primarily of the *fullness* of the reproduction, again of its *faithfulness*, and again of its *individuality* as opposed to the standardized communications of science and business. Last of all, even if I wanted to, I could not hold the word *exact* to a single rational concept apart from values and emotions supplied by the reader. Since you probably assume that this book is not an attack upon poetry, you may already judge that exactness, whatever it signifies, is a good thing, a fine thing. Merely to say that poetry is exact gives us a feeling of certainty and assurance. Now, we feel, we know *exactly* where we are, and we know it "exactly" because of expansive overtones that escape beyond any definition. In giving us the elated illusion of thinking precisely, the word *exact* has become more effective emotionally than rationally.

Language, whenever it is considered closely, appears innately unstable. The significance of a word varies with the memories and intentions of the man who speaks it and with the associations of the man who hears it. Never twice for any individual does it hold quite the same meaning; vary the context or the tone, and the word, chameleonlike, changes its color. All this, of course, is evident only when words are closely scrutinized. In ordinary talking and writing they seem stable enough. The conventional stopgap phrases, the paddings and repetitions, the expected responses in the old grooves, protect us from the painful chore of exact expression. "Good morning" serves as a greeting even in a drizzle. We would consider as affected a person who attempted accuracy in saluting us with "Dull morning!" or "Pearl-gray luminescent morning!" We are not disturbed by the inexplicable convention of using "Good morning" at the start of an interview and "Good day" at the end. Nor do we mean, once in a thousand times, "God be with you" when we say "Good-by." Our everyday speech is flat, dull, and colorless, because it is simpler to get through existence so. Even in those moments when we wish to give unusual significance to our language, it remains easier to add the desired emphasis by inflection rather than by more careful choice of words.

But poetry is another kingdom, with its own laws and priests and customs. The poet in modern times, for instance, cannot depend upon the inflections of his voice. He must achieve his effects of sharpness solely through the words he selects and arranges. He is aware that poetic language is not mechanically exact in the sense that the caliper measurement of a ball bearing is exact. He sees that a sentence is not equal to the sum of the dictionary definitions of the words that compose it. It is more living, more organic. In literature the reality is the sentence, unified and vital, so that all words in their places function together. In a fine line of poetry it is as irrelevant to speak of adverbs and predicates as to discuss where the neck of the Venus de Milo becomes her shoulder.

And yet, if the poet cannot select his words with mechanical accuracy and finality as a compositor selects type, in what does his peculiar power of using language consist? It lies in its faithful reproduction of his own experience. To say that the language of poetry must be exact is to say no more than that it must truthfully reflect the mind of the poet. The poet knows that language is itself living; he has learned to shape it so that it expresses to other people his own individuality. The poet's readers are the judges of his exactness. They must be satisfied that his words mirror his mind fully, clearly, and without distortion. The reader's pleased conviction that he has caught the unique personal thought of the poet in all its precision and completeness may be only an illusion; it may depend upon tricks of technique; for any poem it may not exist equally in all good readers; and it may not return with equal sharpness every time a single reader turns to a poem. Yet in practice such reservations do not make the standards for judging poetry purely relative, for human nature, in all individuals, is basically unchanging. Let us conclude, then, that whenever an individual consciousness, precise, instantaneous, and complete, seems to be re-created through words in the consciousness of another, poetry is at work.

Words cannot easily be manipulated to reproduce exactly what is in their master's mind. The poet is aware of the deadliness of the well-worn phrase, which expresses nothing but its own inanition. He is also aware of the dangers in too vague a suggestion and too wide an ambiguity, so that exactitude is lost in the mazes of uncontrolled fancy. Between the sandbar of platitudes and the fog-shrouded promontory of personal riddles, he must steer his certain course. There will be no well-marked channel for his voyage—if there were, it would cease to be exploration—but if he is a true poet he will wreck himself neither on sandbar nor promontory, and in the end, he will arrive in port.

Every poet is continually, sometimes painfully, working to become master of his own style. The materials he uses may have belonged to others, but until he appropriates them for himself, they are ineffective. The perfecting of a style comes slowly, after prolonged effort to hush in his own work the voices of others, which unassimilated are invariably hollow and unconvincing. Playing the sedulous ape cannot be more than an exercise in craftsmanship; the cleverest imitation is no more than a kind of ventriloquism. The battle between his own personal language and the language of the world is one that each poet must ceaselessly wage. Yet the eighteenth century presents the struggle most clearly, for at no other period in English poetry has a belief in correct speech received such wide support. Individual utterance encountered strong opposition, for the cultured world insisted upon an elegant uniformity. Many of the poets of the time show clearly the partial emergence of a personal style in spite of the current poetic diction.

The Scottish poet James Thomson may serve as an example. At the risk of making arbitrary distinctions, I should like to try, in a passage from Thomson's "Winter," the experiment of printing in italics the more conventional language, as if the whole period were expressing itself, and in roman type the poet's speech when he is most himself:

> The red-breast, *sacred to the household gods,*
> *Wisely regardful of the embroiling sky,*
> *In joyless fields, and thorny thickets, leaves*
> *His* shivering *mates, and pays to trusted man*

*His annual visit.* Half-afraid, he first
Against the window beats; then, brisk, alights
On the warm hearth; then, hopping *o'er* the floor,
*Eyes* all the smiling family *askance,*
And pecks, and starts, and wonders where he is:
Till more *familiar* grown, the table-crumbs
*Attract* his slender feet. . . . *The bleating kind*
*Eye the* bleak *heaven,* and next the glistening earth,
With *looks of dumb despair;* then, *sad dispers'd,*
Dig for the wither'd *herb* through heaps of snow.

This is uncomfortable writing. *The Seasons,* indeed, cannot be read with consistent pleasure. Thomson had the eye of a poet, and perhaps the heart; he lacked the tongue. He cannot completely focus his attention on describing the wild and rural Scottish scenes he knew; half his mind is bent on placating literary critics by copying the idioms of Milton and Dryden. His imitation of Spenser in *The Castle of Indolence* makes his failure in self-confidence even more apparent. Thomson possessed a vision without an unwavering voice, and a vision without a voice is not poetry. In early eighteenth-century literature, London was the law: Thomson was too much the cultivated Scot of his time to overcome his sense of inferiority before the metropolis to the south.

Robert Burns affords a similar example of the conflict between commonly accepted language and a tongue of one's own. Burns's vacillation between English and Scottish makes unusually obvious that slow discovery of style which all poets must achieve for themselves. No one sensitive to poetry can fail to note that Burns's Scottish poems are much better than his English imitations. Why is this true? Though the fact is obvious, its cause is not easily analyzed. Surely no mere seasoning with a few words in unaccustomed dialect has turned conventional lines into poetry, for the native Scotsman, apart from his patriotism, knows Burns's worth no less than the Englishman or American.

> O, wert thou in the cauld blast

does not become poetry because of an odd spelling of *cold*.
Nor is

> Had we never lov'd sae kindly

poetic because of a Caledonian variation. Yet, inexplicably, it
is true that "cauld" and "sae" are the exact words, and that
to anglicize them would be to weaken the verses. Nor can one
tamper with Burns's idioms and syntax. When scrutiny fails
to explain the reasons back of Burns's power over his own language, we are almost forced to accept absolute poetic language as an act of faith. The empirical evidence of Burns's
gift, however, is abundant and undeniable; and possibly his
successes become more understandable if we remember that
language is *organic*, so that when Burns was thinking in Scots,
a phrase, a sentence, or a whole poem was conceived as a unit,
though from our point of view only one or two small words
are in dialect. Organically conceived, the resulting lines are
therefore satisfying even when their secret cannot be plucked
out.

The causes for failure, at any rate, are easier to discover.
"The Cotter's Saturday Night," no less than *The Seasons*,
could be divided into its two languages, the personal and the
derivative. Its epigraph is a quatrain from Gray's "Elegy." Its
stanza form is Edmund Spenser's. And the first stanza is as awk-
ward and uncertain as a boy in his first dress clothes:

> My lov'd, my honor'd, much respected friend!
> No mercenary bard his homage pays;
> With honest pride, I scorn each selfish end.
> My dearest meed, a friend's esteem and praise.
> To you I sing, in simple Scottish lays,
> The lowly train in life's sequester'd scene;
> The native feelings strong, the guileless ways;
> What Aiken in a cottage would have been;
> Ah! tho' his worth unknown, far happier there I ween!

The sentiments are admirable, their expression abominable. The language is at fault. The words are unsatisfying, conventional; they do not fit Burns. After such hollow speaking, it is surprising that the poem could find, even temporarily, a voice of its own. Burns cannot make up his mind as to whether Scotia has two or three syllables; and the "thrifty wifie" and the "wee-things, toddlin," are ill at ease among quotations from Pope and many a "certes," "I ween," and the like.

Yet in his better mood Burns could issue his own declaration of independence from critics and formalism, writing in the stanza and the diction in which he moved so naturally:

> I am nae poet, in a sense,
> But just a rhymer like by chance,
> An' hae to learning nae pretence;
>    Yet, what the matter?
> Whene'er my Muse does on me glance,
>    I jingle at her.
>
> Your critic-folk may cock their nose,
> And say, "How can you e'er propose,
> You wha ken hardly verse frae prose,
>    To mak a sang?"
> But, by your leaves, my learned foes,
>    Ye're maybe wrang.

Thomson and Burns are two poets who tried to write in a language not their own. Thomson never learned to write it well, and Burns in his best poems abandoned it. Although their Scottish nationality makes their attempts so apparent, it must not be forgotten that in a sense every poet begins by trying to write a language not his own—begins with certain crude convictions that poetry results from sounding like Shakespeare, or from inserting or omitting certain words, or from imitating or avoiding definite rhythms. Gradually, and infrequently, the writer of verse develops his own style of expression and becomes a poet. Each truly poetic language has its peculiar and private qualities. Shakespeare has coupled the lunatic, the lover, and the poet; and in respect to language, the poet may well be considered related to the idiot in that each lives a life distinctly his own. The poet is moonstruck by his own invented speech.

The best word, the inevitable word, may come in a flash, or may require long and painful search. Dorothy Words-worth records that her brother made himself almost ill in seeking for an epithet that would describe the song of the cuckoo. The stanza

> While I am lying on the grass
> Thy twofold shout I hear;
> From hill to hill it seems to pass,
> At once far off, and near.

had appeared in print in at least five different versions between 1807 and 1845. The habits of poets in correcting their verse vary from unrevised first and careless raptures to revisions that make Horace's nine-year rule seem precipitate. Some poets correct countless times before the final printed form; and others, even after publication, never willingly reach a final version. But the craving is clear—the hunger for the right word, the search that does not end before success. The interlineations and changes in the Trinity College manuscript of Milton's poems, the metamorphoses of Keats's lines, the ceaseless shiftings made by Wordsworth and Coleridge and Tennyson, all testify to this quest for exactness.

Often an original version will strike a wrong emotional tone, as in Tennyson's 1833 draft of Iphigenia's death:

> One drew a sharp knife through my tender throat
> Slowly, and nothing more.

The solemn and sentimental "tender," the atrocious image in "slowly," and the vapid anticlimax of "and nothing more" Tennyson would probably have discovered for himself with-

out the laughter of the critics. And although he never perfected the final phrase, by 1853 he had caught exactly the
right tone for the rest of the passage, in an image at once intense and impersonal:

> The bright death quivered at the victim's throat,
> Touched; and I knew no more.

One of the landscape stanzas in Tennyson's "The Palace of
Art" in 1833 ran:

> Some were all dark and red, a glimmering land
> Lit with a low round moon,
> Among brown rocks a man upon the sand
> Went weeping all alone.

Later he particularized the "some" landscape paintings to
"one"; he focused more quickly upon loneliness by an earlier
insertion of the solitary foreground figure; he cut out the "all
alone" echo to keep his sharp picture from blurring into "The
Ancient Mariner"; and he canceled entirely the dull third line,
whose diction and imagery had been about on a level with
Doctor Johnson's parody:

> I put my hat upon my head
> And walked into the Strand,
> And there I met another man
> Whose hat was in his hand.

Furthermore he saw that "round" added little to the moon,
changed the adjective to "large," and made the quadruple
alliteration of *l*'s climactic at the close. This, then, is the 1842
version:

> One seemed all dark and red—a tract of sand,
> And someone pacing there alone,
> Who paced for ever in a glimmering land,
> Lit with a low large moon.

The search for exact expression is evident in a single revised
line from Keats's sonnet "On First Looking into Chapman's

Homer." All through the poem, the thrill of discovering, suddenly and unexpectedly, a new region of literature is illustrated with images of an astronomer and of Greek and Spanish voyagers. The second quatrain runs:

> Oft of one wide expanse had I been told
> That deep-brow'd Homer ruled as his demesne:
> Yet did I never breathe its pure serene
> Till I heard Chapman speak out loud and bold.

The richness and majesty of Homer's thought Keats expresses in the first eight lines in such words as "gold," "realms," "states," "kingdoms," "fealty," and now "demesne." The effect of the poem depends upon Keats's conveying his sense of the spaciousness of Homer—coming to a climax in the comparison to the illimitable and newly discovered Pacific. And in the four lines quoted above, the extent of his discovery Keats indicates in the word "expanse," which he further realizes in the spatial adjectives "wide" and "deep." Logically, of course, "deep" qualifies "brow'd," which in turn qualifies "Homer," so that the famous bust of Homer with its high, wrinkled forehead and the thoughtful set of its eyes may perhaps rise in our memories. Less logically, the word "deep" may suggest the depth of Homer's thought. Yet these more obvious meanings cannot prevent "deep" from tangling in association with "wide," for the language of poetry is not primarily either grammatical or intellectual, but psychologically *organic*, its words rooted and twisted inextricably together. The positive nature of his discovery Keats presents in his eighth line:

> Till I heard Chapman speak out loud and bold.

The monosyllables convey his certainty in crescendo. It is not only "speak" but "speak out," not only "loud," but "out loud," the diphthong echoing. And the whole idea of spaciousness is focused in the seventh line (the third of the quoted quatrain), in the image of the great extent of the sky, which is nevertheless so apprehensible, so much a "living air," that it may be breathed. Every word in these four lines is telling, and strengthens effects gained elsewhere in the sonnet. In the original draft of the poem, however, Keats had written as the seventh line:

> Yet could I never judge what men could mean.

As a prose statement of part of his argument, this is satisfactory. But it is dull and unimaginative and therefore fails hopelessly to convey his feelings on first looking into Chapman's Homer. It is not poetic. The language of poetry transfers to the reader, freshly and faithfully, the consciousness of its creator. All the great lines, all the inspired revisions of weak lines, serve to bear this out.

Logical statement, then, is not necessarily, nor even usually, the most effective method of conveying an exact impression. We must go even further in our consideration. Other elements must be taken into account apart from the definite denotations of words and their power of suggesting illuminating comparisons. In the following rushing choric stanza from Swinburne's *Atalanta in Calydon* consider the one word "bright":

> When the hounds of spring are on winter's traces,
> The mother of months in meadow or plain
> Fills the shadows and windy places
> With lisp of leaves and ripple of rain;
> And the brown bright nightingale amorous
> Is half assuaged for Itylus,
> For the Thracian ships and the foreign faces,
> The tongueless vigil, and all the pain.

Certain readers with a passion for consistency have objected to the adjective. They have pointed out that it is inexact, that the nightingale is in point of fact a rather dull-colored bird, and that even apart from ornithology, if the nightingale is brown she is not bright, and if she is bright she is not brown, for you cannot have it both ways at the same time. Swinburne, of course, is notoriously deficient in visual observation. But he had an ear. The word "bright" may be defended on the ground that it marks an exact hearing of the song of the nightingale. Swinburne, like Wordsworth listening to the cuckoo, may have been keeping his ear on the object. To a fresh ear, the turbulent notes of the nightingale may suggest vitality and ecstasy far more than they suggest the conventional lament and dolor. The song of the nightingale *is* bright, we might argue, or was bright to Swinburne; in another line of his,

> Fierce noises of the fiery nightingales,

he evokes a more actual bird than does Milton in his sonnet which opens

> O Nightingale, that on yon bloomy Spray
> Warbl'st at eve,

or Arnold in "Philomela," which ends

> Eternal Passion!
> Eternal Pain!

Swinburne hears nightingales; he does not merely remember a story about Philomela and Tereus. The quality of the song, then, Swinburne finds fierce, bright, and fiery. In the *Atalanta* stanza, his adjective is perfectly placed.

Even apart from its sharp aural imagery, the word "bright" is effective. Its accentual weight is great enough to bear its emotional import. In a stanza of mixed two- and three-syllable feet, it is the only strong syllable in a position where a weak syllable might be expected. And considered purely as sound, it welds the preceding and following words as no other possible word in the English language could. The two-letter alliteration with "brown," the internal rhyme with "*night*-ingale," utilize every element of sound in the word "bright" to afford a transition from one word to the other. Such attention to pure sound can have almost no intellectual meaning. Emotionally, however, the relation of sounds in poetry, no less than in music, may arouse the pleasure of perceiving an organic harmony, with parts repeated, or varied, or related. In an additional sense, therefore, words may be considered exact when they aid in reproducing a state of consciousness through their sheer sound.

No one has spent more time than Gerard Manley Hopkins in finding words not only precise in intellectual content but tied together by sound. In his sonnet, "To R. B.," Hopkins uses the image of the maternal care which a poet's genius devotes to its creations. He writes:

> Nine months she then, nay years, nine years she long
> Within her wears, bears, cares, and combs the same.

The transitions from one verb to the next, either by means of rhyme or alliteration, are invariable and deliberate. In publishing this sonnet for the first time, however, Robert Bridges, to whom it was dedicated, dared to change "combs" to "moulds," presumably on the score that a mother could not comb the hair of her child while it was in the womb. On the same ground, of course, one might object that she could not "wear" something within her, and might therefore change that word too. The emendation by Bridges destroys much of the sense of tender and loving care which the word *combs* calls up, and to that extent is a less accurate word. And certainly the change takes away the tightly knit organization which the march from one verb to another on pure principles of sound has built up. Hopkins was also no doubt aware of the *m* sound in "combs" and "same." Bridges, in brief, sacrifices emotional accuracy and the organization achieved through aural harmony in favor of a literal-minded consistency. His change replaces the exactness of Hopkins' description with a humdrum fact which any child might know.

The mere gravitation of words toward each other because

of sound is not sufficient in itself. It is at best a secondary device for reinforcing mutual relationships in thought, and cannot be successful when thought content is made subsidiary. Swinburne's refrain, for instance,

> Villon, our sad bad glad mad brother's name,

is a relative failure because the adjectives are weak in describing Villon. Choice of them appears dictated solely by the rhyming dictionary; if *dad* and *cad* were adjectives, Villon might have turned out to be also a father and a bounder. But in the poems of Hopkins, usually, the words seem perfectly chosen for their sound because, first of all, he has been rigorous in choosing them for their intellectual and emotional content. Occasionally, as in "Peace," he teases and twists words, and we get a line such as

That piecemeal peace is poor peace. What pure peace allows . . .

in which we feel that in spite of its exactness of thought for Hopkins, the verbal quibble is dominant for the reader. But more typical is the opening line of the same poem

When will you ever, Peace, wild wooddove, shy wings shut . . .

in which the adjectives transform the dove, conventional symbol for peace, into a living part of Hopkins' emotion, and which haunts us also because of the accentual rhythm and the shuttling back and forth in alliteration and assonance that weaves the words together. His famous sonnet, "The Windhover," compares his joy at seeing the flight of a hawk against the morning sky to his joy in realizing Christ's beauty and bravery. Both experiences are sudden illuminations, and the poem ends with two further examples of sudden fire breaking forth. The octave of the sonnet is a triumphant experiment in selecting words that will exactly convey—in this case almost mimic, through long-drawn sounds—the sustained flight of a bird. And the last sentence of the poem, in which

> blue-bleak embers . . .
> Fall, gall themselves, and gash gold-vermilion,

contains three beautifully exact verbs, not only because "gall" is the perfect bridge (again through rhyme and alliteration) between "fall" and "gash," but also because they support his central theme of a sudden intensity following dullness, possibly make us think in "gash" of the *ash*es of the fire, and suggest, in their associations with the accidents of flesh and blood, Christ's sacrifice on the Cross which is behind the whole sonnet and which, in the final word, gains almost the intense colors of a medieval altarpiece.

The element of pure sound, therefore, since it suggests or reinforces underlying ideas, plays an important part in the choice of the right word. An ear sensitive to poetry cannot disregard the mere sound of the words themselves. In determining the rightful language of a poem, rhythm and accent are almost as important as alliteration and assonance. Pope shows how it may be done in a well-known passage of the *Essay on Criticism* from which one couplet may serve as example:

> When Ajax strives some rock's vast weight to throw,
> The line too labours, and the words move slow.

The words in the first verse are obviously chosen to slow down the movement. Some actual striving on the reader's part is required to pronounce such combinations of consonants as *xstr*, *vss*, *ksv*, and *stw*. Each line is also made heavier and slower by the addition of two extra accented syllables where weak syllables might be expected. Pope and Keats in their characteristic thought appear meditative, deliberate, in contrast with the impetuous charioteers Dryden and Shelley. It is no accident that their verse is made up of words which cannot be read as rapidly as the careening and catapulting lines of the other two poets, for, in this choosing of words, always, and with implications far beyond simple onomatopoeia,

> The sound must seem an echo to the sense.

Milton, of course, from whom Pope learned almost as much as from Dryden, is one of the great masters of expressive rhythm. The boundless Chaos which Satan must traverse with difficulty is made immense in the immense line:

Rocks, caves, lakes, fens, bogs, dens, and shades of death.

Again we find the unpronounceable combinations of consonants retarding the movement, and eight heavy syllables weighing down a line that demands five. In contrast to such a verse, a line from the description of the fragile bower in Eden—

Mosaic; underfoot the violet—

with only three heavy syllables, scarcely appears to be written in the same meter. Milton works rhythmical miracles through such variations upon his blank-verse pattern. Rhythmical effects are technical effects. Nevertheless, the rhythm, though it conveys no more than a fraction of the total import, intellectual and emotional, in any passage, definitely helps to make that meaning acceptable to our imaginations.

The importance of the right rhythmical choice is almost better illustrated by examples of meters at odds with their subjects. Critics have pointed out often enough that the closed and balanced couplets of Pope's Homer do not convey rhythmically the sweep and flow of the *Iliad*. The seven-beat couplets of Chapman's Homer might superficially seem better able to suggest their original in rhythm, but in spite of Keats, to open Chapman is to start an endless jogtrot in what turns out to be the meter of a monotonous ballad. Other critics deplore the rapid movement of the anapest ($\smile \smile \prime$) in Wordsworth's "Poor Susan," and surely his desired effect of nostalgic reverie is shattered by such rhythms as:

Green pastures she views in the midst of the dale,
Down which she so often has tripped with her pail.

Browning's ingenious double and triple rhymes that must fall off in one or two unaccented syllables usually produce comic effects because of this tumbling movement, no matter what the intellectual content of the words may be. The meter, therefore, that rightly makes the droll "Pied Piper of Hamelin" droll unfortunately tends to make the serious "Flight of the Duchess" droll also. A longer roll of horrid examples need not be called. It is enough to suggest that even Shakespeare could not have written his tragedies in limerick stanzas.

Speaking of rhythm has necessarily turned the discussion from words to words-in-combination. The ideal word in poetry must be the best possible word for rational content, for suggestion through imagery, and for pure sound. It must enter into rhythmical combinations with other words in such a way that the rhythmical pattern reinforces the desired end. And finally, it must harmonize in style with its fellows in any particular poem, must give them value and derive value from them.

These rules of exactness in poetic expression make every poem its own standard and every poet his own lawgiver. They are absolute in that a standard of possible perfection is assumed for each poet, and for each of his poems, and for each of the words in each of his poems. But they are relative in that this absolute standard of perfection is applicable only to each successive, unique poem.

If this is true, then any theory of correct poetic diction is false when it assumes that certain rules apply mechanically to *all* poems. Exactness in poetry does not imply invariability of statement (such as "Two plus two equal four"); it implies maximum expressiveness in a particular context (such as "We are such stuff as dreams are made on" in Shakespeare's last play *The Tempest*). And poetic language will be designed to express the consciousness of an individual poet—all its elements in their subtle relationships—through such varied technical possibilities as we have looked at already in illustration.

Every poem, therefore, is untranslatable and irreplaceable. Every poet achieves his own expressive language. He can no more write like Shakespeare and be a poet than he can look like Shakespeare and be himself. Rules which are supposedly universally applicable would in consequence destroy, rather than create, exactness of poetic expression. The exactness of poetry is the faithful reproduction through language of a person's whole mind.

These general observations may best be felt by considering specifically John Dryden, since he is unmistakably a poet in his own right but also a critic in an age when the idea of universal correctness tended to destroy the spirit of poetry. Dryden himself believed that in purifying the English language he was working toward precision; more probably he was strengthening the formal rules of art at the expense of exact, individual expression. Historically, English poets became acutely aware of the question of simple and unshifting statement in mid-seventeenth century. The Elizabethans had used language as a newly discovered toy, playing with its possibilities, piling clause on clause for the sake of rhythm, linking antiquated with novel words, native with imported, in redundant confusion. But the decorum of French literary style and the trend toward rationalism set up standards of regularity and clarity for English prose. The Royal Society, chartered by Charles II in 1662, has been accepted as the great popularizing body for the new ideal language; John Dryden is its great champion. Englishmen are accustomed to laugh at the attempts of the French Academy to establish a "correct" French language. Yet that is what Dryden tried to do for English poetry, by precept and practice. There was to be a just, and a highly selective, language for poetry, the use of which would improve the writings of any poet. Briefly, there was only one right way of saying anything, regardless of who was saying it. Dryden was second to none in his homage to the genius of the past. But he felt deeply that his own world had discovered correct speech. To present-day readers, who have learned to believe in the inadequacy of *all* translations, Dryden's versions of Juvenal, Lucretius, Horace, Vergil, Ovid, and Boccaccio may

appear harmless exercises. But when he turns to English literature, modernizes Chaucer, perfects Shakespeare's *Antony and
Cleopatra* in his *All for Love*, and transforms *Paradise Lost* into
a rhymed drama, his effrontery seems sheer brass. A few examples may show how the exact personal speech of any great
poet vanishes when another poet attempts to say the same
thing for him.

The argument in the following pages is that Dryden's versions are bad Chaucer, bad Shakespeare, and bad Milton; but
that frequently they are good Dryden. His language fits his
own thought because he has changed the thoughts of earlier
poets, but it is inexact in expressing the thoughts of those poets
themselves. And, when his tricks and trade-marks of speech
are appropriated by his contemporaries and successors, they
become almost lifeless. The language of a genuine poet, like
his own voice, cannot be duplicated.

Chaucer opens his "Nun's Priest's Tale" with a description
of a poor country widow in which pathos blends inextricably
with realism:

> A povre wydwe, somdeel stape in age,
> Was whilom dwellyng in a narwe cotage,
> Biside a grove, stondynge in a dale.

Dryden insists on a more formal balance. The three lines become four, even at the cost of padding. The details given by
the Nun's Priest, which in Chaucer are introduced as casually
and simply as in extemporaneous storytelling, must now be
marshaled, so that the widow's age is set off against her poverty,
and both attributes are made dependent upon a noun, with
disyllabic adverbs dependent upon the two monosyllabic adjectives. Interest has shifted to technique, to the flow, balance,
and pauses of the couplet, away from the spirit of the lines.
Chaucer's fine pathos in the *narrow* cottage gives way to obvious commonplace, and the naturalism of his third line is

transformed to pastoral sentiment, in which solitary cottages
stand in dells and are by convention carefully built:

> There lived, as authors tell, in days of yore,
> A widow, somewhat old, and very poor;
> Deep in a dell her cottage lonely stood,
> Well thatched, and under covert of a wood.

As the description proceeds, Dryden is compelled to abandon
Chaucer's line

> Full sooty was hire bour and eek hir halle,

which gains its poignancy through mocking contrast with the
bowers and halls of romance. His equivalent is again sentimental:

> Her parlour-window stuck with herbs around,
> Of savoury smell, and rushes strewed the ground.

Chaucer's honest poverty rings with conviction and understanding:

> Attempree diete was al hir phisik,
> And exercise, and hertes suffisaunce.

Dryden's approximation seems perfunctory, and ends, oddly
enough in Dryden, with a discordant anticlimax:

> Her poverty was glad, her heart content,
> Nor knew she what the spleen or vapours meant.

In lines such as these, in the whole long passage, Chaucer's
sure and delicate portrait is made conventional in its late-
seventeenth-century overpainting. The poor old widow, who
lives only in Chaucer's words, has withdrawn. Instead, there
is a dowager behind a parlor window and under well-thatched
eaves. Dryden held that a translator should modernize; he
tried, therefore, to write as Chaucer would have written had
he lived in the seventeenth century. But by no effort can

Dryden make the fourteenth century into the seventeenth. Still less can he metamorphose Chaucer into himself. "Hertes suffisaunce" and "spleen or vapours" belong not only in different worlds but also in different minds. The lines of Dryden's portrait have their own virtues, but Chaucer's original picture has vanished.

Dryden asked for, and secured, Milton's permission to write a rhymed drama, *The Fall of Man*, based on *Paradise Lost*. But in "tagging" the blank verse of Milton's epic, he turns its asymmetric undulations into the formal figures of a rhymed minuet. The long flow and the echoing sounds of Satan's address to his lieutenant,

> If thou beest he; But O how fall'n! how chang'd
> From him, who in the happy Realms of Light
> Cloth'd with transcendent brightness didst outshine
> Myriads though bright . . . ,

Dryden reduces in scope and intensity to:

> If thou art he! But ah! how changed from him,
> Companion of my arms! how wan! how dim!

Satan's resolved acceptance of Hell

> Is this the Region, this the Soil, the Clime,
> Said then the lost Arch Angel, this the seat
> That we must change for Heav'n, this mournful gloom
> For that celestial light? Be it so . . .

becomes apt and pat and glib and relaxed as

> Is this the seat our conqueror has given?
> And this the climate we must change for heaven?
> These regions and this realm my wars have got;
> This mournful empire is the loser's lot.

After the boundless dignity and expanse of Milton's Hell, this creation of Dryden's appears to be some peaceful province in acrostic land. Even Dryden's famous phrase, "All the sad variety of hell," loses many of its poetic implications in its context, for there Dryden collapses into an epigram Milton's imaginings about the eternal restlessness of evil, the vast and various infernal climates, with their frozen and their fiery alps. For Dryden, Hell's variety is the mere difference between wet and dry:

> In liquid burnings, or on dry, to dwell,
> Is all the sad variety of hell.

Dryden's best efforts, therefore, cannot duplicate Chaucer's eye and heart. They cannot reduce Milton's infinity to ingenious argumentation within the narrow room of the couplet. The point is important, for it must never be forgotten that in final judgment a poem consists of its own words in their own order, and can never be equaled by its glosses, or translations, or criticisms, or prose paraphrases, or values determined by some standard outside itself.

Yet giving illustrations at such length would be laboring the case unnecessarily were it not for the other half of the argument: granted that Dryden's attempts are bad Chaucer and Milton, nevertheless they are fairly good Dryden. He was unable to reproduce his predecessors; he gives us, however, a good glimpse into his own mind and style, much as Van Gogh copying Delacroix or Rembrandt interests us because of the revelation of his own personality. Whatever Dryden touches he turns into Dryden. He has a genius for finding the words that express exactly his powerful if commonplace mind. His confident rhythms and his uninvolved syntax, his obvious balancing of one element against another, throw more light upon his personality than the incidents of his life. We may agree, therefore, with Bonamy Dobrée who says: "What Dryden aimed at was precision, finality of utterance, saying all that could be said upon a subject in the most concentrated way. His is the gift, or rather, one should say, the hard-won capacity, of expressing exactly what he means." But also we may still hold that Dryden's chief trait was a sensible clarity, and that therefore *exactly* what he meant must be expressed in general or typical statements and within the limits of a selected, purified vocabulary, comprehensible to all well-bred, rational, social human beings. Within this framework—given, in other words, Dryden's own mind and his own intentions—"The Cock and the Fox" and *The State of Innocence, and Fall of Man* are not bad translations so much as adequate original poems, the words of which exactly express Dryden's particular consciousness.

Successive critics have made Dryden an idol or a target. Much of this praise and blame is beside the point, since it disregards the central fact that each poet must faithfully express himself, not someone else. Unless there is no such thing as personality, therefore, the fixed style in poetry—*any* fixed style— is an illusion. It is as absurd to assume that all poets should write somewhat like Dryden as it is to argue that no one who writes at all like Dryden (including Dryden himself) is a poet.

No word is necessarily poetic or unpoetic in itself. Wordsworth's belief in the common language of common men no more affords a general rule for poetry than Dryden's search for elegance, clarity, and elevation. Both poets advocate a selective process in singling out the words that are to be built into a poem. This selective process, however, must always be done by the individual poet. He himself must be judge and jury. When he allows his vocabulary to be dictated by the great artists of the past, or by contemporary convention, he fails to express himself, and his verse grows vague.

Here, as example, is one of two stanzas published in the 1830's by Felicia Hemans, but in large part dictated, one might say, by Sidney and Shakespeare and the Elizabethans.

> Come to me, gentle Sleep!
> I pine, I pine for thee;
> Come with thy spells, the soft, the deep,
> And set my spirit free!

> Each lonely, burning thought
> In twilight languor steep—
> Come to the full heart, long o'erwrought,
> O gentle, gentle Sleep!

When this poem is compared with "The Indian Serenade" or "To Night" by Shelley—from whom also Mrs. Hemans so obviously borrowed—its lack of precision is evident. It expresses nothing, except perhaps the mistiness of the poet's mood and her wish that she might be expressive. The unconscious realization of an empty mind may account for the protestations and repetitions which attempt to convey certainty and conviction. But apart from the echoes of other poets, this short two-stanza lyric—I spare the reader the other stanza—has literally nothing more precise to say than: Come, come, come, come, come, gentle, gentle, gentle, gentle, gentle, gentle Sleep!

Even the great figures of the rational and social eighteenth century had championed, in their own ways, individual precision of speech. Pope attacks conventional diction when he levels his wit against the whole trite tribe of poetasters:

> While they ring round the same unvaried chimes,
> With sure returns of still expected rhymes;
> Where'er you find "the cooling western breeze,"
> In the next line, it "whispers through the trees":
> If crystal streams "with pleasing murmurs creep,"
> The reader's threatened (not in vain) with "sleep."

His famous definition of true wit in art—"What oft was thought, but ne'er so well expressed"—is a defense of exact expression, particularly when he further defines it as something "that gives us back the image of our mind."

Thomas Gray, in maintaining that "the language of the age is never the language of poetry," defends the enriching of poetry by foreign idioms and derivatives, even by words invented by the poet, and cites not only Shakespeare and Milton as "great creators this way" but even collects twenty examples of startling and unconventional words from Dryden himself, "whom everybody reckons a great master of our poetical tongue."

And Samuel Johnson, the last of the line, in spite of his belief in generalized precepts and his attacks on perverse originality, can lash out lustily against jejune thought and speech. His criticaster, Dick Minim, is the tiny creature he is because he cannot leave the well-traveled ruts of other people's opinions. And in his *Life of Milton*, however mistaken Johnson's own hostile criticism of "Lycidas" may be, it is based on rebellion against the form of the pastoral, which he finds "easy, vulgar, and therefore disgusting: whatever images it can supply, are long ago exhausted." Although Johnson may warn us against counting the streaks of the tulip, in the most memorable lines from his own poetry he speaks with his own accent:

> How, when competitors like these contend,
> Can surly virtue hope to fix a friend? . . .

> Fate never wounds more deep the generous heart,
> Than when a blockhead's insult points the dart . . .

> Yet hope not life from grief or danger free,
> Nor think the doom of man reversed for thee . . .

> There mark what ills the scholar's life assail,
> Toil, envy, want, the patron, and the gaol . . .

> With these celestial Wisdom calms the mind,
> And makes the happiness she does not find . . .

Johnson, no less than Dryden, shows that the idiosyncratic use of words need not depend upon startling particularized expressions. These famous couplets from *London* and *The Vanity of Human Wishes* are expressed as general moral precepts. Yet from them, and from the complete poems, emerges a definite personality of sullen power and melancholy nobility, so that once more surly virtue walks the city streets among the block-heads.

Oddly enough, one of the most original of English poets got his unmistakable effects without a wide departure from the conventional vocabulary of his day. William Blake, long before he created his private mythologies, was infusing new and mysterious significance into ordinary words and combinations of words. The tiger, the lamb, the worm, the sunflower, the chimney sweeper, take on extraordinary vitality when Blake sees them suddenly, arbitrarily, almost with explosive force, as symbols of his own fantastic inner world. A. E. Housman speaks of the mysterious grandeur of Blake's lines, their sug-gestiveness uncondensed into definite thought, the unreasonable excitement his words set up in some region deeper than the conscious mind. Such phrases superficially seem to belie the principle that the words of poetry must be exact. But Hous-man also says that Blake "gives us poetry neat," that he writes "pure and self-existent poetry." And this is true because Blake's phrases reproduce so precisely his own mind. In such a line as

> The lost traveller's dream under the hill,

to search for rational denotations is to destroy its poetic pre-cision. The process is comparable to condemning Blake's water colors and drawings because they are neither photographic nor academic. The line above becomes more precise when we see it as part of a meditation on the spirit ruling the world:

> thou art still
> The son of morn in weary night's decline,
> The lost traveller's dream under the hill.

And finally it gains a complete precision—though not one of its individual words is startling or unusual—when the whole poem including its title is remembered:

## TO THE ACCUSER WHO IS THE GOD
## OF THIS WORLD

Truly, my Satan, thou art but a dunce,
And dost not know the garment from the man.
Every harlot was a virgin once,
Nor canst thou ever change Kate into Nan.

Though thou art worship'd by the names divine
Of Jesus and Jehovah, thou art still
The son of morn in weary night's decline,
The lost traveller's dream under the hill.

Now it has become Blake, and Blake alone.

No one speaks with a more individual voice than Blake; yet out of their context his words are conventional, generalized, and far from arresting. Blake is a living argument, therefore, that the use of vague words, which he manages magnificently, must not be confused with the vague use of words. The language in the following stanza from "To the Muses" would be acceptable to the most rigid Augustan:

Whether in Heav'n ye wander fair,
Or the green corners of the earth,
Or the blue regions of the air
Where the melodious winds have birth.

Yet the verse is not dead, but vibrant, and in English poetry it could no longer be said that

The languid strings do scarcely move!
The sound is forc'd, the notes are few!

In new combinations of the old words, the village green echoes again, the Muses return to England, and once more she can listen to the voice of the Bard. And the voice speaks as naturally of love and simplicity—

So sung a little clod of clay,
Trodden with the cattle's feet—

as of fear and grandeur:

The eternal gates' terrific porter lifted the northern bar . . .

Why an ear, a whirlpool fierce to draw creations in?

In most of his poems Blake shaped the accepted "poetic diction" of the eighteenth century to the molds of his own original and frenetic thought. Nothing could be further from the famous principles laid down by his contemporary in the preface to *Lyrical Ballads*. Wordsworth regards the poet as not different in kind from the ordinary man: Blake was considered mad. Wordsworth attacks "what is usually called poetic diction": Blake as a rule adopts it. Wordsworth avows that he has taken pains to avoid "those arbitrary connections of feelings and ideas with particular words and phrases, from which no man can altogether protect himself": yet this phrase describes Blake's poetic process, and indeed, with certain modifications, the poetic process in general.

It is worth remembering that Wordsworth's observations were in the nature of a defense of his own revolutionary style, a preface to a particular volume of "ballads." Like Dryden and Milton before him, he tended to transform his particular practice into general rules. His instincts were sound: why should he have written "The Old Cumberland Beggar" or "The Idiot Boy" with the "gaudiness and inane phraseology of many modern writers"? During the year in which Wordsworth and Coleridge first were neighbors, Coleridge tells us, they talked frequently of "the power of exciting the sympathy of the reader by a faithful adherence to the truth of nature"—discussions which must have been on this question of exactness in poetry. And no observations on precision in poetic language are worth more meditation than Wordsworth's dictum that the words of a great poem appear to be inevitable, and Coleridge's deceivingly simple statement that prose is composed of good words in good order, poetry of the best words in the best order.

The combining of compatible words is the essence of style. Robert Bridges has given us the only law governing a poet's vocabulary: that the words should not clash with each other (unless, indeed, they are designed to clash, in the light of a larger harmonious effect). He cites as ridiculous out of its context the line from "Lycidas":

>And, O ye dolphins, waft the hapless youth!

Yet he praises it for its consonance in the elegy itself. Few lines could be found less poetic in themselves than:

>Is the night chilly and dark?
>The night is chilly, but not dark.

Near the start of Coleridge's "Christabel," however, they are in keeping with the rough, balladlike measure, and help set the mood. The reputation of many poets, indeed—Milton, Herrick, Landor, Housman, Frost—rests, more than one might believe on first thought, upon their unerring taste, their accurate selection of the proper words to support and strengthen each other. The hostile reader must go far in *Paradise Lost* to ferret out the bad puns of the rebellious angels during their momentary triumph in Heaven, or the elephant in Eden who "wreathed his lithe proboscis," or Eve preparing a repast in the Garden:

>No fear lest dinner cool.

Such lapses (and even here, only the last is strictly a lapse from a fitting vocabulary) constitute what Pope has called the art of sinking in poetry. When they occur, it is as if changeling words, excellent though they might be in some far distant home, had found the wrong cradle. Wordsworth, for instance, accurately sets the tone—in colloquial sentence structures as well as words—in the opening lines of "The Thorn":

>There is a thorn; it looks so old,
>In truth you'd find it hard to say,

> How it could ever have been young,
> It looks so old and grey.

But the vocabulary wavers when "overgrown" in stanza one becomes "o'ergrown" in stanza two, and such words and phrases as "manifest intent," "espy," "a beauteous heap," "hand of lady fair," and "beauteous dyes" begin to intrude.

Arnold with some justice criticized the early-nineteenth-century poets for parts that are superior to their wholes, for the purple patch, the fine phrase, the arresting word, which beggars the rest. There can be no exactness in disproportion or incongruity that is not deliberate. The words of a poem must get along with each other. Mere verbal consistency is in itself an indication of the certain vision, the exact expression, of some idea. And when such harmony is achieved, whether it be the tortuous elliptical thought of Shakespeare's later plays or the simplicity of Wordsworth's "The Solitary Reaper," the language of poetry has become exact.

In all probability this first quality of poetry is the most difficult of them all to analyze. May not a second-rate mind, for instance, express itself with extreme sensitivity? Perhaps. If it does, then the *expression* is poetic, though the *mind* expressed be negligible. Conversely, readers frequently feel, and writers frequently assert of their own experience, that powerful and profound thoughts have not found adequate words. When this happens—when a poem arouses an *accidental* sense of fumbling, strain, incompletion, blurred vision—then a successful poem has not been achieved. Exact expression is not the only requirement for poetry, but it is the first. It is the first discovery regarding the nature of poetry because the immediate impression which a poem makes is that of style. Style is the man; poetry is the speech of a man. It cannot be completely defined, but it can be immediately recognized—noble or trivial, gay or grave.

So far, we have followed the poet in his search for a language, not only the general language that fits his race or nation or locality, but the particular language that fits his own temperament. We have seen how the words of the poet strive for exactness in many ways: in imagery, in feeling, in thought, in rhythm, in the sound of the words themselves, and in compatibility deliberately achieved. And we have considered various examples of exactness in a brief chronological survey which spent most time on the period from Dryden to Wordsworth, when the language of poetry is often thought to be not individual, but conventional. Yet even in that period the poets express themselves with freshness and truth. Each by his own road arrives at that exactness of utterance which is of the nature of poetry.

This quality of exact expression may be found in poems which make no pretension to high seriousness. There is no uncertainty in the selected details, the suggested pictures of this short poem by William Allingham:

> Four ducks on a pond,
> A grass bank beyond,
> The blue sky of spring,
> White clouds on the wing;
>     What a little thing
> To remember for years—
> To remember with tears!

A scene forms, a mood is created, memory colors experience, bringing the significance of the past into the present. The *language* of poetry can do no more—has, indeed, no more to do. Even in such a small poem, language has achieved exactness.

# CHAPTER TWO

# POETRY
# IS INTENSE

EXACTNESS of language alone cannot produce poetry. The world we live in is "exact" in the sense that it is made up of precise particulars. Yet the world we live in is not the same as poetry, though poetry grows out of our experience in the world. The multitude of sense impressions that endlessly surround us, our very whims and daydreams—all these are unique in that they are as they are and cannot be otherwise: individual to each of us, continuously present, and unescapable. Fully to describe any moment of existence would require a small volume, if it could be done at all. Here as I write, I might begin with an ant on the flagstones, a little yellow flower among deep-red leaves, smoke from a cigarette thrown in the grass, sound of a rushing stream, of a car braking down the hill, of the beating of carpets. These details are fortuitous, and do not cover a thousandth part of the material now present to my senses. Furthermore, a complete catalogue of them would not be poetry. Its very length would destroy immediacy; its succession of unrelated details would kill the sense of unified existence.

Even if it were desirable, complete description of an instant is impossible. I cannot convey to you in words the shape, size, and position of every blade of grass before me. To say that the little yellow flower here is a fifth of an inch across would probably do less to reproduce it than to say that the ant on the flagstones could cover it. Finally, it is as hard to be impersonal as to be complete. The word "little" itself may begin to call up emotions, to interpret the yellow flower in human rather than botanical terms; and I would probably find it hard to pay as much attention to telephone wires as to the robin sitting on them, or to describe the bridge below me with as much care as I would the person crossing it.

We live in the midst of multiplicity as easily as we do because we have learned to disregard it. If we were perpetually and equally aware of all our sensations and emotions and thoughts, life would be unbearable. Yet the moments of awareness seem the important ones, so that Marcel Proust can construct his gigantic novel by using as keystones a few sharp small fragments of experience with all their implications and connections. These sudden moments, these poignant sights and sounds, these flashes of insight, are the stuff of poetry. For any act of artistic creation requires effort, and the monotony and continuity of the days, unless the sense of monotony and continuity itself becomes intense, do not afford sufficient impetus to induce anyone to describe them. Experience, therefore, of at least a certain degree of intensity, is the necessary soil out of which poetry grows. Such intense experience may cause anyone to write. If the writer is a poet, he will be able to convey his intensity, at least in part, to his readers. This is what interests us here, for the nature of poetry is less a question of the genesis of a poem than of its qualities, once it is created. This chapter, therefore, will be limited to the intensity which readers may feel for themselves as they experience actual poems.

Since the language of poetry is exact, how does intensity of experience usually find exact reflection in the poem? Let us look again at the little poem by Allingham at the conclusion of the previous chapter. What makes it effective? Surely not the inclusion of all details. The first four lines present a scene, the last three comment upon it. Yet we do not know whether the pond is on a farm or a village green, whether or not there are trees near it, whether the banks are steep or flat. Out of all points of the compass, the author looks in a particular direction; out of all seasons of the year, he has chosen spring. Out of all springs he remembers one particular spring, and one day, one hour, one moment of that spring. The scene and time are particular, then, but they are not described to the last detail. The comment, also, limits itself to suggestion. The spring day, though seemingly unimportant, remains in the author's memory, and remains with tears. The mood is particularized, but not accounted for. Do the tears rise from unhappy far-off things, or from remembrance of fortunate times in days of misery? It does not matter. The scene matters, and the mood matters. If they can be created with a minimum of detail and comment, their poignant immediacy will increase.

A strait economy of selection focuses the attention; many poets rely for their effects of intensity on the power of a single keen suggestion. A heavy weight of details does not usually increase the illusion of reality, but rather leads to bewilderment. Poems attempting to describe natural objects, a difficult task at all times, most frequently fail because they are overloaded with data. They stifle us under a ton of feathers. The *Gawain* poet devotes ninety-six lines to Gawain's accouterments and ninety-two to the Green Knight's first appearance; actually these detailed pictures are less effective than the few lines Chaucer devotes to his young squire, fresh as the month of May, with his long wide sleeves, embroidered like a meadow of fresh white and red flowers, or the knight with fustian tunic smudged with the rust of armor. Cowper's *The Task* is well named for the long stretches that present rural and domestic life in all its minute fragments: fewer parts would have made a greater whole. Because he will not omit any observed scene

that he remembers, Thomson makes *The Seasons* more an
exercise in persistence than a poem. Art errs in trying to reproduce everything at once. As an actual experience, Thomson's "Summer" necessarily falls short of summer itself; as a
work of art, on the other hand, because it attempts the literal
and the complete rather than the suggestive, it falls short of a
few verses from Theocritus:

Nay, but beneath this rock will I sing, with thee in mine arms,
and watch our flocks feeding together, and, before us, the Sicilian
sea.

Too long a catalogue risks being more like a telephone di-
rectory than a poem. Do Whitman's longest geographical lists
make America seem great, or merely overstuffed? Do the enu-
merations in Henley's and Auden's poems produce momentum
or flatness? And is not Homer's catalogue of the Grecian ships
in itself less akin to poetry than it is to Burke's *Peerage?* Medieval and Renaissance poets seem to have believed that they
could show that princes fall, that this world is woeful, that
saints are good, that magistrates need mirrors for their con-
duct, only by bringing all possible examples into their in-
terminable collections. But the human imagination, the instrument of poetry, works at its best in a powerful immediate leap
toward apprehension; it fails to assimilate countless disjoined
fragments calling for, without impelling, long-continued attention. The method of exhaustive realism, because it tires
and blunts the imagination, actually fails to achieve its end. A
certain selection of details is necessary in all literature. In poetry
this necessity is even more marked, for selection helps to re-
create the force of emotion or conviction that brings a poem
into being.

Although effects of concentration are present in all good
poetry, they are achieved in ways so various that we may
easily forget that the law of intensity is universally binding.
The simplest way, of course, is the centering upon a single detail, or a few related details. Here is a four-line poem which,

though anonymous, has already survived hundreds of years, simply because it is good:

> Western wind, when will thou blow,
>     The small rain down can rain?
> Christ, if my love were in my arms
>     And I in my bed again!

Two lines of description, two of emotion. And for description, the eliminating of everything but the wind and the rain. Then, for the sake of sharpness, the two adjectives—the "western" wind, the "small" rain. "Small" alone calls up the whole of England's climate and counties, and justifies in a word the sub-title given it in *The Oxford Book of English Verse:* "The Lover *in Winter* Plaineth for the *Spring.*" The words are exactly chosen, even to the sound of the *w*'s in the first line and the droning *n*'s in the second. But more than that, the poem has been made intense by a rigorous narrowing down to two simple elements.

An anthology of the best poetry descriptive of nature would show clearly that economy in choosing details most frequently meets with success. Spenser sometimes makes little etchings or pastels in a few lines, such as the first glimpse of Abessa in the *Faerie Queene:*

> at length she found the troden gras
> In which the tract of peoples footing was,
> Under the steepe foot of a mountaine hore;
> The same she followes, till at last she has
> A damzell spyde slow footing her before,
> That on her shoulders sad a pot of water bore.

And Wordsworth is a master of this effect, as if he could never call away his mind's eye from a solitary man or woman against a mournful landscape. His pictures are powerful because the figure is single, and the landscape dominated by one mood. The highland reaper, the old leech-gatherer of "Resolution and Independence," the idiot boy below the

moonlit waterfall, Martha Ray beside the stunted thorn tree
on the mountainside, Michael by the unfinished sheepfold—
all are variations upon a persistent single vision, done with a
few vividly realized details. In *The Prelude* it is the same: the
lone boy in the stolen boat below the one peak, the grave in the
mountain churchyard, the skater pausing as the frosty hills
wheel past, the old soldier resting by the wayside, the desolate
woman in flying cloak on the moor. Even his dreams here fall
into the pattern, as in that fantastic allegory of the Arab on
his camel against the vast expanse of desert and of flood. The
lyrics in lighter vein employ the same technique of concentration upon a single object. Complete landscapes expand from
a central focus, delicately, imperceptibly, so that innumerable
daffodils "beside the lake, beneath the trees," stretch "along
the margin of a bay." Beyond the small celandine, or the
cuckoo, or the butterfly, or the green linnet, or the daisy, rise
the shifting panoramas of English countrysides in shower and
sunshine. The selected foreground objects, the titular themes,
hold the pictures together and give them certainty.

Wordsworth was aware of what he was doing, and writes
with scorn of those who, trying to create a picture in words
by mere enumeration of details, fail to create the organic unity
which he himself felt in nature and which his friend Coleridge found in man's own consciousness. Even when, as in
Book XIV of *The Prelude*, his purpose necessitates a lengthy
description—the ascent of Snowdon on a misty night, the
breaking through clouds into the upper moonlight, the sea
of mist at his feet, the mountain tops like islands, and the
farthest clouds towering like the last promontories—Wordsworth works for intensity through coalescing all details into
the conception of a mighty being, much as "Tintern Abbey"
reaches its most intense moment in the exalted

> I have felt
> A presence that disturbs me with the joy
> Of elevated thoughts.

When, therefore, his grandest passages cannot be simplified by mere suppression of details, Wordsworth tends to compress the multiple details, once given, into a single final dominating mood.

The poems of A. E. Housman, almost without exception, select and arrange a few simple pictorial elements with the surety and skill of a Chinese painter. Opening *The Shropshire Lad* at random, we come across such lines as:

> Far in a western brookland
> That bred me long ago
> The poplars stand and tremble
> By pools I used to know.

This stanza has been stripped to essentials. Embroidery might have blurred it. The poet, then, keeps his eye on the object so intently that he discovers essential traits which a few words may reveal. To catalogue all the accidentals on the same level is not to see the object at all. The school of Imagist poets at their best, for instance, and the Chinese landscape poets before them, come close to high seriousness precisely because of a passionate selectivity. Their poems achieve tension through the disciplined exercise of the eye's unswerving scrutiny.

So far we have been considering the principle of selection, the commonest device for making poetry intense. The illustrations have been confined to the relatively simple transferring of sensory impressions. Yet the principle is no less effective in describing spirit and emotion. An emotion, in contrast with a "problem," for example, seems to the human mind simple. The stronger the emotion, the simpler it seems. Milton is speaking of the intensity of poetry, and hinting at means for achieving it, when he writes of poetry, distinguished from logic and rhetoric, as simple, sensuous, and passionate. An extended description destroys the passion by annihilating the simplicity.

On the other hand, an attempt to describe emotion too directly may end in disaster. Thus, Tennyson makes himself ridiculous when he opens his adolescent poem "Fatima" with the line:

O Love, Love, Love! O withering might!

The indirect expression of the same feeling which he achieves in "The Lady of Shalott" by telling a story with an ironic ending is incomparably more effective. Whatever the poet may feel, he usually produces effects of sentimentality and bathos when he states too directly, or too fully, or in too loud a voice, his emotions. "The least that I could say of my sufferings," writes Alfred de Musset, "would break my lyre as if it were a reed." But many poets, even the best, do not realize the delicacy of their instrument, do not always lead their skeptical readers into a new world by subtle indirections and gentle hints. The emotion may be genuine enough when Keats writes

I stood tiptoe upon a little hill,

or Shelley confides that

I shrieked, and clasped my hands in ecstasy,

or conservative Tennyson, distrusting the radical French, sneers at

The red fool-fury of the Seine.

But the technique is bad. It plunges direct to an extreme. It demands sympathy from the reader instead of arousing it.

Far better to suggest the emotion in terms not too direct, after a picture or situation has been presented so vividly that an intensity results which could not possibly be produced by such words as "grief," "joy," and "despair." Such suggestion of emotion *after* careful preparation is exemplified in Allingham's poem about the duck pond (quoted at the end of the first chapter), and also in the anonymous poem about the western wind and the small rain, and in Housman's poem on the pools and poplars:

> *Here* I lie down in London
> And turn to rest *alone*.

Wordsworth, in "She dwelt among the untrodden ways," describes his beloved Lucy, and only in the last lines cries out:

> But she is in her grave, and oh,
> The difference to me!

And Dante, before or after his sharply cut descriptions, often complains in true poet's fashion:

> *Ah, quanto a dir qual era è cosa dura!*

> How hard a thing it is to tell what it was!

These last two examples are vague in statement with a purposeful cunning. The poet *does* manage more than helpless ejaculations, he *does* explain, no matter how hard it may be. But he employs—all these poets had already employed in their poems—image and symbol and suggestion and indirection. Keats begins the "Ode to a Nightingale" with the commonplace statement, "My heart aches." Nobody would now believe him if he had not made the feeling more precise and intense through selected comparisons in the next lines, and even more poignant in the developed idea of the evanescence of ecstasy and beauty, an idea that fills the poem to the brim.

The simple and direct statement of an emotion, therefore, is in itself seldom poetic. It rises to poetry only after some process of selecting and combining elements has created in the mind of the reader something vivid and fresh. We seem to be approaching the consideration of metaphor in poetry. And, indeed, in actual practice metaphor is principally used to create the intensity that poetry cannot dispense with. What is the effect of metaphor, of simile, of using one thing in place of, or compared to, or in association with, another? The sun, let us say, has been seen thousands of times, and has been called by name. Suddenly someone sees it as the burning eye of God, or the chariot of the horses of the sky. The comparison compels us to consider it closely, to weigh both members of the equation, to see the sun afresh. Such new awareness is the invariable effect of a good metaphor. The metaphor itself implies a process of selecting certain qualities which exist both in the object and in that to which it is compared. It is as if two circles overlapped, and the area within their intersecting arcs were to be subjected to intent inspection. If I say, "Love is a dove," I am not referring to love as the creative principle of the universe, nor to its self-forgetfulness. Neither am I referring to the color of a dove's eyes, or the shape of its tracks in the dust. I am concentrating on the common qualities of the two. I probably have in mind a certain tenderness associated (though in different senses) with both, and possibly that power to soar in flight which made Plato compare the soul to a wing. A metaphor, in other words, centers the attention on certain aspects of a subject. The comparison need not be logical. Often a poet's most intense and effective coupling of spirit and matter comes purely through association. In as psychologically acute a portrayal of grief as has ever been written, Rossetti makes an ordinary word the symbol of his emotion because of an accidental happening:

> The wind flapped loose, the wind was still,
> Shaken out dead from tree and hill:
> I had walked on at the wind's will,—
> I sat now, for the wind was still.

> Between my knees my forehead was,—
> My lips, drawn in, said not Alas!
> My hair was over in the grass,
> My naked ears heard the day pass.

> My eyes, wide open, had the run
> Of some ten weeds to fix upon;
> Among those few, out of the sun,
> The woodspurge flowered, three cups in one.

From perfect grief there need not be
Wisdom or even memory:
One thing then learnt remains to me,—
The woodspurge has a cup of three.

It is worth noting that although the deepest concern of the poem is grief, the title is "The Woodspurge." And though that grief is imparted keenly, the method has been to narrate and describe: only the next to the last couplet looks at the emotion directly.

Metaphor, then, in its wider senses, succeeds because it avoids the attempt to cover a subject by complete and direct statement. It singles out certain aspects, which, thrown into relief, gain intensity because they *are* singled out, dwelt upon, and described through parallels. A spiritual state—a mood, an emotion, a vagrant thought or a conviction—eludes direct reproduction in words. Consequently the metaphors of poetry usually suggest the intangible in terms of the tangible, which can be more sharply described. The best comparisons are the subtlest, but their effect may be most easily caught, perhaps, in a series from *Sohrab and Rustum*, since Matthew Arnold is here consciously using the conventional extended "Homeric simile." In the first of these comparisons, he is describing the birthmark on Sohrab's arm, glowing against the pale flesh; Sohrab is dying, and to preserve the tone of pathos, the simile as it is elaborated still suggests delicacy and frailty:

Then, with weak hasty fingers, Sohrab loos'd
His belt, and near the shoulder bar'd his arm,
And shew'd a sign in faint vermilion points
Prick'd: as a cunning workman, in Pekin,
Pricks with vermilion some clear porcelain vase,
An emperor's gift—at early morn he paints,
And all day long, and, when night comes, the lamp
Lights up his studious forehead and thin hands:—
So delicately prick'd the sign appear'd . . .

The pathos of irretrievable time may be illuminated by a visual simile:

> tears gather'd in his eyes;
> For he remember'd his own early youth,
> And all its bounding rapture; as, at dawn,
> The Shepherd from his mountain lodge descries
> A far bright City, smitten by the sun,
> Through many rolling clouds;—so Rustum saw
> His youth.

The most extended simile in the poem is also the most complex in suggestion. Unknowingly Rustum has mortally wounded his own son. Here are spilled blood, and death, and tragic ignorance, and uneasy premonition, and parental love, and grief, and separation, and loneliness, and irrevocable loss. Arnold does not state them directly. Instead:

> As when some hunter in the spring hath found
> A breeding eagle sitting on her nest,
> Upon the craggy isle of a hill lake,
> And pierc'd her with an arrow as she rose,
> And follow'd her to find her where she fell
> Far off;—anon her mate comes winging back
> From hunting, and a great way off descries
> His huddling young left sole; at that, he checks
> His pinion, and with short uneasy sweeps
> Circles above his eyry, with loud screams
> Chiding his mate back to her nest; but she
> Lies dying, with the arrow in her side,
> In some far stony gorge out of his ken,
> A heap of fluttering feathers: never more
> Shall the lake glass her, flying over it;
> Never the black and dripping precipices
> Echo her stormy scream as she sails by:—
> As that poor bird flies home, nor knows his loss—
> So Rustum knew not his own loss, but stood
> Over his dying son, and knew him not.

Obviously, no complete correspondence exists here between Rustum and the eagle. But all the father's emotions have been touched upon in the imagined parallel. We enter by a comparison between two deaths; we close on the theme of ignorance of catastrophe. Possibly the simile is too long as it stands. Nevertheless, it achieves a much more moving effect than an equal number of lines could ever have achieved if they had been directly devoted to describing Rustum's emotions.

A simile may be so complex in itself as to suggest more than one relation to its subject. Milton, when he describes the fallen angels on the lake in Hell, enters upon a comparison thinking of their number; he returns to his narrative thinking of their confusion; within the simile itself he has made the transition:

> Thick as . . . scattered sedge
> Afloat, when with fierce Winds Orion arm'd
> Hath vext the Red-Sea Coast, whose waves orethrew
> Busiris and his Memphian Chivalrie,
> While with perfidious hatred they pursu'd
> The Sojourners of Goshen, who beheld
> From the safe shore their floating Carkases
> And broken Chariot Wheels, so *thick* bestrown
> *Abject* and *lost* lay these.

Often a metaphorical image is not only complex in its relations to the subject described, but is not even directly introduced as a comparison. "Sohrab and Rustum" ends with a magnificent passage—

> But the majestic River floated on—

in which the Oxus flows by moonlight through all its winding channels, loses itself in the reed beds, and finally, with stars above, opens out into the expanse of the tranquil Aral Sea. The passage is not formally a comparison, nor need it be; many of the best comparisons are beyond the province of the rhetorician. But one cannot read the lines about the Oxus and the Aral Sea without thoughts on life and eternity, without a feeling that ultimate calm may follow this momentary turbulence and bewilderment. The inference is not logical. The river is at once individual human life, tangled among the beds of sand, and general human life, flowing on indifferent to particular catastrophes. Yet by means of a carefully chosen picture and its implied comparisons, Arnold has won an intensity that the most serious direct moral preachment could never convey.

If a comparison can be more convincing than a flat statement, then, indeed, an implied metaphor may be more subtly powerful than a direct metaphor. Certainly poets use the veiled approach frequently enough; and if poetic imagination consists in seeing likenesses between things apparently unlike, then the reader of poetry, if he analyzes the reasons for the intensity of any poem, will find it often lies in comparisons that are never directly stated. The interest of Browning's "My Last Duchess" resides in the contest of wills between the proud, possessive Duke of Ferrara and his beautiful young wife. Unable to dominate her fully while she is alive, he has her put out of the way, and coolly adds her portrait to his collection. As Ferrara and a guest descend the staircase, the Duke casually points at a statue:

> Notice Neptune, though,
> Taming a sea-horse, thought a rarity,
> Which Claus of Innsbruck cast in bronze for me.

In these final lines the whole poem is crystallized and compressed into a single image. The effect is comparable to that secured by adding a brief moral at the end of a fable, but is more subtle and convincing. That Browning used such implied comparisons consciously is shown by the end of the companion piece "Count Gismond," which tells how the chivalric Count Gismond strikes down and kills Count Gauthier, who has traduced a lady's honor. The lady, now Gismond's wife, interrupts her narrative in the final lines:

> Gismond here?
> And have you brought my tercel back?
> I just was telling Adela
> How many birds it struck since May.

Careful selection of details is the commonest means of working toward intensity. Metaphor, direct or implied, is a special form of selection, tending to give weight or clarity or heightened feeling to what it touches upon. Yet there are other ways of gaining intensity. One of them is compression, of language, of thought, or of both.

John Donne is the first great English poet consistently to get intensity through grammatical ellipsis. Time, from Noah to the Last Judgment, is compressed into his line:

> All whom the Flood did, and fire shall, o'erthrow.

Again, Donne summarizes the Pythagorean and relativistic philosophy of *The Progress of the Soul* by similar compression:

> There's nothing simply good, nor ill alone,
> Of every quality comparison
> The only measure is, and judge, opinion.

Such sentences as these from Donne almost require expansion to clear up the sequence of thought. And, in Milton as in Donne, the compression natural to inflected Latin has come over into English style. When Milton desires effects of weight and terseness, he relies on Latin constructions and meanings:

> Fall'n Cherub, to be weak is miserable
> Doing or Suffering.

Donne frequently constructs his verses so that the parts of the sentence depend upon the last word for their meaning. Again ellipsis gives intensity to the climactic syllables:

> What if this present, were the world's last, *night?*

> Sleeps she a thousand, then peeps up one *year?*

'Cause I did suffer, I must suffer, *pain*.

He faith in some, envy in some *begat*,
For, what weak spirits admire, ambitious, *hate*.

Even more powerful effects he builds by delaying the completion of the thought while he crowds together compound subjects or verbs:

All whom war, dearth, age, agues, tyrannies,
Despair, law, chance, hath slain.

That I may rise, and stand, o'erthrow me, and bend
Your force, to break, blow, burn and make me new.

Suspense here has created momentum.

Donne's damming up of strong words until they break through in a rush of thought is a favorite trick of Gerard Manley Hopkins:

And, eyes, heart, what looks, what lips yet gave you a
Rapturous love's greeting of realer, of rounder replies?

Hopkins gives great weight to nouns by piling up modifying phrases before them in Germanic fashion. He wastes no connectives. A falcon drawn toward, and etched against, the mottled sky of morning becomes a "dapple-dawn-drawn falcon." To describe a fighter for Christianity in modern times, who is also God's especially chosen instrument, he writes, as if it were a cumulative compound noun:

An our day's God's own Galahad.

And since the phrase "whose least quickenings lift me" contains a final syllable with a falling rather than a "lifting" rhythm, he distorts the sentence order to give each word intensity in accent:

Whose least me quickenings lift.

No one has taken more pains than Hopkins to make his lines nervous by the omission of all somnolent syllables:

Lów-látched in léaf-líght hóusel his tóo húge Gódhéad.

In his effort to get at quintessences, he has squeezed out the lifeless articles and connectives. To express the idea, in "The Windhover," that mere plodding effort causes a plow to shine in its progress down a furrow, he writes:

shéer plód mákes plów dówn síllion
Shíne,

where pronunciation, metrical pattern, and rhetorical accent make every syllable taut, except the last one in "sillion," which rhymes with "billion"—intense because of hyperbole—and "vermilion"—intense in color. Such striving for compression by omitting commonplace words may make a passage enigmatic and not always successful.

Yet Hopkins, however we rate his achievement, has a conscious theory, based on rhythm and grammar, and consistently practiced, for increasing intensity. Few readers put down his work without realizing the vigor of his verse.

Several modern poets, notably W. H. Auden, employ grammatical ellipsis as Hopkins uses it. Sometimes this is done to secure ambiguity for purposes not pertinent to this chapter. But often the ellipsis increases the intensity. Our minds are mesmerized away from the logical progression of thought which complete grammatical structures foster, to a concentrated focusing upon a pure, timeless, static feeling, an emotion undivided and immovable:

> In groups forgetting the gun in the drawer
> Need pray for no pardon, are proud till recalled
> By music on water
> To lack of stature
> Saying Alas
> To less and less.

Apart from all such grammatical devices of compression, intensity in poetry may be created by structures and expres-

sions that appear impulsive and unlabored. Spontaneous expression seems more passionate than careful second thoughts.
And language may be manipulated to give the illusion of first
fine careless raptures. Browning's own roughness and obscurity
are tied up with his freshness, his habit of striking out his ideas
impromptu and rarely bothering to revise them. His paren-
theses, his quick shifts and breaks in thought, his sudden
startling associations, his questions and ejaculations—all these
point toward immediacy and spontaneity in composition.
Donne gains similar effects by abrupt openings and transitions,
and by wrenching the meter to fit the accents of common
speech, so that many of his verses possess the emphasis and
changes in pitch of a living voice. Hopkins also works for freshness by leaving corrections or expansions within the finished
poem itself, which give the impression of immediate speech:

> A bugler boy from barrack (it is over the hill
> There)—boy bugler, born, he tells me, of Irish •
>   Mother to an English sire (he
> Shares their best gifts surely, fall how things will).

Or:

> No, I'll not, carrion comfort, Despair, not feast on thee.

To Browning spontaneity was natural; Hopkins deliberately
feigned it. Conscious or unconscious, however, it is achieved
through tricks of language, and in any poem it results in the
intensity of the immediate.

Let us turn from the word to the idea. Tricks in thought no
less than grammatical and rhetorical devices may create intensity. Compression in language accompanies, or fosters, compression in thought. And compressed thought creates intensity.
Many of Donne's lines already quoted illustrate this, and there
is little need to make a garland of pithy verses and apothegms.
But we might pause a while to consider two ways of com-
pressing thought: the reliance upon quoted passages or familiar

ideas from other authors; and the omission of connecting links, so that apparent incongruities are placed side by side.

A few words may call up their original context in some well-known work, and may suggest a large body of experience; whenever this occurs, the effect of quotations or allusions is obviously powerful. Dante, a magician in securing intensity through compression, scatters the great hymns and psalms and canticles of the Church throughout the "Purgatorio" and the "Paradiso." Usually he gives no more than the opening Latin words, but his design is to call up the entire earlier work by citing a few words from it—the entire work in its relation through centuries to the Christian world.

On a smaller scale G. K. Chesterton secures this same effect in his little four-stanza poem "The Donkey." Here the donkey, who is speaking, is aware that he is a fantastic creature, a monster with absurd voice and ears, a devil's parody, a tattered outlaw of the earth. Yet in spite of the world's derision, he has his secret, which in the last stanza he imparts:

> Fools! For I also had my hour;
>   One far fierce hour and sweet:
> There was a shout about my ears,
>   And palms before my feet.

This brief and effective poem gains all its intensity from its readers' associating the final stanza with Christ's entrance into Jerusalem on Palm Sunday, although that event is never mentioned. We might say without exaggeration that "The Donkey" stands upon the Four Gospels. The more we read, the more we come to realize that the intense richness of modern poems comes from the fertile ground of earlier literatures and cultures and poems and poets in which they are nourished.

In a sense, the use of well-known figures from myth or history is a species of "quotation," taking advantage of earlier thought and association to increase the intensity of a single word or symbol. As the body of English literature grows, and as knowledge of that literature can be more and more assumed, compression by means of quotation—granted that the overtones and implications will be understood—becomes increasingly effective. Who can write a poem today about daffodils without raising the ghosts of Herrick and Wordsworth? A late long poem by W. H. Auden, "The Sea and the Mirror," acknowledges such reliance directly in its subtitle: "A Commentary on Shakespeare's *The Tempest*." When T. S. Eliot and Delmore Schwartz write of Coriolanus, they do not disregard Plutarch and Shakespeare: they assume a knowledge of their predecessors in calculating their effects. More than any recent writer, T. S. Eliot has attempted to secure compression and intensity through quotation and allusion, from such a simple line as Prufrock's

> I am not Prince Hamlet, nor was meant to be

to the succession of esoteric quotations that ends *The Waste Land*, or the complicated epigraph to "Burbank with a Baedeker, Bleistein with a Cigar." And in theory, at least, to introduce into a poem a single, selected, representative phrase which will invoke memories of a whole tragedy or epic or philosophy is a magnificent way to give weight and richness and emotional intensity to that poem.

T. S. Eliot's consistent practice has also made it easier for modern readers to respond to intensity secured through omission of links between thoughts. The very title "Sweeney among the Nightingales" juxtaposes symbols of animality and conventional beauty. The poem presents a modern tavern scene, murderous, fear-struck, sensual, and sordid. A number of sinister figures move mysteriously against an unspecified background. It ends:

> The nightingales are singing near
> The Convent of the Sacred Heart,
>
> And sang within the bloody wood
> When Agamemnon cried aloud,

> And let their liquid siftings fall
> To stain the stiff dishonoured shroud.

Everything here is contrast: "Are singing" and "sang," murderous blood and the sacred heart, the tavern of earlier stanzas and the convent, the loud cry and the shroud, the bird song and the bird droppings. And without explicit comment or comparison, into the main narrative of betrayal by the brute lust of the world, Eliot has inserted suggestions of the story of Christ's bloody sacrifice, of Agamemnon and Clytemnestra, of Tereus and Philomel. For, in Eliot's poetry, the nightingale itself is more than the inviolable voice of beauty singing in a sylvan scene; she is the Grecian woman

> by the barbarous king
> So rudely forced.

Eliot's symbols gain intensity, then, by their very ambiguity and complexity.

Whether the illustrations parallel, or contrast with, the main theme, they serve to intensify it—the more so because Eliot will not set down his thought flatly. His method is comparable to *pointillisme* in painting, which proceeds on the theory that juxtaposed points of color on a canvas will coalesce *within the mind of the beholder* to give an effect of vibrancy impossible in monotone surfaces. Similarly, Eliot expects to keep his poem alive by compelling the reader to think *for himself* of possible relationships and connections between its parts. In "Sweeney among the Nightingales" Eliot has not made his story easy. The course of the action is "indistinct," "veiled," although the central emotions of lust and suspicion and impending violence are intensely realized. But the reader himself must place the characters—Sweeney, the lady in the Spanish cape, Rachel *née* Rabinovitch, the silent man in brown, the host conversing with someone indistinct—and this placing of the characters in what seems to the reader a possible relationship helps to give the poem its life. Nor can he settle down with a complacent feeling that the poem is designed to contrast the sordid modern world with ancient splendor. For there is *present* beauty in the branches of wistaria, and dignity and somber tragedy even today in such mysterious symbols as "Death and the Raven," "Gloomy Orion." And there is horror in the picture of the past: in the crucifixion of Christ, the murder of Agamemnon. Actually, the opposing poles, in Eliot's vision both of ancient and of modern times, are superficial beauty and underlying baseness. But the contrasts are not formally stated; they are implied by means of juxtaposed images.

Violent contrasts may surprise the reader into awareness. Shock technique, in order to jolt us into vivid realization, lies back of such rebellions against the conventional as Shakespeare's sonnet

> My mistress' eyes are nothing like the sun

and Donne's

> Get with child a mandrake root

and Eliot's

> Garlic and sapphires in the mud.

The danger is that instead of coalescing into a comprehensible pattern, the disparate fragments will remain a crazy quilt. At its best, however, such contrast stabs our spirits broad awake. The greater and more abrupt the contrast, the more intense the effect of the fused parts.

Shakespeare is forever using the device. Contrasted characters, contrasted modes of speech, are made more impressive by their mere contiguity. This placing together of dissimilars without comment is in effect a compression, an ellipsis, of thought. Juliet and the Nurse are each outlined more sharply by the presence and speech of the other. Even within a single speech or scene, Shakespeare moves without transition from one plane to another. The great scenes of the last two acts of

*Antony and Cleopatra* shuttle continually between realistic detail and superhuman passion. And Lear's heart-shattering

> Thou'lt come no more,
> Never, never, never, never, never!

is immediately followed by his request:

> Pray you undo this button. Thank you, sir.

The contrast between the two planes, of anguish and of everyday action, destroys neither of them. It creates, instead, the certainty that such suffering is happening to an actual man, at the same time that it intensifies the suffering by showing the great gap between it and the common world. The mixture of the genres in Shakespeare is built on the belief that the contrasting mood of comedy will intensify the effect of the serious scenes. It is a device for securing intensity on the grand scale. Comic relief in Shakespeare should not mean relief from scenes of tension; it should mean throwing the scenes of tension into even bolder and sharper relief by means of contrast.

Directly opposed to the technique of compression and contrast as a device for securing intensity is the technique of accumulation, of repetition. It proceeds on the theory that nothing is blacker than black except more black, and that long dwelling upon a theme may produce intensity through sheer momentum. In poetry thematic material may be expanded as gradually, diversely, and successfully as motifs in symphonic music. The narrative flow of the first book of *Paradise Lost* is held up from time to time by similes which make us pause to consider closely what is being described. The similes in the opening section fall principally into two classes, one emphasizing the tremendous size of the fallen angels, the other their tremendous number. The two conceptions play into each other to increase the sense of Hell's infinity. A single comparison for size or number should be sufficient to present the point rationally. But not emotionally, not imaginatively. Milton groups his similes in repeated surges, until if we are not overwhelmed by the first waves, the third wave sweeps us away. Finally, through some one of the many comparisons, we sense Milton's own unrivaled vision of space. If we are not caught by Satan's bulk on the flood, floating like a whale which mariners mistake for an island, we are caught by his spear, taller than the tallest mast of any flagship, or by his shield, bigger than the full moon, even bigger than the moon seen through a telescope. If we fail to grasp the number of the gigantic angels lying on the lake, thick as autumnal leaves on a forest brook, or as the sedgy reeds of the whole Red Sea, then we see them thick as locusts when they fly toward the land, or, when they light on the burning soil, numberless as all the barbarian hordes that ever the populous North poured down on the Mediterranean. The mere delaying over these conceptions, presenting them again and again in new images, intensifies them by a kind of geometrical progression. We are held in a timeless world by the contemplation of some selected theme.

When Milton describes Paradise in Book IV, the grouped suggestions of other Edens rise in fountains:

> Not that faire field
> Of Enna, where Proserpin gathring flours
> Her self a fairer Floure by gloomie Dis
> Was gatherd, which cost Ceres all that pain
> To seek her through the world; nor that sweet **Grove**
> Of Daphne by Orontes, and th' inspir'd
> Castalian Spring might with this Paradise
> Of Eden strive; nor that Nyseian Ile
> Girt with the River Triton, where old Cham,
> Whom Gentiles Ammon call and Libyan Jove,
> Hid Amalthea and her Florid Son
> Young Bacchus from his Stepdame Rhea's eye;
> Nor where Abassin Kings their issue Guard,
> Mount Amara, though this by som suppos'd
> True Paradise under the Ethiop Line

By Nilus head, enclos'd with shining Rock,
A whole dayes journey high, but wide remote
From this Assyrian Garden.

The beauty of Paradise has been made more intense by leisurely, harmonious comparisons. After such delay we return to the main narrative almost with reluctance. Milton is fully aware of the richness that comes from the long-drawn-out dwelling upon a theme. The bare structure of *Paradise Regained* is made sumptuous for a time by the ample descriptions of Roman and Greek civilization; and, at the very end of Samson Agonistes, the severe, unornamented style bursts into a triple simile—"as an ev'ning Dragon," "as an Eagle," "like that self-begott'n bird in the Arabian woods"—to intensify Samson's triumph.

Shakespeare's method of lingering over an important theme until it assumes intensity does not display the obvious consistency of Milton's. Yet Shakespeare uses it so frequently that it can hardly have been unconscious. It might be called the method of varied reiteration. He marshals any phrases, any images, drawn from any of the fields of experience, that will illuminate his theme. As Juliet contemplates drinking the sleeping potion, all words that can conjure up the macabre, uncertain horror of the grave throng round to produce a glaring intensity:

Shall I not then be *stifled* in the *vault*,
To whose *foul* mouth *no healthsome* air breathes in,
And there *die strangled* ere my Romeo comes?
Or, *if* I live, is it not very like
The *horrible* conceit of *death* and *night*,
Together with the *terror* of the place—
As in a *vault*, an *ancient* receptacle
Where for this *many hundred years* the *bones*
Of all my *buried ancestors* are pack'd;
Where *bloody* Tybalt, yet but green in earth,
Lies *fest'ring* in his *shroud;* where, as they say,
At some hours in the *night spirits* resort—

*Alack, alack, is it not like* that I
So early waking—what with *loathsome smells*,
And *shrieks* like *mandrakes torn* out of the earth,
That living mortals, hearing them, run *mad*—
O, *if* I wake, shall I not be *distraught*,
Environed with all these *hideous fears*,
And *madly* play with my *forefathers' joints*,
And pluck the *mangled* Tybalt from his *shroud*,
And, in this *rage*, with some great *kinsman's bone*
As with a *club* dash out my *desp'rate* brains?

The whirling, flashing images gain intensity from the sheer liberality of the hand that flings them forth. They gain also from the contrasting ideas of health and air and greenness and early waking and life. In later plays Shakespeare moves so easily through all experience that there is nothing in the world he may not use in illustration.

Keats, like Shakespeare, clusters images and synonyms around a theme. His poems gain their intensity of sensation and feeling through the richness and number of associations woven into their heavy textures. The first stanza of the "Ode to Autumn" repeats the idea of fecundity in twenty ways. The second stanza presents the figure of Autumn against a succession of landscapes. The third collects and arranges the sounds and songs of the season. Such a multitude of details would sink the thirty-line poem, were the stanzas not organized, sonata-like, into the triple divisions of touch, sight, and sound, dominated by the single autumnal theme. Images and adjectives press as close together in the "Ode on Melancholy," and again thematic organization saves it from chaos. The first stanza summons up all the conventional symbols and trappings associated with melancholy. In contrast, the second stanza marshals examples of ecstatic joy in the presence of beauty. The third stanza, again through many images, presents the conclusion that melancholy dwells not in unrelieved gloom, but in the poignant realization that joy and beauty must pass.

The intensity of Keats's odes comes from the reader's gradual realization that all the rich details are related to a unified central emotion which slowly emerges. Such an organic structure is probably the most satisfying in the end. But the central theme, of course, may be stated at the start, and given power by expanding illustrations. This is the young Shakespeare's method in the direct opening of his eighteenth sonnet:

> Shall I compare thee to a summer's day?

And this is also Elizabeth Barrett Browning's when she writes,

> How do I love thee?   ·

and answers in the rest of the sonnet by counting the ways, which, to be precise about it, are eight in number. Obviously, the effect of the sonnet is not that a catalogue has been made, but that a single emotion has been stamped as precious by variations remembered and recounted with love and joy.

Mrs. Browning has built her sonnet around a question. Although her answers are many, the mood is unquestioning. John Donne develops many of his poems in the form of questions, but his are not always rhetorical. Instead of collecting images around a set theme, he collects hypotheses. The result is intensity, for he has held our minds to a certain question, compelling us to see it from all sides, and to scrutinize all possible answers. His fondness for paradox springs from this same passionate desire to focus the intellect upon some riddle. The paradox shocks us into attention, for how can two opposed answers to the same question be true? Deeper realization of religious faith comes from trying to understand such lines as:

> . . . I,
> Except you enthrall me, never shall be free,
> Nor ever chaste, except you ravish me.

or:

> . . . thy mild Dove,
> Who is most true, and pleasing to thee, then
> When she is embrac'd and open to most men.

These paradoxes are simple, since their point comes from the violent opposition between flesh and spirit. Yet he can build a train of more subtle paradoxes into a sonnet, as in that on the "Annunciation." He addresses the Virgin:

> Ere by the spheres time was created, thou
> Wast in His mind, who is thy Son, and Brother;
> Whom thou conceiv'st, conceiv'd; yea thou art now
> Thy Maker's maker, and thy Father's mother;
> Thou hast light in dark; and shutt'st in little room
> Immensity . . .

Here the effect of repeated impossibilities is to compel speculation on the mysteries of religion. Intensity does not spring from certainty alone. Doubt can be anguished, and Donne can produce profound realization of human blindness by multiplying uncertainties.

Donne's love lyrics, as well as his religious poems, gain sharpness from conflicting and cumulative doubts. Donne can develop a strict argument: "The Extasie" and "A Valediction Forbidding Mourning" are direct and full enough. But he prefers mutually destructive alternatives, which, presented in swift succession, startle us into the realization of the uneasiness of intense passion. All incompatibles must be heaped together as trophies to the ambiguity of his restless mind. When Donne is not building poems on *ifs*, he is juggling with *yets*, *ors*, and *buts*. "The Flea," "The Broken Heart," "The Dream," "The Blossom," "Lovers' Infiniteness" speculate on all the situations which Donne's fertile brain can devise as germane to their themes. "The Funeral," relatively simple, gains its poignancy because Donne cannot decide whether a lock of hair has been given him out of love or pride. Just when he has convinced himself that his mistress meant it to give him strength and governance, he veers to:

> except she meant that I
> By this should know my pain,
> As prisoners then are manacled, when they're condemn'd to die.

He sees himself as love's martyr, recognizes his humility in worshiping the lock of hair, yet in the succeeding lines, in a spirit of defiance, declares:

. . . since you would save none of me, I bury some of you.

The poem has not lost intensity simply because Donne may say of his mistress' gift: "Whate'er she meant by it!"

Donne, of course, is unique. Few men find uncertainty an emotion positive enough to produce poetry. And few have the agile intellect that can develop a theme by means of incompatible ruminations. Yet in his particular manner, even Donne illustrates the general rule that essentially the poetic mood is not so much argumentative as it is emotional, "moody." It does not move through time, but holds time in suspense. Once an emotion has been established, it may be intensified merely by dwelling upon it, much as prolonged contemplation of a crystal ball may lead to a hypnotic state. Obviously the creation of such a mood is far different from the medieval collecting of *exempla* to illustrate a point. The effects stem more from music than from logic.

Of all English poets, Spenser is the most musical. I am not speaking now of his rhythms and the sound of his words, but of his amplifications and variations of a theme, which are comparable only to the development of a movement in music. His "linkèd sweetness long drawn out" in the *Faerie Queene* might lead one to expect verbosity and a resulting flat or unstrung verse. That is not Spenser's effect. The plots of the cantos of the *Faerie Queene* wander more widely and are less important than in most long narrative poems, such as *Troilus and Criseyde* and *Paradise Lost*—although, indeed, in any great narrative poem, the *poetry* does not reside in the bare story. Spenser is less interested in the story than in the moods and tricks and meditations of man's heart, which he transmutes into the phantasms of the *Faerie Queene*. Each book is a separate symphony. No one would scorn Beethoven because he repeats in uncounted echoes the four-note opening theme of the Fifth Symphony; similarly Spenser is not redundant, but is seeking the powerful mesmeric effects of music in building from line to stanza to canto to book without departing from his themes. The stories can hardly be said to progress or reach conclusions, for the characters are only tapestry figures from a fairy kingdom: a dream unfolds, shifts, and returns, through the slow breathings of Spenser's stanzas. Spenser does not create suspense: he compels us, through his deliberate meandering, to breathe an alien air until it has become familiar. And the intensity of this strange world Spenser has created through the slow mill-wheel revolutions of his stanzas. We as readers are brought back with a shock when Una strikes the knife from the hands of the Red Cross Knight, for the voice of Despair has lulled us through so many stanzas that we have accepted his insidious whisperings. So also the Bower of Bliss is spun so cunningly, with such deliberation and patience, that we are caught in its web, as if delights and beauties would never cease; after such luxuries, we wake painfully—Spenser himself seems to—when in a few rude lines Guyon shatters the Bower. The Cave of Mammon, the Garden of Adonis, the Palace of Busirane, the betrothal of Una, the sea journey of Guyon—all are hallucinations that hold us to a mood or a sensation. If the mood is pleasant, lingering over it is its own justification—even if it be no more than the smooth sliding of water, cool liquidity, which fascinates Spenser through 405 lines as he describes with endless figures and glints and flowings the wedding of the Thames and the Medway. Spenser may be a dangerous model, but his own practice affords an example, the best in English, of intensity gained by multiple variations upon a theme.

Repetition, then, may be a means to heighten emotion in poetry. It may take the form of clustered illustrations, as in Keats and Milton, or of grouped near-synonyms, as in Shakespeare, or of related ideas, as in Donne, or of leisurely embellishments of a theme, as in Spenser. These are all repetition with variations.

The repetitions of the same words can also increase intensity. The refrains of ballads give unified emotion to fast-moving narrative, thereby transforming sensational stories into poems. This incantatory power is obvious, from Shakespeare's

> With hey, ho, the wind and the rain

to the

> He was her man
> And he done her wrong

of "Frankie and Johnnie." But repeated words, even when they do not come at regular intervals, can make a snowball into an avalanche. In Shakespeare such repetitions vary from Iago's cynical reiteration, "Put money in thy purse," to Ulysses' mellow meditations on "degree." More subtle effects are secured in the way the "hands" of Adam and Eve, twined or separate, figure recurrently in *Paradise Lost;* or in the use Shakespeare makes of the repeated words "true" and "noble" in his later plays. Many poets, indeed, return to certain words so frequently that the words might serve as *cartes d'identité*. But here we are dealing not so much with words repeated in a single poem as in the whole body of a poet's work, and that takes us beyond our present chapter.

Not only narrative poems, but reflective and meditative poems, may have an intensity of their own. This is no paradox: serious or exalted meditation on any subject demands a certain tension—concentration on difficult thought, excitement in new combinations of ideas and discoveries, annoyance or exultation as we lose for a moment, or hear clearly, some whispered intuition. Wordsworth in *The Prelude*, Lucretius in his *On the Nature of Things*, afford proof that meditation need not result in flaccidity or somnolence. A good reflective poem possesses in some measure high seriousness. And what does "high" mean if not intense? Awareness, alertness, bold new thought, a wider consciousness—these are the signs of intensity in meditative poetry.

Intensity, then—intensity in some form—is a necessary element in poetry. Exactness is not enough. Quite possibly—are there not examples?—a man might put down on paper words so weak and jumbled and platitudinous as to reflect exactly the torpor and incoherence and automatism of his own mind. But the quotidian dullness of a deep-sea fish, if reproduced with absolute accuracy, would not be poetic. Some heightening of emotion is necessary. And although the methods of achieving this are almost as numerous as the poets themselves, although they may vary from compression to expansion, from omission of detail to repetition, from shock to incantation, from contrast to consonance, nevertheless the result is the same throughout the long company of poets, and the exact expression of their pens becomes poetry because it has also taken on intensity.

# CHAPTER THREE

# POETRY
# IS SIGNIFICANT

BENDING above her bed, looking upon his wife by a single flame before he sacrifices her life to her honor, Othello says:

> Put out the light, and then put out the light.

The line is famous. But it is not famous for its simple words or its seeming redundance. It is famous for its meaning. "And then put out the light" obviously means: "Then kill Desdemona." But beyond this rough equivalent are many implications, nobler and more delicately precise. The image of light is expanded through the whole speech; the word itself occurs five times in seven lines. To the Moor, the material illumination of the torch or candle or rushlight in the bedchamber seems rare enough to be called a "flaming minister" (even here it waits upon Desdemona); yet in comparison with the "cunning'st pattern of excelling nature," it is nothing. Once the light of her life is quenched, Othello ruminates,

> I know not where is that Promethean heat
> That can thy light relume.

The adjective suggests the daring of Prometheus—the plucking of fire from the sun—as well as his pity for mankind. The

light has become infinitely precious: it is beauty and life and
love in one superlative woman, white as snow, sweet as a rose.
Yet vital beauty and warmth must be sacrificed to ideals of
chastity and justice, even while Othello weeps for it.

> This sorrow's heavenly;
> It strikes where it doth love.

As the passage develops, the significance of "then put out the
light" grows clearer and more complete. Ultimately, the line
is notable, not because of the exactness of expression (although
the image of light is perfectly chosen and expanded), nor because of the intensity of the emotion (although words could
not do more to touch the heart), but because of the *significance*
of the emotion expressed. Great spiritual forces are in conflict;
it is blindness to pass them by, for Shakespeare sees them so
clearly that he has conceptualized them in the scene: chastity,
deceit, repentance, justice, love, cruelty, sanctity, grace, mercy,
fear, guilt, sacrifice. Their interplay, not as abstract forces, but
within individuals in a specific situation, creates the precision
and intensity of poetry. But the final worth, the deepest joy the
line conveys, comes from the nobility of the thought itself
in its full context, when we see melodrama transformed into
tragedy, and revenge, passion, jealousy sublimated into an act
of holiness and purification. The line

> O Desdemona! Desdemona! dead!

contains emotion as intense as

> Put out the light, and then put out the light.

But comparable as the two lines are in technique and in strength
of feeling, the second—in its full context—is incomparably
greater poetry because the thought back of it is of more worth
to human life.

Such an argument, let us grant at once, links morality and
art. I do not see how they can be separated in experience, no

matter what distinctions may be made in theory. The argument makes poetry didactic. So it is. The belief that art and ethics depend upon each other runs counter to much recent thought and strikes at the autonomy of esthetics, that latest born of all the children of philosophy. We must therefore not accept this conclusion too hastily, but examine its foundations in the history of poetry and poetic theory. We must define our terms *significant* and *moral* if we are to reach any agreement on the moral aspect of poetry, or on the proposition that a poet's measure is to be found not only in his technique, or in the intensity with which he conveys his personal experience, but also in the value to the world at large of the experience he conveys.

Briefly, the argument of this chapter runs:

A thing is significant if it is understandable. All poets wish to make themselves understood. The poet "understands" in a distinctive manner: he contemplates the world (and is therefore not primarily a man of action) through his own eyes (and is therefore not an impersonal scientist). Since his outlook is individual and contemplative, he will not often directly assert universal dogmas of practical action. But this does not mean that because his manner of thinking is personal rather than impersonal, localized rather than abstract, his poetry lacks moral significance. The poet deals with the raw material of morality, the acts and beliefs and sensibilities of men; he cannot possibly refrain from passing judgment on the values of those human acts and beliefs and sensibilities. These moral judgments may or may not be explicit; they are always important. A poet does not write just for the pleasure of moving his fingers: he writes to communicate. And what can he communicate, directly or indirectly, that is not touched by his convictions? A poem is neither a crude creed nor an exercise in technique; it is a conveying of personal values and beliefs, and as such it possesses moral significance.

If the quality of intensity accords with the thought of all romantic schools of poetry, the quality of significance is supported by the classical schools. One approach insists upon the importance of emotion, the other on the importance of understanding. In the nature of poetry they need not exclude each other. Indeed, intense emotion brings significant thought into clear outline far more frequently than it crowds it out of a poem. One other contrast: The consideration of poetic exactness, though it acknowledges the importance of communication, is based primarily upon faithfulness to individual experience. The consideration of significance focuses on comprehensibility in terms of common and continuous human life in all ages. Here, therefore, emphasis shifts from the individual and the emotional to the social and the rational.

It has not been fashionable, during the last half-century, to defend the moral purpose of poetry. "Sing, goddess," Homer begins, "the wrath of Achilles!" To some critics, Homer is already outside the pale of poetry in stating his subject so flatly. If we go further and inquire, "*Why* does Homer sing the wrath of Achilles?" they reply, "Must poetry have a purpose?" For them, poetry is its own end. It is contaminated by awareness of anything but its own pure self. It must avoid the ties of life and the standards of life. The Muse descends—for no good reason—and poetry is born.

Yet the high priests of pure poetry are here making it more ineffable than religion. Faith has its theologies, at least, that strive to connect its mysteries with reason; yet the advocates of pure poetry, solipsists speaking from within their own inner shrine, insist that poetry is only itself, and thereby keep their goddess veiled, unapproachable, incapable of apprehension in common terms. The poet as poet, they maintain, can have no commerce with purposeful intellect. He is governed by blind instinct as much as a dog or a bird. He can only say:

> I do but sing because I must,
> And pipe but as the linnets sing.

But is poetry, in its composition or its effect, so far beyond analysis and reason? The poet who wrote the two lines above also wrote in the same poem:

> The high Muse answer'd: "Wherefore grieve
> Thy brethren with a fruitless tear?
> Abide a little longer here,
> And thou shalt take a nobler leave."

Tennyson must have obeyed the Muse's command, for he was able, at last, to write the purposeful invocation and the final prayer:

> O living will that shalt endure
> When all that seems shall suffer shock,
> Rise in the spiritual rock . . .

And if poetry is willful, are we not justified in inquiring: What is the end it wills? Furthermore, is the end nonexistent unless it can be successfully expressed in simple terms? How simply, for instance, can Homer's purpose as a poet be stated? Is the *Iliad* great because it accidentally gives a full picture of early Greek society? Or because in singing the wrath of Achilles it shows the results of anger? Or is it great because it gives us in Agamemnon the example of a good governor, calculated to inculcate in the reader the political virtues, "as Aristotle hath devised," much as the *Odyssey* gives in Ulysses the model of a brave warrior, perfected in the exercise of the Aristotelian "private moral virtues"? This last judgment represents Edmund Spenser's opinion of the poem; he praises Homer for his moral allegory. Spenser held unswervingly to his conviction that the poet's function is didactic. No reader of the *Faerie Queene* can overlook Spenser's belief. To the men of the Renaissance, it was as natural to conceive that poetry must teach as that the world was composed of four elements, the body of four "humours." But their critical application of the belief was naïve and crude. Sir Philip Sidney shared his friend

Spenser's conceptions, and in his *Apologie for Poetrie* has given them classic expression in two important statements: "Poesy therefore is an art of imitation . . . with this end, to teach and delight. . . . " "It is that feigning notable images of virtues, vices, or what else, with that delightful teaching which must be the right describing note to know a poet by." All this sounded familiar to the Oxford or Cambridge Elizabethan. Horace had said that the poet mixed the useful with the sweet, the useful being that which was *morally* useful. And Aristotle, whose descendants they all were, had argued in the *Poetics*, as Sidney understood it, that art was the imitation of human life not as it is, but as it should be. Poetry, therefore, "is more philosophical and more studiously serious than history."

Yet Sidney finds himself uneasy before his own pronouncements. In the first place, his rule that poetry must teach he applies as mechanically as Spenser in his praise of Homer. Thus, in admitting that "the old song of Percy and Douglas" moves his heart more than a trumpet, Sidney writes: "I must confess my own barbarousness." He is able, indeed, to justify the lyric poem only when it sings the praises of God or kindles men to courage. In his faltering defense of the lyric as a type of poetry, therefore, his instinct compels him to mention the old Scottish ballad of Percy and Douglas even when his formal theory hardly allows him to account for it as a good poem. Sometimes his system leads him to disregard actual poetry altogether: he surveys ruefully the little that has been accomplished in English poetry up to the 1580's, neglecting the real achievements in the early Elizabethan lyric. Lyric poetry in general receives less attention from him than the other forms, for its didactic end, in any narrow sense, cannot easily be demonstrated. The madrigalists, the first Petrarchans, the crowd of erotic poets that fill the miscellanies and songbooks with their native joys and imported sorrows, Sidney disregards. He is writing to answer the puritans who felt poetry to be often harmful, frivolous at best. But he is writing as a puritan himself. The lyric form, he therefore declares, should not be scorned, for who knows what wonderful hymns and religious poems may not soon be written in that mode?

Such a conception of morality is narrow and rigid. At this point, however, it is enough to recognize how basic the poets themselves hold the moral elements to be. Chaucer's "Retractation" disowns much of his best work because it does not contain sufficient direct moral or religious instruction. And Spenser, as if hymns in praise of love and beauty were not didactic enough, would like to discard them, he says, in favor of his two new hymns of heavenly love and beauty. Both Sidney and Milton are worried into ingenious arguments by Plato's banishing of most poets from his mathematically moral Republic. The dogmas both of Christianity and of Greek ethics kept the men of the Renaissance from developing a more elastic conception of moral significance. In the light of his own theory, to take an example, how could Sidney justify as didactic his own beautiful sonnet:

> With how sad steps, O moon, thou climb'st the skies!
> How silently, and with how wan a face!

The fancy that the moon is pale because of unrequited love would seem, in Sidney's view, to lie outside the useful, the religious, and the moral worlds. It is "feigning," but it is not feigning an obviously notable image either of virtue or of vice.

Here we come to the second point that makes Sidney uneasy. He is not completely sure that poetry can tell the truth. Neither is his contemporary, Francis Bacon. *The Advancement of Learning* divides human understanding into three parts: history, poesy, and philosophy. But Bacon dismisses the realm of poetry in a few brief paragraphs. Bacon scrutinizes almost with patronizing contempt "this feigned history." The usefulness of poetry, he writes, "hath been to give some shadow of satisfaction to the mind of man in those points wherein the nature of things doth deny." Through its "feigned chronicles, feigned lives," its fables and parables, poetry "doth raise and erect the mind, submitting the shows of things to the desires of the mind." And after a few cursory remarks, Bacon concludes: "But it is not good to stay too long in the theatre."

Thus, to Bacon poetry at best is an opiate and a trivial diversion, the work of professional liars. Sidney himself seems to believe deep down that poetry is skillful deceit. He imagines his opponents—pragmatic materialists like Bacon, say, as well as devout Christians—advancing the argument that poetry "is the mother of lies." His own answer, though ingenious, assumes that his antagonists are right. Sidney maintains that the lies of poetry, unlike ordinary falsehoods, are not harmful, for since they are told deliberately, within an artistic convention, neither the poet nor the reader believes them. "The poet never maketh any circles about your imagination, to conjure you to believe for true what he writes. Because he telleth them not for true, he lieth not." Such a conception considers poetry too superficially, and diminishes its significance. It is a degradation of Aristotle's doctrine of imitation, for it fails to consider that Aristotle does not therefore think of art as secondary, a pale reflection of the truth, but rather exalts it as a more philosophical and higher thing than history, for history is bound by accidents, whereas poetry can imitate spiritual forms and types and permanent essences of the mind by deliberately selecting or creating the incidents and characters which will best embody them. Sidney himself develops this suggested argument of Aristotle's elsewhere in his essay; but he vacillates, he is inconsistent; and in his discussion of truth in poetry he really resigns the field to his enemies.

The position of the Elizabethan theorists as exemplified by Sidney may be condensed into a sentence: they were certain that poetry was morally significant, but their narrow conception of morality led them to disregard, or reject, or misinterpret, actual poems. They applied too mechanically Horace's precept that the artist mixes the useful and the sweet. They felt that the morally useful should be stated directly; then the delightful might be added as decoration, to trick the unsuspecting reader into accepting the lesson. The notion of fusing or blending the two—the organic conception of poetry—received scant attention. The rationalized argument that poetry was philosophy made palatable by a feigned story or rhetorical decoration or illustrative ornament was not disputed. It is evident not only in the critical opinions, but more significantly in the original poems of such leaders, over a long period, as Spenser, Ben Jonson, Dryden, Pope, Doctor Johnson—even Milton. It may account for the splitting of so many of their poems into statements plus examples. And it explains partially Doctor Johnson's preference for general precepts, as if useful teaching proceeded from rules, and rules could not be well established, or suggested, on the basis of the single observed particular. Yet however forthright were their interpretations, without exception the poets held that their art had a serious moral purpose. The fervent moral conception of poetry is unmistakable in Milton's famous sentence: "He who would not be frustrate of his hope to write well hereafter in laudable things ought himself to be a true poem."

The early nineteenth century had its own new conceptions of moral significance in poetry, without ceasing to insist on its importance. The new emphasis upon emotion and imagination in Wordsworth, Coleridge, and Shelley leads us to forget at times their acceptance of the traditional belief that poetry is didactic. It is Wordsworth himself who, while insisting that poetry must delight, says of his own poems, "each of them has a worthy *purpose*"; it is Wordsworth who believes that poets "discover what is really important to men" and who holds that the understanding of the reader of poetry "must necessarily be in some degree enlightened, and his affections ameliorated." And Coleridge, who insists that a poem proposes pleasure for its immediate object, allows that "truth, either moral or intellectual, ought to be the ultimate end." Shelley writes an impassioned defense of poetry on moral grounds, and even makes such remarkable statements as: "It exceeds all imagination to conceive what would have been the moral condition of the world if neither Dante, Petrarch, Boccaccio, Chaucer, Shakespeare, Calderon, Lord Bacon, nor Milton, had ever existed." And Keats's whole career exemplifies the resolution he took in his early "Sleep and Poetry":

> And can I ever bid these joys farewell?
> Yes, I must pass them for a nobler life.

If Matthew Arnold may speak for the mid-nineteenth century, belief in the moral significance of poetry was never more obvious than in his ruling out Chaucer from the top flight of poets on the ground that he lacked "high seriousness." His conception of culture—the study of the best that has been thought and said in the world—makes art and the criticism of art didactic, and the recipient a conscious cultivator of himself.

If the long line of critics and practicing poets from Aristotle to Arnold are so nearly in accord regarding the necessity to poetry of moral significance, how can the recent reaction against such a belief be explained? Partly on grounds of theory. The philosophers have made us conscious of esthetics. Since the days of Immanuel Kant—and, to a slighter extent, of Winckelmann and Lessing—we have assumed that the sense of beauty exists independently. The most forceful modern champion of this belief is Benedetto Croce. For him, the esthetic sense is one of the four independent aspects of the human consciousness; the esthetic critic judges the successful expression, the clarity of an intuition within the artist's mind. He is not concerned with its logical consistency, or its relation to verifiable experience, or its effect upon morals, or even its technique of externalization such as the use made of brush-strokes, of anapests, or of counterpoint.

The philosophers have done admirable work in clarifying our conceptions of beauty. The straight clean thought of Croce sweeps aside many cobwebs. He sees that once an intuition has been objectified in a work of art, it may be judged by moral standards, may be praised as helpful or censured as harmful to society. He warns us, however, that no one should delude himself into believing such a judgment esthetic. In the realm of pure thought, Croce has done much to establish again clear conceptions of the true, the beautiful, the good, and the useful.

But as their doctrines become vulgarized, the estheticians have a harmful effect upon conceptions of art. Art is not philosophy. No poet is purely a philosopher; even less, then, is he purely an esthetician, since esthetics is merely a division of philosophy. The poet does not work solely with beauty, even if one grants that verbal beauty distinguishes his from other products of human consciousness. To seek for the distinctive element in the poet's work is necessary to the philosopher; it is dangerous to the student of poetry, for the *distinctive* element need not be the most important, and emphasis upon it may lead to the neglect of other elements simply because they are shared by other forms of thought. To make a parallel: singling out man's capacity for reason may help to distinguish man from other animals; by itself, however, it is not an adequate conception of man, since it disregards the instincts, sensations, and sheer vital spirits that he possesses in common with other animals. Or again: a critic might conclude that poetry is metrical in contrast to prose. But the exhaustive study of metrics would certainly not lead to a complete comprehension of the nature of poetry. The increased competence in theorizing about beauty, therefore, has tended to warp understanding of a poem in all its aspects. Esthetics is, or should be, a philosophical system; art is a personal experience. They differ as sharply as insurance mortality tables and the death of a friend.

Partly, also, the revolt against the ethical conception of art has developed out of the actual practice of poets. Early theories are modified by later art; they tend to become less acceptable in their simple outlines. And the classic doctrine of moral significance, whose development has been glanced at in this chapter, has outlived usefulness in its mechanical form. The poets of the later nineteenth century were tired of the glaring didacticism of earlier ages; they distrusted the romantic hysteria and emotionalism that trailed in the wake of the French Revolution. They wished neither to shout morals nor to wring the heart. However it affected its contemporaries, such a stanza as the following from the *Faerie Queene* would fail to move the generations of Flaubert, or Pater, or Anatole France:

> What man is he, that boasts of fleshly might,
> And vain assurance of mortality,
> Which all so soon as it doth come to fight
> Against spiritual foes, yields by and by,
> Or from the field most cowardly doth fly?
> Ne let the man ascribe it to his skill,
> That thorough grace hath gained victory.
> If any strength we have, it is to ill;
> But all the good is God's, both power and eke will.

It is too antiquated, too obvious, too naïve in its manner of presentation. It creaks. Yet not the ethical import, but the art, makes this stanza bad. The significance of a poem cannot be expressed in the same fashion as the significance of a sermon, a mathematical demonstration, or a political speech. To realize this truth, however, is not to conclude that a poem may be enjoyed thoroughly as a poem apart from its significance. Yet that is the tendency back of some of the most influential critics of the last hundred years. Walter Pater, in spite of his underlying moral preoccupations, emphasizes the importance of style —the manner of expression—rather than significance—the matter expressed. Such emphasis leads to distortion; it is ceasing to regard the nature of poetry in all its simultaneous manifestations. A minimizing of the significance invariably present in poetry may even be read into Pater's profound remark: "*All art constantly aspires toward the condition of music.* For while in all other kinds of art it is possible to distinguish the matter from the form, and the understanding can always make this distinction, yet it is the constant effort of art to obliterate it. . . . Art, then, is thus always striving to be independent of the mere intelligence."

The arguments of A. C. Bradley, A. E. Housman, and George Moore, because of their very consistency, are not open to attack. But also they are not very helpful. Each in his own way, these men define poetry by naming it over again. It is perfectly true that poetry is not identical with whatever else it may resemble; nor is it the same as the sum of its analyzable parts. Logically, poetry is only poetry. But that proposition can be of use to the initiate alone, the poet himself within the inner sanctuary. A rainbow is only a rainbow, yet surely thinking of its seven arbitrary colors in an established order may help us to remember it.

The theorists of pure poetry, however, urged on by adoration or by logical consistency, weave a circle around the art. The world cannot enter its domain, nor can it speak with the voice of the world. Since poetry cannot be explained or commented upon without falsifying its essence, the critic of poetry is transformed into an anthologist, no more and no less. He can only point.

Bradley's "Poetry for Poetry's Sake" presents a basic truth with eloquence, for, after all the talking is done, it is well to remember that poetry is itself and not something else. But how can one use this knowledge? How can one's understanding of and sensitivity to poetry be increased by this undeniable equation? The reader of a new or a difficult poet will not be aided by Bradley's statement: "He meant what he said, and said what he meant." Neither is it particularly helpful in distinguishing between a pure poem and adulterated or inferior products to learn that "if we insist on asking for the meaning of such a poem, we can only be answered 'It means itself.'" Bradley repudiates the art-for-art's-sake theory that minimizes the importance of content or "substance." He insists, however, that "in a poem the true content and the true form neither exist nor can be imagined apart." Yet if content and form were not in some manner distinct in his own mind, his statement would be meaningless. If thinking *about* a poem as well as directly experiencing it were not enjoyable and profitable, there would be no literary criticism and no Chair of Poetry at Oxford for such men as Professor Bradley to fill. Analysis of art is natural. Since Bradley considers that the "substance" of a poem cannot be scrutinized apart from the poem itself, he is forced to set up his own special terms and refer to "subject matter" as that which is separable from the poem. Content and form are inseparable; and yet, he says, the "moral" or the "idea" of a poem "perhaps in one instance out of five thousand . . . may be found in so many words in the poem." How has he discovered, in the other 4,999 instances, the moral or idea except by reading the poems themselves? Each poem must have generated its own significance clearly in Bradley's mind if he can be *certain* that its significance cannot be found neatly stated in the poem "in so many words." Surely here Bradley is making special distinctions in his use of words in order to speak *about* poetry and insist at the same time that one cannot speak about it, that there is only "the thing itself."

Bradley, then, is less convincing and constructive in this essay than in his *Shakespearean Tragedy*, which deals with poetry for moral philosophy's sake. Such critical procedure is justifiable, provided it is made with full consciousness of its own narrowed scope. More often than not, the close scrutiny of a single constituent element—and a separable significance is one element of a poem—makes the whole more comprehensible. It is, indeed, hard to find a poem which mysteriously defies all comment. Housman's famous lecture on "The Name and Nature of Poetry" takes the stand that poetry cannot be approached intellectually, that it is a shudder, a bristling, a swelling of the gorge rather than a product amenable to analysis.

Yet in support of his physiological conception of poetry, Housman quotes as "nonsense," or as "poetry neat, adulterated with little meaning," poems which would be so regarded only by someone supporting an extreme and paradoxical position. To excise the meaning from poetry is indeed difficult. Examples of pure poems, or of pure poetry even in selected stanzas or lines, are rare as phoenix eggs. George Moore, working with Walter de la Mare, admits his anthology of pure poetry is a tour de force; such a collection is clearly less a representation of the poetic spirit in general than an illustration of a limited theory and particular tastes.

And of the pure poetry which the apologists have themselves selected, may we say with truth that it is divorced from rational import, that it is understandable only in itself? If the purest and choicest lines cannot avoid significance—even moral significance—the lesser lines, inferior because tainted by the prosaic desire to be understood rationally, will certainly possess it.

We must, therefore, look at some of the most celebrated instances in an effort to determine whether poetry can ever exist apart from a significance which can be detached and stated, more or less successfully, in rational terms. The exponents of pure poetry have a fondness for proper names, on the theory that such names cannot express the intellectual concepts of generic nouns. On the contrary, proper names often convey many related ideas, both particular and general, precisely because they do have numerous specific associations. The one word "Caesar" may suggest Alps, antiquity, empire, and epilepsy—a whole card index of objects and ideas.

The Abbé Brémond quotes as an example of *la poésie pure* a famous line of Racine's:

La fille de Minos et de Pasiphaë.

Surely this was neither written nor is best understood as a splendid collection of syllables of indefinite import. Its effectiveness increases as we realize more and more clearly what its words suggest: that one Minos was ruler of the underworld, but this particular Minos was King of Crete; that Minos broke his deep vow of sacrifice to Neptune; that Pasiphaë as a result fell prey to Neptune's anger through his instrument, the sacrificial bull; that the offspring of this union, symbol of overpowering animal passion, was the Minotaur; that "the daughter of Minos and of Pasiphaë" is more than a line of poetry: she is Phaedra herself, wife of Theseus, with her uncontrollable love for her stepson Hippolytus. Phaedra is what she is because of the black tangle of her fated family. Far from being meaningless, the whole tragedy of the houses of Minos and Theseus, with all its moral judgments, is present by implication in that line, not in spite of, but because of, the proper names.

Even when the names are not familiar, they may assume meaning in a poem.

> Techelles,
> Usumcasane, and Theridamas,

have little enough specific meaning, isolated, to satisfy the most ardent defender of pure poetry. But in their place, with Marlowe's Tamburlaine speaking to his three lieutenants, planning his first great conquest, they give dimensions, the support of barbarous sinews, to the dream of empire in distant places:

> Is it not brave to be a king, Techelles,
> Usumcasane, and Theridamas?
> Is it not passing brave to be a king
> And ride in triumph through Persepolis?

The processions of proper names in Spenser, in Marlowe, in Shakespeare's history plays, in Milton, are never paraded merely for their sound, but always with a deliberate intention of increasing some significant conception of the splendid, the spacious, or the exotic.

Housman praises as "ravishing poetry" Shakespeare's song

in *Measure for Measure* at the same time that he calls it "non-sense":

> Take, O, take those lips away
>   That so sweetly were forsworn
> And those eyes, the break of day,
>   Lights that do mislead the morn.
> But my kisses bring again, bring again;
> Seals of love, but seal'd in vain, seal'd in vain.

It is difficult to believe that Housman can be wholly serious when he finds these lines devoid of meaning. The structure itself shows intellectual organization. Beauty versus betrayal is repeatedly balanced: "so sweetly" against "forsworn"; "break of day," "lights," "morn" against "mislead." Then, too, there is the more important setting off of the treacherous physical passion of the first four lines—the sweet lips and bright eyes—against the trustful emotional constancy of the last two —"kisses," "seals," "love"—made unmistakable by the pivotal repeated "but" and the certain climax "in vain." Nor is the moral judgment vague: the delight of the senses must be taken away, must be forgotten; love, sealed with its own loyalty, must be brought again, must remain. Within its own circumference the poem stands as clear in statement. In its place in the play for which it was written, the clarity of its argument and its ethical values are even more apparent: this is the song sung by the page to Mariana, faithful still to Angelo who has deserted her. And in its place in Shakespeare's thought, it is but one more variation on the theme he could never forget: of the phoenix of human beauty and the turtledove of endless devotion:

> Love is not love
> Which alters when it alteration finds.

To think that of all people Housman, who voices the same theme with bitterness and scorn, could have missed the significance of the song, is to think him as dense as he evidently considered his audience. If this be pure poetry, then where is impure poetry to be found?

The mysterious songs of Blake's which Housman cites have some significance even to those who are not initiates into Blake's coherent visions; and surely to admit that we cannot fully state the meaning of the poems themselves is not to conclude that they are therefore without meaning. To show the inexplicability of poetry, Housman quotes two versions of the Forty-ninth Psalm, in the Book of Common Prayer and in his own Bible. The first he considers poetic, the second unemotional. Yet this is merely evidence of the exactness of poetry, the rightness of the right words. The *significance* of the Psalm is the great, needful, organizing principle in determining the best words and their best order; and it is doubtful whether tears would have come to Housman's eyes over an exactly similar collocation of rhythmical syllables in an unknown tongue.

For, given the human mind in its workings, the idea of pure poetry is a chimera, the deliberate and difficult creation of the abstracting intellect. In any form of art, expression cannot exist devoid of meaning; it takes a real effort of the will to anesthetize most parts of our consciousness long enough to consider what a pure esthetic state might be. It is true that all art constantly aspires toward the condition of music (that is, toward instantaneous, unified apprehension); but it is no less true that all art aspires constantly toward the condition of meaning. The most rigorous abstract experimenters—Mallarmé or Gertrude Stein—cannot distill poetry until it becomes unsullied by meaning. A Jabberwocky poem, practically considered, is impossible; it is worth remembering that when she got a chance, Alice asked the meaning of "the poem called 'Jabberwocky,' " and Humpty Dumpty, sensibly enough, proceeded confidently to explain. And if Edward Lear's "The Dong with a Luminous Nose" rises into the domain of poetry, it does so not merely because of its rhythms and its aural richness, but because, in the great Gromboolian plain, the Zemmery Fidd, the Jumbly Girl, and the Bong-tree, we sense an elusive meaning which we cannot directly see—like the headlights of a car around a corner, or like, shall we say, a dong with a luminous nose. Instinctively the mind strives to fit together, so that they may be understood, any succession of syllables uttered by a human being, any words written on a page in the traditional shape of a poem.

If Lewis Carroll and Edward Lear irk the intellect because they seem to mean so little, other poets tire because they mean so much. Common sense is not at home in the realms of non-sense or of supersense. But the poets of multiple meanings are not beyond reason, nor is their difficulty a purposeful attempt to conceal significance. The heavy footnotes to an edition of Dante's *Divine Comedy*, the glosses which T. S. Eliot himself appended to *The Waste Land*, are evidence enough that a difficult poem is not designed as a mystery and need not remain so. Poetry may be difficult—indeed, no great poetry is immediately and fully comprehensible—but it is not unfathomable. It cannot be either completely above or below intellectual comprehension. Significance is a part of poetry, though never its equivalent.

Thus far this chapter has been a little sour-faced. The traditional critics, the argument has run, have betrayed poetry by insisting upon too direct a moral significance; the pure-poetry champions by denying to it any moral significance at all. May not both groups be at fault in assuming that poetic significance can be conveyed only by means of direct rational propositions? A more elastic conception of the term "significance," plus a pragmatic consideration of the way in which poetry speaks to us, may help in understanding that poetry must be significant.

In a sense all poetry is didactic. To teach is to impart knowledge. All poetry increases our knowledge, for it is not poetry if it does not affect us, and we cannot be affected without becoming aware of new experience, or more keenly alive to what we have already vaguely known. In the broadest sense, therefore, our simple acceptance of the poetic vision, exact and intense, makes the poet a teacher. And in this sense, paradoxically, direct moral statements in verse teach very little, for the reader is not often convinced by them; they are not, in Wordsworth's phrase, "carried alive into the heart by passion." Man does not live by reason alone, and the poet does not try to convince him—to teach him—by reason alone. He plays upon whatever in man is alive. On the grounds of effective appeal, then, rather than of systematic thought, Milton praises "our sage and serious poet Spenser, whom I dare be known to think a better teacher than Scotus or Aquinas."

But it has already been suggested in this chapter that Spenser's mechanical technique of separating moral precept from illustration weakens his poetry in many instances. Shelley's adverse criticism of Spenser may show the wider conception of poetic significance which this chapter is designed to uphold. Shelley's opinion of the poets as the "unacknowledged legislators of the world" is exalted. But if the poet strives too fanatically for the conclusive word, the unalterable law, he will legislate not at all, or for his own time only. Thus Spenser, because he *was* sage and serious in the extreme, insisted on making his moral drive obvious to his contemporaries, and in consequence lost much of his appeal for later generations. As Shelley says, "Those in whom the poetical faculty, though great, is less intense [than in Homer], as Euripides, Lucan, Tasso, Spenser, have frequently affected a moral aim, and the effect of their poetry is diminished in exact proportion to the degree in which they compel us to advert to this purpose." In most of the *Faerie Queene*, Spenser is one of the great English poets. But in the directly didactic stanzas which he often inserts, he dates. Contemporaneous appeal in a work of art loses its force as the days pass. And a direct statement on moral issues is usually an address to contemporaries. It runs the risk of falling out of fashion, of losing its original significance.

In contrast, Homer, Shakespeare, Dante, and Milton the world has continued to regard as artists of the first rank because the significance of their work, since in large part it is implied rather than openly stated, is fresh, adapting itself to the changing needs of new times. Here again is an organic conception of poetry: a poem is not static—held to one fixed, intellectual meaning for all people and all ages—although such a purpose has usually governed directly didactic poems. Instead, the significance of a true poem shifts and adapts itself, or better, is living and flexible, so that it may be shaped by each reader to his own comprehension. If the crystallization into concepts comes too early or too completely within the poem itself, the result may be lifeless to the reader. Direct didactic statements often occur in long poems, but then they are felt *as poetry* only when they are absorbed into the life of the whole poem; in short poems, the direct statement rarely serves *primarily* the purpose of stating directly. Both of these considerations, however, must be left for illustration to the fifth chapter.

Shelley's remarks on *Paradise Lost* aptly illustrate the truth of this conception of significance. Milton states that his moral purpose is to "justifie the ways of God to men." Many critics have held, though perhaps erroneously, that the weakest parts of the poem are just such formal justifications of God—the long speeches of the Father in Books III and X, Raphael's entire books of theological and cosmological explanations, the repeated arguments about free will and foreknowledge. Yet Shelley finds the significance of the poem in Satan, the magnificent spirit of rebellion against God:

Milton's Devil as a moral being is as far superior to his God, as one who perseveres in some purpose which he has conceived to be excellent in spite of adversity and torture, is to one who in the cold security of undoubted triumph inflicts the most horrible revenge upon his enemy, not from any mistaken notion of inducing him to repent of a perseverance in enmity, but with the alleged design of exasperating him to deserve new torments. Milton has so far violated the popular creed (if this shall be judged to be a violation) as to have alleged no superiority of moral virtue to his God over his Devil. And this bold neglect of a direct moral purpose is the most decisive proof of the supremacy of Milton's genius.

There can be no question here that for Shelley the poem is full of living significance. Yet even Shelley could hardly have argued that Milton consciously aimed at such Devil worship. The opposite case—that the poem demonstrates the littleness of pride and the ultimate failure of rebellion—might be more legitimately argued on the basis of the whole poem, in spite of Blake and Shelley.

Shelley's argument as presented in the paragraph quoted above is important for two reasons. First, he assumes that the significance of a poem may lie deeper than its avowed purpose; that although Milton may make Adam say

Henceforth I learne, that to obey is best,

nevertheless the true spirit of the poet who was Latin Secretary under the Commonwealth, the apologist for regicide in *Eikonoklastes*, is brightest in the speeches of the rebel angel. Many readers, indeed, would agree that *Paradise Lost* touches its heights in passages that show Satan's fervor for liberty, his scornful independence. Second, as Shelley sees it, Milton has not dwarfed his epic speculations by reducing them to a few copybook maxims. The wider significance of *Paradise Lost* makes it possible for Shelley to find in it living truth which would be comprehensible to an age when the fall of the Bastille and the revolt in Greece seemed trumpets of a prophecy, and to an individual for whom atheism and his own type of anarchy were necessities. The profoundest import of a poem, in summary, may differ from the poet's conscious intent; since it is always more than an intellectual proposition, it cannot be stated, like Newton's laws, so that it will not vary; the significance, therefore, no matter what the poet himself had in mind, and whether the scientific critic likes it or not, shifts from reader to reader and from age to age. Although the poem itself does not change, its apprehension depends upon the varying tastes, sensitivities, and beliefs of individuals and of epochs.

It may strike us as ridiculous that the Middle Ages considered Vergil a great poet partly because of a supposed prophecy of Christ's coming which is to be found in the Fourth Eclogue, or that Comrade Walt Whitman has a current vogue among the Communists. Occasionally, also, the individual reader falls into demonstrable error and misinterpretation. But such instances are extreme; men's thoughts agree over a remarkably large area, differing only in superficials. Although it cannot be fully explained, in spite of psychological and epistemological mysteries the miracle of communication through art is continually happening. Once given this normal agreement on fundamentals, a reinterpretation of a poem, a revaluation, or an altercation over some part of its meaning is usually a genuine sign of its vitality.

The critical problem that promises to engage the present century centers on the relation between art and propaganda. The argument of this chapter needs only slight rephrasing to bear upon this question. In the sense that all art is the expression of passionate belief, produced in the hope of being understood and accepted, all art is propaganda, and only those who wish to cut off the artist from serious life would deny it. As a vehicle for achieving practical and immediate action, however, art is relatively inefficient. Action results from rhetoric, not from contemplative art. Once action is brought about, the life usually goes out of a crusading pamphlet or poem. And the intense significance to contemporary readers of the diatribes against Anglican prelates in "Lycidas" or against child labor in mines and factories in "The Cry of the Children" today has vanished.

Largely through theoretical argument, this chapter has so far maintained that all poems possess a wide significance, in an extrarational as well as in a rational sense. Such significance must be further illustrated in this and succeeding chapters; we must in fairness establish some significance in those poems usually supposed to exist without it; we must first of all make sure that subject matter and meaning are not confused. Subject matter does not determine the significance of a poem, for any given material may be used to produce diverse effects. The same red might be found in pictures by the Van Eycks, Rembrandt, and Renoir, for example, yet what it does emotionally to the beholder cannot be determined by its chemistry and physics. Nor do dictionary definitions or historical traditions fix absolutely the meaning of any word in any poem. Othello speaks of Desdemona as "light." Yet here Shakespeare does not use the word, as he does in his early comedies, to suggest by punning interplay woman's brilliance and her fickleness. We are aware, of course, of sharp particularity in the contrasted fairness or "light" of Desdemona and the swarthiness of the Moor. But more than that, in this one play of *Othello*, we feel that "light" is a rare spiritual grace shed upon one human being by the action and character of another. This conception of the worth and significance of human life is deep and unchanging in the mature Shakespeare. How different is Milton's use of the same small word in the opening lines of Book III of *Paradise Lost!*

> Hail holy light, ofspring of Heav'n first-born,
> Or of th' Eternal Coeternal beam
> May I express thee unblam'd? since God is light,
> And never but in unapproached light
> Dwelt from Eternitie, dwelt then in thee.

Again, superficially, we think of Milton in his blindness writing about light. But deeper than such personal pathos, as the long invocation progresses, it becomes apparent that Milton nearly identifies light with wisdom, which springs for him from intelligence. Light is associated with spiritual grace, but it lies within each solitary being. This, too, is consistent with the whole of *Paradise Lost*, wherein light is a sign of virtue, which is reason in control of the individual. And again, how different is Milton's "light" from Dante's *luce!* In Dante it is at once more mystical and more cosmic—an irradiation and a warmth that carries the rapt soul to contemplation of God. The same term, the same raw material, Shakespeare, Milton, and Dante use to express their different dominant meditations: on human ties, on the individual spirit, and on God.

Not only is it impossible to fix the significance of any raw material for all artists; it is also impossible to rule out any subject matter as without significance as it may be used in art. Donne may couple a flea with agile speculations on the Ten Commandments, the sacrament of marriage, and the Trinity. Burns may use a louse to lead up to a broad and humorous interpretation of human life. What is conventionally considered ugly or sordid may be material for expressing the noblest thoughts. Skelton's "The Tunning of Elynour Rumming" presents a filthy alewife and crawling crowds of drunken human vermin to express a strong sense of human weaknesses and human needs, of social injustice and human solidarity. Does the coarseness of Burns's "The Jolly Beggars" reflect liberty and love less convincingly than the more conventional beauty of the Fire-Bringer and of Asia in Shelley's *Prometheus Unbound?* The beggars and madmen in Shakespeare's *Lear*, in Wordsworth's poems, and in the later poems of Yeats are at least as profound and noble symbols of human destiny as the kings and aristocrats in Shakespeare, in Scott, and in Yeats. Long ago, in writing on the sublime, Longinus insisted upon the difference between raw material and the significance given to it by the shaping artist. Beggars and lice and fleas may be repulsive in themselves; they may, however, afford the raw materials for art of the noblest import.

T. S. Eliot has written two lines that may serve as a touchstone:

> I am aware of the damp souls of housemaids
> Sprouting despondently at area gates.

The popular attack upon modern literature for treating so frequently the sordid, the ugly, or the brutal is based on such lines. The material is unquestionably dull and uninviting. But the significance is sharp: certainly the verses bring up vividly the dispirited limbo of city suburbs. They realize the hopelessness of the modern megalopolis; they repeat, in little, Eliot's despairing judgment on present civilization. And without such consistent conviction, such significance expressed in negation, Eliot could never have advanced to his positive belief in the need for tradition and for religious faith.

Many misconceptions arise out of failure to distinguish subject matter from significance. Often the enigma of tragedy puzzles us: why do we delight in representations of cruelty and suffering and loss? Yet here again, though the matter be painful, the content is human capabilities at their highest, and the greatness of tragedy springs not from fateful accidents, villains, and flaws in the hero—the matter—but from the triumph and purification at the end—the content.

And again, satire has a hard struggle in maintaining its position as a legitimate form of poetry. Partly this springs from the element of propaganda in satire, its contemporaneous appeal, so that many satires are now dead simply because they were so effective in their own day. But partly also satire is in low repute as poetry because of the persistent belief that poetry must treat "beautiful" subjects. Readers see the immediate repellent material of which satire is composed; they are so revolted by the surface that they miss the poet's motivation and fail to grasp the underlying significance. It is the unfortunate lot of satire at its best that it must convey a positive moral ideal by portraying its opposite; if we shudder too much at the material, we miss the drive beneath.

Subject matter and significance should never be confused, then, although popular appraisals of art have continually fallen into error on this score. And better critics as well. Late nineteenth-century poets, for instance, had come to see that the beauty of a work of art did not depend upon the subject matter. The same matter, they rightly held, may be shaped into beauty or left in ugliness. But they did not distinguish clearly enough between subject matter and content, and concluded that the content of a poem was likewise of little concern to a poet. Here they were mistaken. To say that subject matter is relatively unimportant is not to argue that content in poetry is unimportant. Not the raw material, but its transformation, is the essence of a work of art. And this transformation demands of the artist far more than mere technical skill; it also requires the shaping influence of his deepest instincts and emotions and convictions. The selection of the subject matter itself often helps to indicate a poet's judgments and standards. Artistic creation, therefore, cannot be divorced from values, especially moral values. The poets of the late nineteenth century tried in their theories to equate unimportance of subject with unimportance in meaning. In practice, however, it is impossible. The Parnassians' chiseled descriptive verse conveys a belief in a certain emotional impassivity, a cool aloofness which gave them their significant name. The Pre-Raphaelites, as their name tells us, held that a primitive and childlike simplicity was better than academic perfection. "Art for art's sake" sounds like a moral slogan in itself, and implies that the "good" artist must be absorbed in his art, or that beauty is the most dependable value or standard in the world.

Even "Kubla Khan," which is perennially brought up as an
example of a poem without a discoverable meaning, possesses
significance. The mere fact that Coleridge took the trouble to
set down the lines on paper and later to publish them shows
that he considered the fantastic visions of some value. The
theory of associative thought, to which both Wordsworth and
Coleridge paid such serious attention, has seldom been better
illustrated, and Professor Lowes has shown the deep wells
of reading and remembrance that were drawn on to produce
this poem. The woman wailing for her demon lover is more
vivid and lasting than the man from Porlock who interrupted
Coleridge's composition. The visionary kingdom of dreams is
given terror and beauty and a rich reality. The very incom-
pleteness of "Kubla Khan" reflects a belief that inspiration
cannot be forced, that poetry does not necessarily have neat
edges. The poem as it remains conveys no less clearly than
Hamlet, though it does not state it so directly, the conviction
that

> There are more things in heaven and earth, Horatio,
> Than are dreamt of in your philosophy.

And if such an appraisal of human life is communicated to the
reader, can it be said that the poem lacks significance?

The selection of details, the mere process of creative activity,
inevitably reveals moral belief, some judgment on man's purpose and functions and duties and qualities. How can a creator
avoid expressing his sense of values? Art, indeed, which must
look at life through a single pair of eyes, is the most natural
channel for moral judgment, for expressing the *value* to the
individual of the speculations made by philosophy and theology, the actions of men, the findings of science. To most men,
to poets as well as to their readers, the prime worth of a poem
lies in its moral significance in this comprehensive sense of
the phrase. And to most men, the poets themselves again included, the more convincing and comprehensive and inspirit-

ing a piece of writing is in its moral judgments, the greater it is as a work of art. A poem, narrowly considered, is merely a manner of saying something. But the success of the manner itself may depend upon the confidence and conviction of both poet and reader that the thing said is worth saying well.

Only perverse ingenuity or impatience or dullness or extreme enthusiasm for some other single element can fail to find moral import in art. And if ethical significance is omnipresent in art, other kinds of significance can hardly be absent: poetry is not poetry if it does not offer us a world that appears fresher, or clearer, or more comprehensive. It must understand and make us understand. It must communicate and convince. Whether its subject be trivial or cosmic, it must interpret. The books of the British Museum were *not* written by myriads of monkeys accidentally striking the keys of typewriters. Even this well-worn hypothetical image is "poetic," since it ironically conceives the actual existence of countless unrelated volumes by uniting them all in a conception of mechanistic purposelessness.

We dream most of our lives away, in the comfortable torpor of accepting what comes next. The laziness of living is seldom disturbed by thinking. Thought is so painful and strenuous that the creative process of poetry would never be undertaken were it not for the goad of some purpose, some belief. The impossibility of establishing an unchangeable significance for any passage of poetry simply indicates that poets express their beliefs in ways different from those of rational argument, not that the beliefs are absent. The poet is the mirror "of the gigantic shadows which futurity casts upon the present"; unlike the critic, he is not concerned with tidying up the past; he is a creator, not a copier; he sees the world anew, but the strangeness of his vision, its idiosyncrasy, does not mean that he is unintelligible. He writes with a purpose, and since he has a purpose, poetry, when it is successfully communicative, must be significant.

# CHAPTER FOUR

# POETRY
# IS CONCRETE

THE SIGNIFICANCE of poetry finds expression in concrete terms. If the general, often the universal, idea is not present, the result is not a poem; no less certainly, if the specific, the immediate, the tangible *thing* is not present, the result is not a poem. In a sense, then, the third and fourth chapters make opposed demands: one insists upon the ideal, the other upon the actual.

This requirement of concreteness necessitates a more complete exercise of man's consciousness than is explicit in the first three chapters. The first quality of exactness demands that a poet express himself personally; it is a way of using language. The second quality of intensity centers on our emotions, as the third quality of significance centers on our intelligence. This present consideration demands that poetry appeal not only to the emotional and intellectual sides of our nature but also to the sensuous. The thoughts and emotions of the poet must be set in a framework of the outside world; they must be expressed in concrete, sensuous terms. Man not only conceives general ideas; he perceives specific things; and poetry will not allow him to abandon either of these capacities. "Poetry," says Doctor Johnson, "is the art of uniting pleasure with truth, by calling imagination to the help of reason." This section will

be devoted to the workings of the poet's imagination in selecting concrete symbols and fixing them in the poem, and also to
the reader's imaginative activity as he experiences, through
reading the poem, what seems to him the experience of its
creator.

The law of concreteness may well be shown by quoting a
short poem by Archibald MacLeish. His "Ars Poetica" is
already well known. Has it gained its reputation because its
*significance* is apparent, or because its *concreteness* illustrates
its argument so neatly?

> A poem should be palpable and mute
> As a globed fruit
>
> Dumb
> As old medallions to the thumb
>
> Silent as the sleeve-worn stone
> Of casement ledges where the moss has grown—
>
> A poem should be wordless
> As the flight of birds
>
> *     *     *
>
> A poem should be motionless in time
> As the moon climbs
>
> Leaving, as the moon releases
> Twig by twig the night-entangled trees,
>
> Leaving, as the moon behind the winter leaves,
> Memory by memory the mind—
>
> A poem should be motionless in time
> As the moon climbs
>
> *     *     *
>
> A poem should be equal to:
> Not true
>
> For all the history of grief
> An empty doorway and a maple leaf

> For love
> The leaning grasses and two lights above the sea—
>
> A poem should not mean
> But be

In this poem, the interplay between significance and concreteness is constant. Mr. MacLeish's argument, of course, is all on
the side of concreteness; but the mere fact that it is an argument points the arrow back toward a rationalized significance.
The antithesis between the two poetic qualities is everywhere
apparent. How, for instance, can one explain the art of poetry
in silence and timelessness, the two qualities which the first and
second thirds of the poem demand? And do not the final famous two lines contradict in practice, because of their explicit
intellectual statement, the very point that they are making?
Perhaps an Art of Poetry is not designed to be a poem in itself.
Yet such a supposition hardly applies to Mr. MacLeish's work
here, for in general his lines on how to write and recognize
poetry illustrate aptly the doctrine which they are expressing.
Significance and concreteness, therefore—"meaning" and "being"—are here in conflict. Their interaction is one of the most
common phenomena in poetry.

Let us look further at these clashes and reinforcements. The
significance of Mr. MacLeish's poem is not hard to get at:
poetry should possess the three qualities of silence, timelessness, and concrete symbolism. To some extent these three
*abstract* requirements are expressed *concretely* by the triple
division of the poem. One might even argue that the concrete
form of the poem on the printed page is a "silent form," as
Keats called the Grecian urn, and that the device of absence
of usual punctuation adds concretely to the idea of poetic "being" rather than grammatical "meaning."

In considering the argument of the first section of the poem,
readers might arrive at differing interpretations of the significance. Possibly Mr. MacLeish, like so many recent poets,

is emphasizing that today most of us get our pleasure from poetry through the eye, no longer through the ear. Or, if our enjoyment still seems to us imaginatively aural, then "not to the sensual ear, but more endeared," the poet pipes to the spirit his ditties of no tone. Possibly, too, Mr. MacLeish is thinking of the permanence of those printed characters, that can magically call up again at any moment that reflection of the creator's experience which we call the poem, so that any recorded copy of great verse might itself be addressed as

> Thou still unravish'd bride of quietness,
> Thou foster-child of silence and slow time.

However we may interpret its significance, Mr. MacLeish has unmistakably given us his first demand in five overlapping adjectives: a poem should be palpable, mute, dumb, silent, and wordless. There can be no doubt that in these lines Mr. Mac-Leish has wished to give a general statement of the necessary qualities, or quality, of a poem. But immediately these ideas —and a quality must necessarily be an idea abstracted from some thing or some things more complex—are illustrated concretely, in images that might have been drawn from Keats or Tennyson or Rossetti, and we have in the first section a globed fruit, old medallions, stone, and birds in flight. This tendency to think of the idea, or the quality, in concrete terms is carried even further by the modifying adjectives and phrases that will compel a more vivid realization of the object imagined as so very quiet. A poem is as silent as a stone. Such a comparison might be overlooked because we have heard the phrase "still as a stone" so often. Therefore, to rouse our attention, the poem is as silent as a particular worn stone; and to make us believe that it is worn the coined adjective "sleeve-worn" (akin to "thread-bare"? worn by sleeves resting upon it? worn out at elbow and cuff, like a sleeve?) turns us to yet another image from concrete experience. And then the sleeve-worn stone is particularized and modified by a tangible ledge, which in turn is modified by a tangible casement, and the whole is modified by an arresting specific detail, designed to catch or convince our imagination: "where the moss has grown."

The other sections develop in like fashion, but in place of the four similitudes of the first section, the second section repeats the same image—that a poem in some way is like the moon—four times. Here again the particular interpretation may vary from reader to reader, although most would probably feel that a poem wakens in the reader's consciousness memory after memory, complex, minute, and exact, just as moonlight, against the motionless, durable, illimitable night, etches out twigs and leaves and innumerable silhouettes. But all readers would agree that the writer is saying a poem is timeless, although even this idea is seemingly given more tangible form by translating it from time to space—"*motionless* in time." Particularly interesting is the device of suggesting timelessness through repetition rather than through change of images. In this section the final pair of lines mirrors the first, so that we are meant to feel, in the changeless concrete image of the moon, that time has not elapsed, or that if it has, it has made no difference, for the end and the beginning are the same.

The third section continues the minuet between meaning and its concrete embodiment. The first and fourth pairs of lines are direct statements, and as such, considered purely by themselves rather than in the light of the whole, are not poetic because they defy this very law of concreteness that the poem is designed to proclaim. Most readers would agree that they present the argument that a poem does not state its meaning directly, syllogistically, logically, rationally; its meaning rather exists in the recognition of unstated, sometimes unformulated, equivalences between its concrete symbols and what they symbolize. In this last section of the poem, the two middle pairs of lines are excellent illustrations of the doctrine of concreteness which Mr. MacLeish has so unconcretely expounded in the first pair and the last. Within a poem we come upon an empty doorway and a maple leaf; in the crucible of our imagination these objects assume a general significance and become "all the history of grief." Similarly, the leaning grasses and two lights above the sea become in our minds the symbols of love. This is the way poetry works. The significance of a poem to any individual reader need be no less sharp than the significance of a mathematical proposition, though within limits this significance may vary from reader to reader as the mathematical proposition cannot do. But the *technique* of expressing significance in poetry demands sharp, specific *detail*. The concrete symbols, the things of this world as we know it —these are the invariable stuff of poetry, as, to the same extent, they need be of no other form of verbal communication. Poetry must operate through such concrete symbols. This is the argument which this chapter is designed to develop.

That poetry has always been concrete is much more obvious than that it always should have been and always should be. Why should meaning in poetry assume other ways of expression than meaning in philosophical or rhetorical or scientific or critical or historical writing? Philosophy and science, for different purposes, deal with general truths; rhetoric has the practical end of convincing the reader or auditor within some limited field; criticism analyzes, classifies, relates, and strives to reach rational conclusions of general validity; history always looks in one direction, and the historian usually feels virtuous only when he is trying to get outside himself. But poetry is more comprehensive than any of these modes of verbal expression. The realm of the poet has none of these limits. He must secure his effects through the full exercise of his consciousness, and since sensuous images are an important part of his imagination, his poems must be concrete.

Nothing in human consciousness is alien to the poet in his contemplation; man lives most of his conscious life accepting the world of things, disparate entities given him by his senses; these concrete objects, therefore, the poet will naturally use to embody the structures in his mind. They are the materials to which the poet, in his desire to make his conception permanent, turns as instinctively as the architect turns to bricks and stone.

In past times, concrete imagery and poetry have always been closely connected. Primitive languages are imagistic; they name concrete things and have few words for abstractions. And the first literary remains in most languages are poetic. There is little point in speculating whether a concrete vocabulary fosters poetry or poetry insists upon a concrete vocabulary. Historically, at any rate, the language of poetry has almost invariably been highly specific. Philosophies and religions in their early stages are tangibly embodied; concepts and forces are visible and walk and speak. Even in a highly developed, mature civilization, thinking in terms of images occurs naturally. Plato's ideas gain much of their power and appeal from the myths which clothe them, for he is indeed the *fabulator maximus*.

There is, then, something instinctive in man that craves the symbol. Chaucer's Pardoner is shrewdly aware that ordinary men take hold of ideas most easily when they are presented as parables, full of people, things, and actions.

> Lewed peple loven tales olde,

he says, and gives as the reason:

> Swiche thynges kan they wel reporte and holde.

Popularly considered, the concrete is more "real," more readily acceptable or believable, than the abstract. The mode of presenting ideas by means of perceivable objects that stand for those ideas is as old as human consciousness—and far older than the consciousness of what was being done and how it was being done. Evidently such imaginative embodiment makes it easier and pleasanter for an audience to grasp ideas, as the rhetoricians and literary critics of antiquity well knew.

Sir Philip Sidney is only following in their footsteps when he speaks of the end of poetry as being "to teach and delight." If the teaching implies that poetry must be significant, the delighting, in Sidney's argument, comes clearly from the imagery. His conceptions may seem a bit mechanical in the light of our more complex self-awareness; but they show unmistakably that the central critical tradition accepts without question as requirements for poetry the qualities of significance and concreteness. The poet, Sidney says, "coupleth the general notion with the particular example." Sidney, indeed, even makes Aristotle's doctrine of imitation seem almost purely physical when, after mentioning it, he immediately defines poetry as, "to speak metaphorically, a speaking picture." And again: "the right describing note to know a poet by" is "that *feigning notable images* of virtues, vices, or what else." Over and over, Sidney returns to this discovery of the poet's secret. The poet "beginneth not with obscure definitions. . . . With a tale, forsooth, he cometh unto you: with a tale which holdeth children from play, and old men from the chimney corner. . . . In men (most of which are childish in the best things, till they be cradled in their graves), glad they will be to hear the tales of Hercules, Achilles, Cyrus, and Aeneas: and hearing them, must needs hear the right description of wisdom, valour, and justice." Elsewhere, with even more confidence in his argument (and again illustrating his principles in his own practice), Sidney breaks out:

Anger, the Stoics say, was a short madness. Let but Sophocles bring you Ajax on a stage, killing and whipping sheep and oxen, thinking them the army of Greeks, with their chieftains Agamemnon and Menelaus, and tell me if you have not a more familiar insight into anger than finding in the schoolmen his genus and difference. . . . Even in the most excellent determination of goodness, what philosopher's counsel can so readily direct a prince as the feigned Cyrus in Xenophon? Or a virtuous man in all fortunes as Aeneas in Vergil? Or a whole commonwealth, as the way of Sir Thomas More's *Utopia?*

Turn at random to the poems or their fragments quoted throughout this book—poems quoted to illustrate other arguments—and you will see how universal is this quality of concreteness. Shakespeare, in "Take, O, take those lips away," conveys the ideas of beauty and betrayal by means of lips, eyes, dawning, lights, and seals, and by such concrete, easily visualized *actions* as taking away, bringing again, and misleading. Browning's "My Last Duchess" presents the Duke of Ferrara's desire for domination and possession in the final image of the rare bronze statue of Neptune taming a sea-horse. And in the little poem quoted at the conclusion of the first chapter, William Allingham materializes the poignancy of memory in such stage properties as a pond, four ducks, a grassbank, clouds, and the blue sky of spring.

The interplay between significance, which may be stated roughly in other words than those of the poem, and its illustration or embodiment in the poem itself is steady throughout poetry. Yet various poets drive this team of horses with a difference. Some are more clearly aware of the white horse tending toward the realm of ideas, where significance exists quintessentially. The others are first of all aware of the black horse of the corporeal world. Poets may therefore be divided roughly into two classes—those who begin with a proposition which they proceed to illustrate, and those who begin with a specific experience which they proceed to interpret. If we do not regard these tendencies as fixed categories, we may distinguish between the poets who proceed by deduction and those who proceed by induction.

Characteristically, Alexander Pope builds from abstract observation to particular illustrations. The *Essay on Man* affords many examples of the typical movement of Pope's poetic thought, such as the following eighteen lines (with my own analytical gloss):

PROPOSITION:       The bliss of Man (could Pride that blessing
                   find)
                   Is not to act or think beyond mankind;

RESTATEMENT:       No powers of body or of soul to share,
                   But what his nature and his state can bear.


ILLUSTRATIONS:  1. Why has not *Man* a microscopic *eye?*
                   For this plain reason, Man is not a Fly.
                   Say what the use, were finer optics given,
                   T' inspect a mite, not comprehend the heaven?

                2. Or *touch*, if tremblingly alive all o'er,
                   To smart and agonize at every pore?

                3. Or quick effluvia darting through the brain,
                   Die of a rose in *aromatic* pain?

                4. If nature thundered in his opening *ears*,
                   And stunned him with the music of the spheres,
                   How would he wish that Heaven had left him
                       still
                   The whisp'ring Zephyr, and the purling rill?


CONCLUSION:        Who finds not Providence all good and wise,
                   Alike in what it gives, and what denies?

Here the drift from an initial general thought to a more specific
embodiment is constantly evident. Even in the first four lines,
the second couplet tends to make more specific the thought of
the first couplet; and the next four lines are similar in the increasing particularity of the thought. After the general proposition, follow illustrations based upon the "powers of body,"
as if the "powers of soul," not being so directly connected with
the material world, could not be adequately illustrated in a

compressed argumentative poem. The very organization itself, which makes use of four of the five conventional senses, indicates that Pope's verses spring from ordered thought rather than from observed experience: first he has the abstract idea of the five senses; then he imagines examples. After the illustrations, the conclusion. The thought is as formally organized as the rhythm of the couplets themselves; the images do not dictate the general idea; they are called in to serve it. What is true of Pope is true generally of English poetry from Dryden to Wordsworth. The poems *originate* in general controlling ideas, whether of argument (*Religio Laici*), or of topic (*The Seasons, The Grave*), or of form (satire, heroic drama, eclogue).

Conversely, an actual scene, a fleeting emotion, a sudden single incident may germinate the poem. Wordsworth at his most characteristic well illustrates this other type of poem. The poem springs from powerful emotion, usually growing out of a particular experience; but it is emotion recollected in tranquillity—that is, the experience is brooded over until it acquires significance. Thus one feels that the concrete experience of "The Daffodils" preceded the general idea that the store of our memories sustains us—not that it was called to mind in order to illustrate the general idea. The same idea comes at the conclusion (not at the beginning) of "The Solitary Reaper"—

> The music in my heart I bore
> Long after it was heard no more

—and even there it is not stated directly. Many people speak of Wordsworth's poem "Resolution and Independence" as "The Leech-gatherer"; for here too the poem is obviously generated by the old man by the lonely pool on that day of sunshine after rain, when the air was filled with the noise of birds and waters. Only as a kind of epilogue to the experience itself does the generalized significance of the actual title develop.

Wordsworth begins with the world of eye and ear; he ends in thought. This characteristic may explain his unusual and repeated use of the word *form* throughout his poems to designate *idea:* his ideas did actually come to him first as forms—the peak striding after him, or any other incident or picture of his childhood in *The Prelude*—and only through meditation, or through poetic craftsmanship, or both, does he turn his percepts into concepts. Wordsworth continually progresses from object (the concrete) to idea (the significant). Writing in "Tintern Abbey" of the "beauteous forms" of nature, he confesses:

> I have owed to them,
> In hours of weariness, *sensations* sweet,
> Felt in the *blood*, and felt along the *heart;*
> And passing even into my purer *mind*,
> With tranquil restoration.

It is not profitable to argue that Pope's characteristic method is preferable to Wordsworth's, or Wordsworth's to Pope's. Some critics have maintained that to begin a poem with a general idea—Pope's usual method—is to make the concrete illustrations mere decorations, arabesques, prettifications. On the other hand, opposed theorists have maintained that the nineteenth-century poets' regard for detail has left them blind to general significance, which, if it is present at all, seems tacked on as a postscript. Arnold is not the only critic who has held that the Romantics cannot see the tree for the leaves.

Neither of these positions, however, satisfies current doctrine. Modern critics are well aware of the quality of concreteness in poetry and, at least in their analyses of specific poems, of the quality of significance. But the conception of the organic nature of poetry leads many to hold that poetry is inferior whenever imagery and significance are in any way separable. The practice of Yeats and of Eliot, the serious study of the Symbolists and the Metaphysicals, have in various fashions given

authority to this theory. Admirable in itself, it does not provide
an exclusive formula for poetry. Pushed to an extreme it leads
perilously near some such critical observation as: A poem is
a poem is a poem is a poem. Man is no less a single organism
because we can speak now of his head and now of his feet,
now of his mind and now of his body. And a poem may retain
its unified nature even after being critically dissected into
seven distinct qualities.

One further point. Granted that the components of a poem
must fuse into a whole, at what point must this fusion take
place? May not the reader, as often as the poet, make the
fusion? Older poems often follow the pattern of an Aesop's
fable: a story is told, a picture created, an incident sketched,
and finally a moral presented. Yet the *total* effect of this conclusion, which frequently might appear able to stand by itself
like an old proverb, is that of arriving at the end of a search,
or of giving weight and value and dimensions and worth to
the preceding tapestry or panorama. Isolated, the direct general statement is not poetic; within the poem, it may assimilate
relevant concrete elements and may thus become poetic in
effect.

Keats, for instance, tends to begin and end poems with something very like a prose statement, and to work them up to
an internal climax in which the concrete symbol fuses with its
abstract significance. The reader experiences these changes
from prose statement to imaginative vision every time he reads
Keats with alertness. The opening of *Endymion* progresses
in each phrase from flat statement toward sensuous expression
of a delicate intuition:

> A thing of beauty is a joy for ever:
> Its loveliness increases; it will never
> Pass into nothingness; but still will keep
> A bower quiet for us, and a sleep
> Full of sweet dreams, and health, and quiet breathing.

Similarly, the first lines of the "Ode to a Nightingale" work imperceptibly from a simple, flat assertion toward rich, complex, concrete suggestion:

> My heart aches, and a drowsy numbness pains
> My sense, as though of hemlock I had drunk,
> Or emptied some dull opiate to the drains
> One minute past, and Lethe-wards had sunk.

Not until the middle of the fourth stanza—"Already with thee!"—is Keats caught up by the nightingale, and then the poem proceeds in trancelike ecstasy. The thronging images heighten imaginative experience by giving it a body. The last stanza marks the return from imagination to actuality:

> Forlorn! the very word is like a bell
> To toll me back from thee to my sole self!
> Adieu! the fancy cannot cheat so well
> As she is fam'd to do, deceiving elf.

And in the last lines, the fading song of the nightingale, past meadows, stream, hillside, and valley glades, embodies this departure of ecstasy, and leaves Keats questioning in a dull world, as if to exemplify poetically—that is, concretely—Shelley's dictum that "the mind in creation is as a fading coal, which some invisible influence, like an inconstant wind, awakens to transitory brightness."

There are, then, innumerable ways of combining the significant and the concrete. Either may generate the other; or they may coexist inextricably. It is enough if we recognize the presence both of significance and of concreteness, and allow the poet, provided somehow he attain a final impression of unity, to combine his elements as he pleases.

Let us accept, then, the proposition that poetry conveys thought by means of imagery. And let us confine ourselves at the start to obviously imagistic examples. What *kind* of images are best produced in the specific medium of rhythmical words?

How do they gain their effect? Do they shift from reader to reader, or do they remain fairly stable and invariable?

It is almost immediately evident that poetry cannot reproduce phenomena exactly. Its "images" are not really comparable to the visual equivalents produced in a mirror or the audible equivalents produced in a telephone receiver. Poetry cannot model from the life, cannot reproduce its original as faithfully, say, as Rembrandt's Saskia represents Saskia herself. The medium of poetry is sound; yet even in this limited range, the sounds of our speech are not of much use in imaging other sounds taken as "life models." Thus, Verlaine's famous

> Les sanglots longs
> Des violons
> De l'automne

is really not a very exact mimicry of the sound of violins, although it is about as much as language can do. If we collected an anthology of similar passages in which poetic sounds are meant to echo actual sounds—Tennyson's "The mellow ouzel fluted in the elm," Dryden's "the double double double beat of the thund'ring drum," James Whitcomb Riley's "The husky, rusty rustlin' of the tossels of the corn," Poe's bells and Southey's waters of Lodore and all the others—we might admire virtuosity on display, but could hardly be impressed by any exact equivalence between the verbal sounds and the actual sounds they are designed to represent.

Such images as I have mentioned above are auditory images. The sounds the poet wishes to produce are therefore held fast to the accepted pronunciation of the words he uses. These images, then, though they are not perfect echoes, are at least fairly stable. In imaging other senses than that of hearing, even this relative fixity tends to disappear.

A poem is not only heard; it is, perhaps too frequently, seen as letters on a page. Certain recent poets have even made experiments because they have been aware of this fact. But I have not found the right way to use concrete imagery when I have set up on the page, as a poem entitled "Versailles," the following arrangement of words:

| TURF | TURF | TURF | TURF | TURF |
|------|------|------|------|------|
| PARTERRE | PARTERRE | STEPS | PARTERRE | PARTERRE |
| PALACE | PALACE | LOUIS | PALACE | PALACE |
| PALACE | COURTYARD | COURTYARD | COURTYARD | PALACE |
| WALL | COURTYARD | COURTYARD | COURTYARD | WALL |
| WALL | WALL | GATES | WALL | WALL |

And the ingenious experiments of the seventeenth century, of which George Herbert's poems in the forms of a pair of angel's wings and of an altar are the best-known examples, are curious rather than convincing as images.

If within the specific media of poetry—the sound of words, or their appearance on a page, or both—words are inadequate for exactly reproductive imagery, they must be even more unsatisfactory in creating images of smells, tastes, or tactile sensations. Keats, of course, has wrestled with this difficulty as persistently as any English poet. Such lines of his as

> him whose strenuous tongue
> Can burst joy's grape against his palate fine

come perhaps as close as words can come to conveying a taste; yet even here the sensation is not principally conveyed by direct reproduction, but indirectly through tactile sensations, and these tactile sensations themselves are indirectly suggested by words implying action, such as "strenuous" and "burst." Similarly the thought of one of Donne's most famous religious sonnets is carried by tactile images of straining fighters. It opens:

> Batter my heart, three person'd God; for, you
> As yet but knocke, breathe, shine, and seeke to mend;
> That I may rise, and stand, o'erthrow mee, 'and bend
> Your force, to breake, blowe, burn and make me new.

Yet here again, any tactile images of struggle and effort are
not directly "covered"; they arise partly through sound—
in the force and heaviness of the extra accented syllables; partly
they spring from the motile suggestions in "batter," "over-
throw," "bend," "break," and "blow"; and partly they may be
generated by our emotions of sympathy as we imagine ourselves so beset and battered. The truly poetic significance of
a complete poem seldom rests in a direct general statement; it
must spring from concrete images. But now we seem to be
forced toward the conclusion that the images themselves are
seldom direct reproductions of the phenomena they supposedly
describe. How, for instance, can words hope to describe an
odor directly? Only by ingeniously arresting our attention
and compelling us to dwell on what is imaged.

When Robert Bridges in *The Testament of Beauty* wishes
to give us the scent of a summer garden, we read:

> 　　　　　　　　　The imponderable fragrance
> of my window-jasmin, that from her starry cup
> of red-stemm'd ivory invadeth my being,
> as she floateth it forth, and wantoning unabash'd
> asserteth her idea in the omnipotent blaze
> of the tormented sun-ball, checquering the grey wall
> with shadow-tracery of her shapely fronds; this frail
> unique spice of perfumery, in which she holdeth
> monopoly by royal licence of Nature,
> is but one of a thousand angelic species . . .
> 　　　　　　　　　Legion is their name;
> Lily-of-the-vale, Violet, Verbena, Mignonette,
> Hyacinth, Heliotrope, Sweet-briar, Pinks and Peas,
> Lilac and Wallflower, or such white and purple blooms
> that sleep i' the sun, and their heavy perfumes withhold
> to mingle their heart's incense with the wonder-dreams,
> love-laden prayers and reveries that steal forth from earth,
> under the dome of night: and tho' these blossomy breaths,
> that hav presumed the title of their gay genitors,
> enter but singly into our neighboring sense, that hath

no panorama, yet the mind's eye is not blind
unto their multitudinous presences:—I know
that if odour wer visible as color is, I'd see
the summer garden aureoled in rainbow clouds,
with such warfare of hues as a painter might choose
to show his sunset sky or a forest aflame;
while o'er the country-side the wide clover-pastures
and the beanfields of June would wear a mantle, thick
as when in late October, at the drooping of day
the dark grey mist arising blotteth out the land
with ghostly shroud. Now these and such-like influences
of tender specialty must not—so fine they be—
fall in neglect and all their loveliness be lost.

Here is long dwelling upon scent. But only perfumes—never
words—can directly reproduce the odors of roses. The in-
tangibility of odors is realized in such describing words as "the
imponderable fragrance," "her *idea*," "multitudinous *presences*," "such-like *influences*—so *fine* they be." In these phrases
the usual tendency of poetry is reversed, and concrete sensations are made distinct in tenuous abstractions. The intellect
is called in, in an attempt to give bounds and sharpness to a
floating persistent sensation, when the jasmine's "frail unique
spice of perfumery" is defined directly (though the definition
itself falls back upon concrete imagery) as "but one of a thousand angelic species." The passage also shows a hope that the
mere *naming* of flowers may suggest their odors: "these blos-
somy breaths . . . hav presumed the title of their gay geni-
tors"; in other words, Bridges hopes the reciting of their floral
names, by some process of poetic magic, may summon up
their perfumes (though even here "breaths" are not necessarily
apprehended only through the nose).

Again, Bridges is conscious of the limitations of the sense
of smell, the "sense that hath no panorama." Immediately, in
sheer defiance of this realization, Bridges proceeds to suggest
smell in terms of multiplicity of sights, although he has just

made the point that the sense of smell is neither multiplex nor capable of seeing. And just as he had hoped to realize more completely the "frail unique spice" by giving visual details— "*window*-jasmin . . . her *starry cup* of *red-stemm'd ivory*" —so now the symphony of garden odors, by day, dusk, and night, is whispered in terms of color and outline. In this passage, therefore, *odors* are presented *indirectly* by dwelling upon *intellectual* distinctions and definitions and by reference to *sights;* the intellectual and visual elements themselves are presented *indirectly* through *words*, since the words are either the "sounds" of the poem or its "sight" upon the page, where the word "Violet" looks quite different from the violet itself. In short, smell is presented in terms of sight, which is presented in terms of sound. If images of sight are successfully created, memories of an associated scent may be aroused. Once again, then, poetry cannot present even images directly. Its power rises in spite of—perhaps because of—the limitations of its medium; and its power is the power of suggestiveness. The writer, the reader, of poetry must always "by indirections find directions out."

The movement of Bridges' thought—from scent to sight— might indicate that visual images are more easily apprehended than those depending upon the other senses. This is so frequently taken for granted that popular usage limits the word "image" to visual images, forgetting that it may legitimately apply to any of the senses, and beyond the senses to intellectual imagery and emotional imagery as well. Our capacities for seeing, in relation to the other senses, seem more constantly and consciously used, more definite and more complex. Even when this is admitted, it remains true that visual images cannot be exactly denoted by means of words, and despite all care on the part of creator and of auditor, the same words read to fifty people may produce in their minds fifty different pictures. Many vividly pictorial lines become ambiguous upon analysis, or gain their power through associations made by the individual reader.

Donne opens a religious sonnet with:

> At the round earth's imagin'd corners, blow
> Your trumpets, Angels! And arise, arise
> From death, you numberless infinities
> Of souls, and to your scattered bodies go!

The second sentence happens to create in my own mind a sharp visual image: what could the poet have done to keep me from seeing, specifically, Signorelli's great Last Judgment fresco in the cathedral at Orvieto? In practice, the words of a poem invite the reader to search through his remembered experience for the right picture. The picture implicit in Donne's second sentence at least gains a minimum fixity because it points at a scene which has become somewhat conventionalized and familiar in religious art. But what agreement among readers might we expect to find in the pictures the first sentence flashes upon the mental screen? Suppose we assume agreement as to the clothing, coloring, and posture of angels; grant also that "trumpets" will suggest neither bugles nor tubas, but an "angel's horn" of purest Fra Angelico contour. Still—does "round earth" make us see a circular disk or a sphere? And if we *see* either of these, then what can we possibly see in the word "corners"? Is the adjective "imagined" inserted to acknowledge that neither a circle nor a sphere has corners, or to carry the mind's eye beyond material limitations to a view of the whole world? Above all, what has the poet done to suggest the point of view from which we are looking? Are we standing on a flat earth looking at angels in the sky or on the horizon? Or are we off in space looking at angels in space surrounding this little O, the world? And how many angels are there? For some odd reason, most readers would agree upon four, possibly thinking of the four quarters of the globe. Other readers, accustomed to the frequent map images in Donne's poetry, see the whole picture as a flat map, with angels at the four corners, or sometimes, defying what Donne explicitly writes, in the middle of each of the four sides.

The individual pictures these lines call up, therefore, vary widely. Let the reader try a similar short passage on his friends. From asking many students and amateurs of poetry what mental pictures Donne's lines aroused in them, I know how wide the divergences can be. Even more remarkable, many persons insist that they read or hear these lines with enjoyment and what seems to them full appreciation without any sharp visual image in their consciousness. To what extent this is possible or desirable must soon demand our attention.

But first, let us apply the practical criticism of I. A. Richards to the question: how concrete is concrete imagery? A detailed answer to this question is worth our time, for it has not often been considered seriously. Let us take a laboratory example to show in extended comments by readers, first, that visual images called up by any fragment of poetry may vary from vagueness to extreme clarity; and second, that the clear images themselves may have little in common. Here are the first two stanzas of Housman's poem "Reveille."

> Wake: the silver dusk returning
>   Up the beach of darkness brims,
> And the ship of sunrise burning
>   Strands upon the eastern rims.

> Wake: the vaulted shadow shatters,
>   Trampled to the floor it spanned,
> And the tent of night in tatters
>   Straws the sky-pavilioned land.

I asked thirty undergraduates (and did not give them much time to reflect): What do you *see* mentally upon reading these lines? No other question was asked, but many specific questions arise upon close scrutiny of the verses. The possible image that the imperative "Wake!" might call up was overlooked by almost everyone. The first question that actually developed came from the use of the word "dusk." Is not this usually associated with evening rather than dawn, as Housman himself emphasizes in the word "returning"? And if so, have we a picture of day-fall or darkening night superposed upon a picture of day-spring or brightening light? And if this is true, can the imagination hold, or merge, simultaneous pictures? Out of thirty men, nine, unprompted, made some reference that showed they had evening twilight as well as morning twilight in mind—a sunset in reverse. "Dusk returning" seems effective, then, to this extent: possible superposed pictures are either disregarded or received easily and with pleasure. Since no man criticized the image adversely, it would appear that the imagination ordinarily accepts superposed pictures without cavil, perhaps without analysis.

But the thirty comments stop there: few men, for example, attempted to connect the movement of the dusk with the movement of water that dominates the rest of the stanza; and few, therefore, expressed opinions as to whether that "returning" movement was oscillating (like the go-and-come of waves) or rotating (like high-tide going around the earth). Only in misinterpreting the second stanza did one man introduce this idea of rotation—in imagining the trampled shadow of night as falling below the horizon to the other side of the earth. Yet some conception is necessary here in order to get a clear picture of the dusk brimming up the beach of darkness. If "returning" means repeating what has happened in previous dawns, then the light is brimming up again in the east. If, however, one may return only from where one has been, then the dusk must flood back from the west, where it was last seen. Our decisions here will largely condition what we visualize in "beach of darkness." Here there was no agreement. Most commentators did not specify an image. Half of those who did saw the black eastern horizon as the beach: "Dusk here is described as though it was rolling over the land, termed here a beach of darkness, towards [!] the morning." The other half saw the dark sky receding into the west as the beach: "The sleeper sees dawn as another twilight, advancing toward the night as waves to a shore." "The picture shows the light approaching as the tide approaches upon a beach. The beach seems to recede before the silvery light of first sunrise." Others, who felt the *rising* light of dawn, introduced images of their own—paraphrases which do not make the Housman picture particularly sharp: "Here is silver gray of the dusk brimming up over the shadowed beach, which effect seems to be a diffusion of the grayness of the dark and the sandiness of the beach." Or: "Molten silver rising out of dark empty cup and brimming over its edges." "The silver curtain of night gradually retreats before the sun, as a mist evaporates before the approaching heat of that orb."

"The ship of sunrise . . . strands" produced relatively complete agreement on a picture of the sun, or the sun in sharply outlined clouds, just touching the eastern horizon. The whole stanza impressed many through its organized sea imagery—so much so that there were many irrelevant additional pictures supplied, such as "white foam" and "sparkling sea"; and at least four men stated definitely that the poet himself is standing on a beach looking out over a sea to the east.

"Vaulted shadow" was not particularly effective in calling up pictures, although it did suggest cathedral imagery to two men who carried it out, in spite of Housman, through the rest of the stanza. "Vaulted" together with "trampled" led one surrealist to write: "The sense impressions are those of the realm of Darkness and sleep which we are leaving:—as though we were within a monstrous eggshell being crushed by a giant foot." There was general agreement on a picture of patches of shadow on the earth, as if fallen from the sky, in the last two lines. Not very frequently were any of Housman's subtleties in rhythm or word choice appreciated as consciously as in the following comment: "The impact of the imagery is con-

tained more in the words 'strands' and 'straws' and is felt
rather than consciously realized at first reading. The ship strikes
a snag. . . ."

Differing interpretations of "straws" determined three distinct groups of pictures: (1) the idea of *disorganization* predominated—scattered like straw; or (2) *outline* was foremost
—shadows long and straight as straws were cast on the land;
or (3) *color* was foremost—yellow. The first interpretation
was the commonest, doubtless controlled to some extent by
the trampled shadows and the tattered night, and almost certainly by the overtone of "strews" in Housman's unusual verb:
one man even said—conscious of the association?—"very much
as straw is strewn over a threshing floor." The overtone is
effective, for eagle-eyed editors have made it difficult for me
to get the *durior lectio* of "straws" set up at all, since "strews"
is so much more serviceable as a transitive verb. When the
image of color predominated, men usually disregarded the
grammatical relation of "straws" to the tattered tent of night
and found that the sun was producing long yellow gleams on
the land, or straight rays through the sky, or glints on scattered
cloud forms above; so that a few with an intense sense of color
took "sky-pavilioned land" to indicate the sky itself, tattered
with golden stratus clouds, rather than the earth beneath with
its new pavilion of sky. Sometimes a comment wavered between various pictures, as if the reader felt two or more at
once: "The heavens shake and fall in tatters from the impact
of light, of sun; not dispersed completely, the darkness straws
the land, streaks of light tearing it to pieces." Do the lights or
the shadows constitute the straws in this man's picture?

What causes such varying pictures? The poet, the reader,
or the limitations of the medium? I have so far included only
interpretations that might be defended; but often the reader
is seriously at fault. Such a comment as: "The first image is
only of the sun coming up after a black night—something like
that which occurs on the Gulf Coast in the winter"—repre-

sents unimaginative reading in its first half and, probably, auto-biography in its second. Some comments were organized around a single approach suggested by, or added to, the poem. This man concentrated on colors, and supplied one or two of his own: "Deep blue in the west, turning to gray as the eye proceeds eastward; then streaks of yellow and finally a brilliant fiery red." And this man produced an excellent impression at once sharp and generalized; his comment will explain the paradox: "White light growing in intensity. A silhouette against brilliant background of rather diffused color. Heavy shadows spread at one's feet but light above. An image of a field with highlights of color and brilliance interspersed with darkness, and the sense of an extended horizon which gathers brilliance as it goes into the distance." Again, with unswerving gaze a man persisted in his own mis-seeing: "The awakened is greeted by the cool white morning mist. The mist lies on the land (darkness) like water against the shore of the pond or sea. The sun rises over the misty horizon as out of water—continuing the mist-water image. The darkness which was shore to the mist gives way to light as of strands along the water."

These last three complete comments, at any rate, build around a single impression. What, however, does a man actually *see* of Housman's dawning in a comment which breaks up, word by word, the second stanza into images of a glass dropped and shattered on a floor, a blanket, a torn and ragged garment, and a pavilion "adorned·in the colorful medieval times of a tourney"? It would be dangerous to jump at the conclusion that this last reader is better at fanciful equivalents than at organized vision, for the comments as a whole suggest that powers of visualization differ from individual to individual not only in their intensity but in their constituents and their range. Between the poles of insensateness and overfecund fancy such a complete comment as the following may be taken as the norm, among thirty readers, for this passage:

"The pale light of breaking dawn with the sun poised on

the horizon as if hesitating before showing her full self. The vaulted black of night is broken and fallen to earth, leaving the sky to the sun's coloring, while yet the earth beneath remains in shadows—the broken remnants of night."

This picture is not remarkable; it leaves much to be desired; but it is not silly, and it shows the average visual impression Housman's stanzas actually made. The comments were written under circumstances which were casual and everyday, so that no reader was trying to show off his brilliance, or to wring, after profound thought, the last possible image from the lines. The remarks, therefore, may not show how poetry should be read; they do show how it *is* read. No reader seemed dissatisfied either with Housman's data or with his own interpretation. Our imagination is evidently such stuff as can accept inconsistencies either within a poem or within its own musings.

Should, and could, Housman himself have given his images more stability? Often ambiguity arises which, even in an artist as careful as Housman, seems unintended, and to that extent inartistic. Many of us may feel that the visual, extragrammatical suggestions in "strands" and "straws" were deliberate on Housman's part and prove effective imaginatively. Ambiguity in itself, however, is not inevitably a virtue in poetry. For instance, is it not probable that Housman saw one phenomenon only in his "beach of darkness" and would have been taken aback, as artist, to find half the world thinking of a dark sky retreating into the west when he thought of the black eastern rim of land, or vice versa? Even here the important point is the extraordinary assimilative power of the imagination—or should we say its fortunate lack of analytical consistency? Whichever of the above interpretations of the beach of darkness is "wrong," no reader was made unhappy, or uneasy, or uncertain in his own mind, because he held it.

Is the medium of poetry the cause of such varying images? Very largely. A panorama in words, a still life or a portrait in audible or written symbols, is not even a translation of an

original. It is a field of suggestions, of clues and signs and riddles and conventions and patterns, upon which our powerful
and mysterious imaginations feed and exercise. That there
should be any agreement at all as to what a totally new combination of words may suggest visually is in itself amazing. Any
absolute fixity of imagery among all readers is manifestly impossible, nor is it in poetry desirable. If each mental picture is
fairly clear, and agrees reasonably closely with the average intelligent reader's picture, it is a satisfactory visual image in
poetry. The distinction between time arts and space arts is too
intellectualized; for it is an unquestionable fact of experience
that poetry can and does create illusions of visual space. But
on the other hand, we must guard against considering poems
or any of their parts exactly as if they were paintings or sculp-
tures or buildings. The media are different; and if a poem cannot get the precise, unvarying effects that any painting can, it
nevertheless achieves effects of its own. For instance, the comments quoted here at such length show that the mind's eye be-
holds without discomfort, or feels that it is beholding, more
than one picture at a time, even when those pictures are sun-
dered in time, or in space, or in compatibility.

More important, poetry can actually produce moving pictures—pictures that blend into each other, or change through
time. Yet we are so accustomed to think of "pictures" as static
that we are inclined to freeze the images of poetry. Not more
than one or two of the thirty readers of Housman's stanzas
were aware that the picture was developing *in time* through
at least three distinct stages: the gradual brightening, the sudden appearance of the sun, the more extended falling of the
shadows to the earth. Such a comment as the following was
unique in its realization of the capacities of poetry for continuing a changing picture through time:

"The vault of shadows (in the second stanza) is shattered
by the light, because the light streaks the darkness. The light
does not approach as the tide when it has once appeared, but

shatters the vaulted shadow and finally destroys it altogether."

The visual images in our minds, then, vary from one person to another in sharpness and "visibility"; several may exist simultaneously without bewildering us, as if they responded less to laws of space than to undetermined laws of consciousness; they change or lose their outline more easily than steam vapors; except by an effort of will they are not subject to rational control, but respond easily to—are even created by —associative thought, daydreams, the phantasmagoria of the imagination; so that an idea suggests an image, and that image begets, or shifts into, a further image, in a train of shapes which the *poetic imagination* readily accepts, no matter how annoyingly accidental and capricious they may seem to the tidy mind.

Consider, as an example of crowded and varied visual imagery, part of the famous speech of Shakespeare's Ulysses to Achilles, in which the argument is simply that you cannot rest on your laurels but must continually strive in order to keep honor bright:

> Time hath, my lord, a wallet at his back,
> Wherein he puts alms for oblivion,
> A great-siz'd monster of ingratitudes.
> Those scraps are good deeds past, which are devour'd
> As fast as they are made, forgot as soon
> As done. Perseverance, dear my lord,
> Keeps honour bright. To have done is to hang
> Quite out of fashion, like a rusty mail
> In monumental mock'ry. Take the instant way;
> For honour travels in a strait so narrow
> Where one but goes abreast. Keep then the path,
> For emulation hath a thousand sons
> That one by one pursue. If you give way,
> Or hedge aside from the direct forthright,
> Like to an ent'red tide they all rush by
> And leave you hindmost;
> Or, like a gallant horse fall'n in first rank,

Lie there for pavement to the abject rear,
O'errun and trampled on. Then what they do in present,
Though less than yours in past, must o'ertop yours;
For Time is like a fashionable host,
That slightly shakes his parting guest by th' hand,
And with his arms outstretch'd as he would fly
Grasps in the comer. The welcome ever smiles,
And farewell goes out sighing. Let not virtue seek
Remuneration for the thing it was!

At the beginning, the relations between image and idea are stated with the directness of an equation: "Those scraps are good deeds past." The image is elaborated: the scraps are "devour'd" as fast as they are made, and this visual image of the monster eating is immediately explained in terms of the idea: good deeds are forgot as soon as done. By the time Shakespeare has drawn his conclusion that perseverance in good deeds can preserve honor for the hero, the image has shifted to brightness, and this suggests the rusty mail, which in turn suggests the monument (and possibly overtones of admonishing, pointing at?) Now the idea of past and present *time* suddenly shifts to the familiar image of traveling through *space*, possibly through association in the double meanings of "Take the instant *way*." As Shakespeare so frequently does, he now clusters synonyms for "way": "strait," "path," "direct forthright," "pavement." The idea in "emulation" changes the image of the journey into one of pursuit, and then of the speed of a race, where the image of the rushing sons suggests two further images to explain the original—that of a tide breaking a barrier or rushing past it, and that of the fallen horse trampled on. Here the idea of first-and-last leads to the next comparison between present and past, which now takes the form of visual illustration in vertical (no longer horizontal) space in the word "o'ertop." Suddenly, without any sense of incongruity, the initial image of Time, the traveler, reappears by magic as a fashionable host whose actions are vividly described: again,

one visual illustration is made more effective by adding another
to illustrate the first: "his arms outstretch'd *as he would fly*."
This image of the host is so powerful that the mere ideas of
the present deed and the past deed, the "welcome" and "farewell," may be personified with the utmost economy, and we
see figures in motion and with expression in their faces and
actions:

> The welcome ever smiles,
> And farewell goes out sighing.

"*And therefore*," Shakespeare seems to add mentally, virtue
must remember that human forgetfulness precludes a just re-
ward for merit. Yet even the final argument in this passage is
cast in the active, visual world of trade: someone is seeking
remuneration. In a short passage the images have shifted,
blended, and suddenly or arbitrarily jumped. Shakespeare takes
as his province all existence, actual or fancied. We girdle the
earth in twenty minutes, and while Ulysses reasons with
Achilles, we contemplate beggars and the feeding of mon-
sters, old armor in a tomb or chapel or hall, a journey that becomes a pursuit and turns into a battle, trampled horses and a
fashionable entertainment. And this without any real sense of
bewilderment or strain. For if the visual imagery in poetry is
protean, at least like Proteus also it retains through all metamorphoses its own vitality.

Visual imagery shifts quickly and may not be too precise
for any particular reader in any particular passage. How,
then, does the poet assure himself that he will produce the
single effect he aims at? Largely through a type of imagery we
have so far not considered: imagery of feeling or emotions.
Somewhere in his writings, Aldous Huxley maintains with
justice that "feeling-images" are the most common of all types
of image in poetry. Swinburne's ballade refrain,

> Villon, our sad bad glad mad brother's name!

whatever we may think of it as poetry, is characteristic of this poetic process of striving to re-create an emotion—that is, to set up emotional images. If Swinburne's line were effective as poetry, every one of the four adjectives would rouse an emotion. The very word "brother" probably does more to establish an emotional image of fraternity and sympathy than a visual image of a man. Language has always been used to convey emotion—much more frequently than to transfer controlled thoughts or pure sensations; and we consequently have the illusion, at least, that we have absorbed an emotion from any poetic attempt at communication. These emotional images, for whatever reason, come nearer to producing a single stabilized effect than do sensory poetic images. Readers of the first two stanzas of Housman's "Reveille" would be in fair agreement as to the emotional content. And if the whole poem were read, the mood of the first two stanzas would be even more definitely determined. Any reader may test in himself the sharpness of emotional images by trying to describe the feeling any poem sets up in him. Usually he can satisfy himself; in the cases where he is at a loss, he will often find that he is dissatisfied not because the emotion in the poem is vague, but because it is so clear and particular that he cannot himself find the right words to describe it adequately.

The indefiniteness of *sensory* images within a poem, therefore, does not limit their practical effectiveness, for such images ordinarily serve in the shaping of the *emotional* image or mood of the poem, and this emotional image is usually found to be more precise. For example, in *Paradise Lost* we may not all have the same mental images of Satan in Pandemonium, or of the chariot of the Messiah, or of the taste of Eden's fruits and the ashen apples of Hell; but these, and all the other concrete sensory images of the poem, are combined in such a way as to produce a dominating emotion for the whole poem so sharp and unique for most of us that we reject any general descriptive phrase for it—such as "reverent exultation at the justice and mercy of God"—as inadequate to the sharpness of this emotional image.

When tradition, convention, and imitation pall, poetry becomes sophisticated or perverse. Significance and concreteness are essentials, and usually the concrete is employed to body forth the significant. But this common process may be reversed, and a concrete situation may be illuminated or given body by the subsidiary use of ideas, even in their most obvious form of intellectual arguments. The metaphysical poets made this reversed process into a regular device, which explains why they are metaphysicals and why also they are poets. Dryden, for instance, attacks John Donne for perplexing "the minds of the fair sex with nice speculations of philosophy when he should engage their hearts and entertain them with the softnesses of love." Here Dryden is limiting the possibilities of poetry by insisting that each type must remain within certain conventional bounds—that amatory verse, for example, should be only sentimental and tepidly sensuous. But Donne takes a concrete situation (himself and a woman, usually with details of time and place suggested) and intensifies the emotion by arguing or speculating about it. The concreteness of particular existence and the generalization of thought are both present in his poems; but now he is turning the usual poetic procedure upside down: he compels us to dwell on a concrete experience by embellishing it with arabesques made out of abstractions.

As an illustration, consider the three stanzas of John Donne's poem, "The Flea":

Mark but this flea, and mark in this,
How little that which thou deny'st me is;
It suck'd me first, and now sucks thee,
And in this flea, our two bloods mingled be;
Thou know'st that this cannot be said
A sin, nor shame, nor loss of maidenhead,

Yet this enjoys before it woo,
And pamper'd swells with one blood made of two,
And this, alas, is more than we would do.

Oh, stay, three lives in one flea spare,
Where we almost, yea more than married are.
This flea is you and I, and this
Our marriage bed, and marriage temple is;
Though parents grudge, and you, we're met,
And cloistered in these living walls of jet.
   Though use make you apt to kill me,
   Let not to that, self murder added be,
   And sacrilege, three sins in killing three.

Cruel and sudden, hast thou since
Purpled thy nail, in blood of innocence?
Wherein could this flea guilty be,
Except in that drop which it suck'd from thee?
Yet thou triumph'st, and sayest that thou
Find'st not thy self, nor me the weaker now;
   'Tis true, then learn how false, fears be;
   Just so much honor, when thou yield'st to me,
   Will waste, as this flea's death took life from thee.

Here Donne, starting from the unique concrete data of himself, his mistress, and the flea that has bitten them both, develops a distinctive but indescribable mood that mixes desire and humor, forthright passion and cynicism, pleading and taunting, and manages to develop and sustain this mood by intellectual arguments that entail such conceptions as justice, the Trinity, the sacraments, and speculations concerning quantity sophistically developed by analogy. The abstract and the concrete, the intellectual and the tangible, are not easily separated in Donne's mind; one grows from the other, and neither can be said to come first. If the "three-person'd God" can batter Donne's heart, conversely the lock of woman's hair about his arm, the "bracelet of bright hair about the bone," may be his "outward soul."

The concrete element may be hidden, but almost invariably it is present in some important way, even in short fragments of poetry. Dante's famous line,

> *E 'n la sua volontate è nostra pace,*

> And in His will is our peace,

at first glance seems to contain little more than the abstractions "will" and "peace" related by means of the colorless verb "is." But the innocuous preposition "in" (if we accept this as the correct reading) makes the idea implicitly spatial: entities are included *within* a larger entity. The entities, moreover, are persons, since they experience consciousness in that they feel the emotions of willing and of accepting. The two pronouns introduce God and Christian believers; in its context the scene, speaker, and audience are indicated in specific detail. And the high spirituality of Dante's conception develops poetically in the subsequent compressed line,

> *ell' è quel mare al qual tutto si move,*

> it is that sea to which all moves,

where the complex idea, that God's will is the source of all his creatures' existence and their ultimate haven, is expressed in the specific image of the sea and the implied image of all the rivers.

No final rule, then, may be laid down as to the manner in which the concrete element may enter poetry, though it ordinarily takes the form of an actor or an image to carry a thought. It is an invariable characteristic of poetic thinking, and upon analysis, any poem will prove to have an indivisible part of its vitality in this quality of being concrete.

*CHAPTER FIVE*

# POETRY
# IS COMPLEX

A POEM is like a person. Though it has a family tree, it is important not because of its ancestors but because of its own individuality. The poem, like any human being, is something more than its most complete analysis. Like any human being, it gives a sense of unified individuality which no summary of its qualities can reproduce; and at the same time a sense of variety which is beyond satisfactory final analysis. When we have discovered that all poetry is exact, intense, significant, and concrete, we have simply prepared the way, by naming disparate qualities, for a more comprehensive fifth quality: poetry is complex.

The law of complexity, therefore, is a result, rather than a cause, of poetic creation. Under some other Solon, in another country, the laws of poetry might be nine in number, or five. But when they were finally stated, the law of complexity would inevitably emerge. Some poets have even taken it as the primary law, and there are many modern writers who have attempted deliberately to make their poetry complex. They write complex poetry in accordance with conscious theory, and might almost be grouped as the New Metaphysicals. Other poets, such as Eliot, the early Auden, and the later Yeats, seem to strive for a complexity which to uninitiated readers verges on willful obscurity and bewilderment. Apart from deliberate theorists, enough English poets from Donne to Hopkins are complex by nature and reflect their nature in their works. The influence of Shakespeare's subtle, ranging, comprehensive mind, to cite the salient example, tended to make complexity in English poetry an expected trait.

Such instances are obvious. This chapter makes the more sweeping claim that *all* poetry is complex. Degrees of complexity exist, of course. But even the most seemingly simple poem secures its effect *as poetry* by complex means and associations. Conversely, to reduce any poem to a single mood, poetic device, or statement is to destroy it *as poetry*. A poem has not the simplicity of a machine; it has the complexity of a vital organism, of a person.

First of all we must look again at Milton's famous statement that poetry is "simple, sensuous, and passionate." Here, however, Milton was contrasting poetry and ornate rhetoric. Poetry, as opposed to rhetoric, is simple in its statement of intellectual arguments. Any good sermon or political speech or legal brief far surpasses a good poem in the number of its logically organized divisions and subdivisions. But the intellectual content, the argument, of a poem is no more the whole poem than the tag lines of La Fontaine are his fables, or the rough little quatrains before each canto of the *Faerie Queene* are Spenser's complete poem.

Let us grant that the main intellectual content of a poem may be stated more tersely than the proof of a geometrical proposition or the main points of a speech by Edmund Burke. Nevertheless, Euclid and Burke may be summarized with finality; an intellectual paraphrase of a poem, on the other hand, usually does not exhaust even its intellectual possibilities. "The high forms of literature," as Allen Tate says, "offer us the only complete, and thus the most responsible, versions of our experience." Poetry moves on many levels simultaneously. Dante in his *Convivio* holds that writings may be understood in four senses—the *literal*, the *allegorical*, the *moral*, and the *anagogic*, which might be called the spiritual or mystical sense. As an illustration of the "anagogic, that is, above or beyond sense," he cites "that hymn of the prophet [114th Psalm] which says that when the people of Israel went out of Egypt, Judaea became holy and free. Now, although this is obviously true according to the letter, the spiritual meaning is nevertheless true also: that when the soul makes its exodus from sin it becomes holy and free in its own nature."

Now all this may seem no more than the speculation of a medieval mind at home in theology and metaphysics. Let us see, therefore, how Dante's quadruple interpretation works out in a short and superficially simple poem by A. E. Housman, which we have already looked at in the Prologue.

> Into my heart an air that kills
>     From yon far country blows:
> What are those blue remembered hills,
>     What spires, what farms are those?
>
> That is the land of lost content,
>     I see it shining plain,
> The happy highways where I went
>     And cannot come again.

Few people would stop with the literal meaning, which indeed goes beyond credibility. How can a wind from any country blow into a man's heart? It cannot blow even into his lungs. An allegorical meaning is obviously necessary, and is directly supplied, as when Housman states that the "far country" over which the air blows is the "land of lost content." Ethical judgments also are implicit: emotion is assumed to be of value; past youthful happiness, "in harmony with nature," seems praiseworthy; present awareness of one's lot scarcely less so. And if one sought for an anagogical meaning, it might be that the clear realization of sorrow and its springs, and the transmutation of such killing emotion into the permanent forms of art, afford in some sense a triumph over the ills of existence.

All these meanings need not be stated baldly, nor in these particular terms; nor has Dante's fourfold division exhausted the possible intellectual meanings of the poem. They do represent, however, the types of multiplex meanings which a reader of sensitivity and experience expects and derives from a poem. The poem will not have for him a single simple key; the literal meaning, as in Housman's lines above, is usually the least satisfactory; and the further a reader progresses toward meanings difficult to formulate, the closer he seems to be to the heart of the poem. This is not to say that poets and their readers worship the mystifying and inexpressible. It is to say that poets have ways of conveying experience which are not the ways of logic, that significance may exist in human consciousness which the intellect can grasp and express only clumsily and in part. Usually, therefore, rationalists and literalists and men of common sense are enemies of poetry, for in attempting to offer simple substitutes for its complexity, they destroy its nature. The very chapters of this book, combining to form what might be called *The Seven Laws of Poetry*, are incompatible, if taken literally, with the law of complexity, which denies that poetry can be reduced to seven laws, or in reality analyzed into separate qualities at all. Once the complexity of poetry is realized, no one is in danger of believing that such a book of critical essays as this completely explains poetry. The most that criticism can ever do is to help a reader to see more, or to see more clearly, or to see once again.

The greatest beauties of poetry are always just beyond the reach of paraphrase. The critic may point toward them, but they can be realized only in the poem itself. Yeats has said, with the profundity of a true poet: "It is so many years before one can believe enough in what one feels even to know what the feeling is." A poem can be no more than an attempt toward such ideal crystallization of experience. Qualitatively it represents intense living; quantitatively it demands of the poet years of thought and preparation and practice in creation. To assume therefore that a paraphrase, even when it is sympathetic and intelligent and painstaking, will give answers and clarity which the poem cannot supply is woefully to mistake the nature of poetry and the purpose of criticism.

A poem, then, has intellectual content, usually simple so far as the logical formulation of any one of its arguments is concerned. Its intellectual content is nevertheless multiplex, and various meanings may coexist. Poetry resembles the invention by which many different telegraph messages may be sent at the same time over a single wire. The sum of the paraphrases of its different meanings, however, must not be considered equal to the poem itself, for the closer they get to the plane on which the poem is most alive, the less adequate they become as translations. We must, therefore, realize that a poem may send out many messages, and yet also recognize the impossibility of our decoding those messages completely. As in learning a foreign language, only time and practice and the assistance of others enable us to live directly in a poem, without translating it for ourselves into the more familiar language of practical reason.

So far I have limited myself, largely under Dante's guidance, to the multiple meanings which a poem may reveal when it is rationally interpreted. But this does not begin to exhaust the complexity of a work of art. I. A. Richards believes that we must consider four types of meaning in a poem before we can hope to understand it. All four of Dante's divisions would fall under the first of Mr. Richards' categories, its *sense*. His other three types of meaning are its *feeling*, its *intention*, and its *tone*. In Housman's poem the feeling balances between stoical restraint and bitterness, between love of Shropshire at one-and-twenty and regret over the pastness of the past. The feeling, no less than the meaning, is far from simple.

The "intention" of the poem can only be guessed at. If we accept Housman's own speculation with regard to the genesis of poetry—that a poet secretes a poem much as an oyster secretes a pearl—then the irritating grain of sand in Housman's case was his feeling of contentment lost, and the intention of the poem was to protect himself from the sharp, killing edges of this emotion by rounding it off in a work of art. Housman's frequent intention of cursing an evil world is not particularly evident here, though some readers might sense it. Three of his other characteristic purposes—finding refuge from the "blackguard" who made the world in the panorama of nature, in the nobility of endurance, and in the perfection and permanence of art—are recognizable in varying degrees.

The "tone" of the poem, or more specifically, the poet's attitude toward his reader, is not forced. Housman is meditating within himself. The first pair of lines describes a mental state, but for no one's particular benefit. The second pair asks questions; but even when he asks the questions, Housman knows the answer he gives in the second stanza, so that at most this could be considered only a dialogue within one man's mind. But Housman's self-revelation assumes sympathy from the reader (who, if unsympathetic, would immediately brand the poem as sentimental and romantic)—that fellow feeling and understanding which Housman extends to "luckless lads" like himself in the last poem of *A Shropshire Lad*. The tone of the poem, then, is that of one Shropshire lad talking trustfully to another, or to himself. As Richards has pointed out, it is extremely important to the appreciation of a poem that we sense the attitude of the poet toward his reader. Yet nearly always the tone is passed by without notice; when we do notice it, we find the poet cunning past man's thought and the poem growing in complexity.

Thus to Dante's quadruple meanings in a piece of imaginative writing we have added the four types of Mr. Richards. And these complicated systems of interpretation may be applied, as we have seen, even to a short lyric poem of eight lines.

But let us forget, for the moment, these formal systems. Let us take three short poems of different types, presenting respectively a simple thought, a simple sensation, and a simple emotion. Let us deliberately choose three poems by Pope, Herrick, and Burns for their apparent simplicity, and study, in the light of this fifth principle, their actual poetic complexity. If such brief and seemingly uninvolved lyrics are found to be complex in their poetic effects, longer and more ambitious poems might reasonably be assumed to accord with the underlying principle.

Pope's early "Ode on Solitude" should serve very well as a starter: its theme is simple and didactic; in its first form, Pope wrote it at such a tender age that it can hardly contain profound or mellow philosophy, except what the young translator lifted from Horace. Yet even here, in so far as one feels the twenty lines as poetry, the effects are complex.

> Happy the man whose wish and care
> 　A few paternal acres bound,
> Content to breathe his native air,
> 　　In his own ground.
>
> Whose herds with milk, whose fields with bread,
> 　Whose flocks supply him with attire,
> Whose trees in summer yield him shade,
> 　　In winter fire.
>
> Blest, who can unconcern'dly find
> 　Hours, days, and years slide soft away,
> In health of body, peace of mind,
> 　　Quiet by day,

Sound sleep by night; study and ease,
    Together mixt; sweet recreation;
And Innocence, which most does please
    With meditation.

Thus let me live, unseen, unknown,
    Thus unlamented let me die,
Steal from the world, and not a stone
    Tell where I lie.

The first stanza calls up judgments as to what constitutes happiness. Pope answers them by equating happiness and contentment—his familiar theme of "Hope humbly, then"—by suggesting the Aristotelian ideal of a life in which desire and duty are in harmony, and, through conventional imagery and excellent rhythmical and aural effects in the second and fourth lines, by appealing to patriotism, to a love of the soil, to the sense of tradition—in short, to fatherland in a triple sense. The more we consider this simple short stanza, the more we see that emotions, to be more fully developed later, already dominate the poem—particularly admiration for rustic simplicity and the sense of kinship with the land.

The second stanza, again through conventional imagery, suggests the completeness of such a life, though this general idea is not directly mentioned. Life is made to seem safe, certain, full: a pleasant and expected round. Before the stanza has run its course, food (in its double aspect of meat and drink), clothing, and shelter are all mentioned. And rustic content, we are told, persists in all seasons of the year.

The ideas of the continuity, the completeness, and the peace of such a life are developed by various means, particularly by formal balance, in the succeeding stanzas. Pope's lines cannot be appreciated as poetry without alertness to such governing motifs and their complex interplay.

The possibilities of any good poem—even of a mediocre poem—cannot be exhausted by analysis; yet two further aspects of the "Ode on Solitude" are worth mentioning. The first is the atmosphere of the whole poem: no countryman is speaking. This is a townsman's dream of the golden age. Pope is a Londoner, Horace a Roman; and the adverse criticism of sophisticated life, though never stated openly, counterbalances the idyl of rural acres. The emotion underlying the whole becomes the nostalgia of a highly civilized man for the peaceful, simple, humble, natural life—the same idealization of That-which-one-has-not that touches Gray's pictures of the rustic hamlet, or Theocritus' scenes of Sicilian reapers and fishermen.

The second aspect, allied to the first, is the sudden shift from general reflections to the personal application in the last lines. The emotions that have been hidden under didactic precepts in the other stanzas suddenly become direct and poignant, and as Pope rings his own changes on the theme of Shakespeare's sonnet,

> No longer mourn for me when I am dead
> Than you shall hear the surly sullen bell
> Give warning to the world that I am fled
> From this vile world, with vilest worms to dwell . . . ,

it becomes clear that under all the fine precepts of the rest of the poem lies a deep self-pity. The poem, then, is crystallized in the last stanza, and, reread, is felt to be, not a collection of flat moral maxims, but the utterance of a particular individual in a particular place and time, an utterance with the sharpness and complexity that constitutes poetry.

Complexity is no synonym for profundity. A poet like Robert Herrick does not bother his head too much about the cosmos. Yet Herrick, whose poetic skill lies in his lightness, does not lack complexity even in his most delicate lyrics. Take this complete little poem:

> Whenas in silks my Julia goes,
> Then, then, methinks, how sweetly flows
> That liquefaction of her clothes.

Next, when I cast mine eyes and see
That brave vibration each way free,
Oh, how that glittering taketh me!

Without trying to break a butterfly upon a wheel, one might note that this poem is certainly more than "Upon Julia's Clothes." It is also, and primarily, upon Julia, and upon "*my* Julia." Herrick manages to convey the sense of immediate delight, of catching the moment, in his "Then, then," and in the ejaculation of the last line, which has some of the breathlessness (achieved, also, in the same way) of Shakespeare's daffodils that take the winds of March with beauty. And what of that striking and much commended word "liquefaction"? It is, of course, excellent for the silk he is describing. But it is so unusual that it may startle the reader with a fine delight into meditating that Herrick lived in the century of the Royal Society and its physical experiments, or that Herrick was an Anglican cleric who had heard of the liquefaction of the blood of saints, or that Herrick relished the fine savor of the classics and knew how and when to introduce a Latin polysyllable. Moreover, in the light of the whole six lines, "liquefaction" is the key word to establish a water image—of lake, or river, or sea, or of all of them. Together with "flows," "vibration," and "glittering," "liquefaction" sets up in the background the innumerable laughter of the waves. The liquid imagery suggests gaiety and movement, but also imparts to Herrick's dainty Julia a classic dignity and grace, so that light as they are, the six lines are subtly stamped by remembrances of Greek and Roman lyrists. In other poems Herrick uses such jocund references to grave and spacious things deftly. Julia's cherry-ripe lips soon become plantations on a cherry-isle; and Anthea, "who may command him anything," is in a short poem a saint, a lawgiver, and an executioner.

The instinctive singers, then, have their own ways of compelling complex states of consciousness in short lyrics. As a final example we might choose a song by Burns:

Ye flowery banks o' bonie Doon,
   How can ye blume sae fair?
How can ye chant, ye little birds,
   And I sae fu' o' care?

Thou'll break my heart, thou bonie bird,
   That sings upon the bough;
Thou minds me o' the happy days
   When my fause luve was true.

Thou'll break my heart, thou bonie bird,
   That sings beside thy mate;
For sae I sat, and sae I sang
   And wist na o' my fate.

Aft hae I rov'd my bonie Doon,
   To see the woodbine twine,
And ilka bird sang o' its luve,
   And sae did I o' mine.

Wi' lightsome heart I pu'd a rose,
   Frae aff its thorny tree;
And my fause luver staw my rose,
   But left the thorn wi' me.

The worn word "little" of the third line suggests in its context a complex state of mind—an expectation of sympathy, a sense of tenderness and sentience in all nature. The fifth line is probably the finest poetically. Burns thought so, for he repeated it. If the poem had gone no further than

     Thou'll break my heart, thou bonie bird,

its complexity would already have attained expression through suggestion and inference. The remainder merely keeps the emotion of heartbreak before us by giving in more detail its cause. Yet how this complexity is achieved is hard to determine. One remembers another poet who expressed anguish,

listening to the song of a bird, and who kept that anguish before his readers by dwelling upon its sources. Keats says "my
heart aches"; Burns, "Thou'll break my heart." The difference
between *ache* and *break* and the efficacy of each word in its
respective poem are almost sufficient proofs of the complexity
of poetry. Keats in the "Ode to a Nightingale" goes on:

> 'Tis not through envy of thy happy lot,
> But being too happy in thy happiness.

The idea of the painful transiency of beauty and joy, filling
so many of Keats's best poems, here explains his heartache.

Burns's heartbreak, on the other hand, rises not from passing ecstasy but from contrasting moods and times; and although
he takes the rest of the poem for amplification, he has already
made the antithesis in the first stanza between nature's freshness and his own heaviness (or the heaviness of the girl who
perhaps is speaking the poem). Although Burns's lyric centers on a single emotion, that emotion is not simple; furthermore, it is held before the reader not by appealing directly to
his emotions, but by presenting pictures and situations to the
senses and assuming that their logical relations will be understood. The contrast in the first stanza is between the external
joy of flowers and birds and the internal care of the poet. In
the second and third stanzas, the joy of nature is associated with
the past joy of the poet, so that the contrast develops into an
opposition between past happiness and present unhappiness.
The theme becomes:

> That a sorrow's crown of sorrow is remembering happier things.

The dominant emotion of the poem, therefore, depends upon
the interplay between two other emotions—delight in love
and anguish at betrayal. The heartbreak would not be so sharp
if past joy had never been experienced. Stanza four extends the
poet's (or the girl's) past happiness through time and nature
and makes it more nearly universal, so that the painful emo-

tion of the moment seems more nearly unbearable; the whole contrast is crystallized in the final stanza, no longer in terms of time, but of space, by the image of the rose and the thorn.

A rose is love; a thorn is betrayal, deceit, falsity, anguish. If one accepts for poetry the laws of concreteness and of significance, poetry is inevitably complex. That is to say, a poem will handle the visibles and tangibles of the world; it will be seeking general significances. At the very least, then, poetry is complex to the extent that it presents ideas in terms of things. The statements of poetry convey their deepest significance obliquely, indirectly. Such poetic thought—and it cannot be simple—is so much a part of us that we must consider closely before we realize that no bonny bird smaller than a vulture could literally break Burns's heart; that we are not supposed to take as an historical fact Burns's plucking a rose which later the false lover stole; that in finding spiritual equivalents for the stealing of a rose and the leaving of the thorn experience almost forces us to think of the poem as spoken by a girl; and that dramatic imagination on Burns's part, rather than actual belief, leads him to suggest that flowers should cease to bloom and birds to sing when he is full of care.

The complexity of poetry is most clearly evident in the very form that is often considered the simplest or the nearest to prose—in narrative poetry. It is a mistake to consider a narrative poem merely as a rhymed story. Such a naïve approach destroys appreciation of it as poetry. Even the shallowest narrative poems of Byron and Scott and William Morris have some interest beyond the actions of barons and adventurers and kings. Spenser does not write the first book of the *Faerie Queene* in order to tell what happened to a knight with a red cross on his shield; he writes it because he has faith in the English people, abhors Roman Catholicism, has witnessed the enervating corruption of a courtier's life, has felt the seductiveness of physical beauty and the horror of despair, and believes that contemplation of the Christian virtues may lead an erring mortal to repentance and salvation and truth. In the Red Cross Knight, he states explicitly, "Holiness" is figured forth; in Arthur, "Magnificence."

The practice of allegory in medieval and Renaissance times, it might be argued, tends to show that poetry is *duplex*, but not necessarily *multiplex*. Might one not stop with the assumption that poetry usually embodies one general conception in one specific figure, translating a fixed idea into a fixed image? This is not enough. We have seen that even in Dante's ordered mind four levels of interpretation were formulated, so that the understanding of poetry was more than the game of translating an actor or an action in the story back into one simple concept. Few people, in actuality, who have felt a poem powerfully would be content to accept a single interpretation for it. One might just as well suppose that one has adequately characterized Washington as a truthteller, or Hamlet as a procrastinator. Nevertheless, the common error of believing that a poem is a mechanism persists. If we think of it as a living organism, we are on the right track, and are less liable to accept a dogma or a platitude as the full meaning of the poem itself. We have not necessarily known little or thought little about a friend because we refuse to sum him up in a neat phrase. If we remember that a poem suggests more than it can possibly state, that it generates living and therefore shifting thought, we see in what sense a poem may possess intellectual and moral significance and at the same time may be something more than any or all meanings attributed to it by a single sensitive reader. The words of scientific or philosophical prose have the power to tie down; the words of poetry have the power to set free. In the interpretation of a poem, therefore, the limitations of prose should never be imposed too rigidly in the mistaken assumption that the critic is helping the poet to say something that was not clear in the poet's mind. Simplification leads to falsification.

Allegory, in this light, is hardly more than a start toward

poetry. The simplest allegory is a kind of intellectual equation between two members; as such it is the slightest possible step toward establishing that organic unity and that organic complexity which are the essences of poetry. How, then, may a richer unity-in-variety be achieved? Through symbols. Within the last hundred years, the practice of symbolism has been crystallized into theories of Symbolism. But it has always and everywhere been a natural part of poetic technique. The myths of the Greeks, thousands of years old, furnish good examples of vital complexity in meaning. And who would suggest that even now the final and profoundest truths have been expressed about Prometheus or Oedipus or Achilles or Adonis? Hamlet and Don Quixote and Don Juan, says Señor de Madariaga, are examples of our modern myths. We have them in abundance. Every narrative or dramatic poet creates his own myths, although the problem of his and the reader's beliefs in his creations is possibly the most difficult enigma in the criticism of poetry. Far from having a precise, unshifting significance, frequently the vitality and scope of these mythical creations vary directly with the fluidity of their outlines. Hamlet and Falstaff may be Shakespeare's greatest characterizations in tragic and comic modes partly because no two people have exactly agreed on what they symbolize.

Because among poets writing in English, William Butler Yeats has theorized more clearly about symbolism and practiced it more successfully than any other, he shall be our guide. His attack upon allegory and his defense of symbolism upholds intuition and imagination above the rational faculty. "Symbolism," Yeats slowly came to feel, "said things which could not be said so perfectly in any other way, and needed but a right instinct for its understanding; while Allegory said things which could be said as well, or better, in another way, and needed a right knowledge for its understanding." Elsewhere Yeats writes: "A symbol is indeed the only possible expression of some invisible essence, a transparent lamp about a spiritual flame; while allegory is one of many possible representations of an embodied thing, or familiar principle, and belongs to fancy and not to imagination: the one is a revelation, the other an amusement." Because of the power of symbols, the poet becomes prophet and priest:

I cannot now think symbols less than the greatest of all powers whether they are used consciously by the masters of magic, or half unconsciously by their successors, the poet, the musician, and the artist. . . . Whatever the passions of man have gathered about, becomes a symbol in the great memory, and in the hands of him who has the secret, it is a worker of wonders, a caller-up of angels or of devils.

One need not accept Yeats's belief that any significant past event or emotion passes into the Great Mind, lives on in the Great Memory, and may be evoked by symbols. It is enough if present experience may be evoked by symbols. Whatever may have been the source and development of this conviction in Yeats, it rests firmly upon the poet's knowledge that a poem must be at once completely unified and capable of reproducing a complex state of consciousness. Realizing this, we must also realize that the ensuing attempt to get at Yeats's symbols is a kind of vivisection, a falsification or weakening of their actual effect as poetry, undertaken on the assumption that analysis may subsequently make it easier to read his verse *poetically*— that is, to accept his conviction that the symbol and what is symbolized are inseparable. In its final effect, then, the symbol is not to be considered as a translation into concrete terms of something abstract. The Symbolists of Yeats's stamp believe in a kind of poetic transubstantiation: for them the wafer is not a wheaten fragment that serves to arouse musings upon Christ's sacrifice and the Christian communion; it *is* the body of Christ while still being a wafer.

The complexity of Yeats's symbols and their obscurity in his early poems may best be shown by quoting one such poem,

## "The Lover Mourns for the Change That Has Come upon Him and His Beloved and Longs for the End of the World":

Do you not hear me calling, white deer with no horns?
I have been changed to a hound with one red ear;
I have been in the Path of Stones and the Wood of Thorns,
For somebody hid hatred and hope and desire and fear
Under my feet that they follow you night and day.
A man with a hazel wand came without sound;
He changed me suddenly; I was looking another way;
And now my calling is but the calling of a hound;
And Time and Birth and Change are hurrying by.
I would that the Boar without bristles had come from the West
And had rooted the sun and moon and stars out of the sky
And lay in the darkness, grunting, and turning to his rest.

Yeats's extended note on this poem shows not only the difficulty of the symbols, but also his hesitation in attaching them to single beings or ideas:

My deer and hound are properly related to the deer and hound that flicker in and out of the various telling of the Arthurian legends, leading different knights upon adventures, and to the hounds and to the hornless deer at the beginning of, I think, all tellings of Oisin's journey to the country of the young. The hound is certainly related to the Hounds of Annwoyn or of Hades, who are white, and have red ears, and were heard, and are, perhaps, still heard by Welsh peasants, following some flying thing in the night winds; and is probably related to the hounds that Irish country people believe will awake and seize the souls of the dead if you lament them too loudly or too soon. An old woman told a friend and myself that she saw what she thought were white birds, flying over an enchanted place, but found, when she got near, that they had dogs' heads; and I do not doubt that my hound and these dog-headed birds are of the same family. I got my hound and deer out of a last-century Gaelic poem about Oisin's journey to the country of the young. After the hunting of the hornless deer, that leads him to the seashore, and while he is riding over the sea with Niamh, he sees amid the waters—I have not the Gaelic poem by me, and describe it from memory—a young man following a girl who has a golden apple, and afterwards a hound with one red ear following a deer with no horns. This hound and this deer seem plain images of the desire of the man "which is for the woman," and "the desire of the woman which is for the desire of the man," and of all desires that are as these. . . .

Once the reader begins to associate, as Yeats does, the hound and deer with the young man who pursues a girl holding a golden apple, how many other images of desire—of Paris and the three goddesses, of Atalanta's race, of the golden apples of the Hesperides, of Eve herself in the thornless garden—may tangle themselves in his mind! And all this, of course, tends inevitably to make the poem richer and more suggestive and more complex.

In speculating on the possible associations which Yeats's poem might arouse, we have moved from his highly personal and esoteric associations to more familiar elements and incidents in our cultural heritage. Such a movement may be noted in the development of Yeats's own poetry. Increasingly he turns to more recognizable material for his symbols, as if his theory that *any* intense event lives in the Great Memory were more a speculation than a belief. Blind Raftery and Mary Hines, therefore, who may live in the Great Memory but do not live in ours, give way to Homer and Helen, or to Solomon and Sheba, who strike a response from us all.

Yeats, however, never abandons his personal symbolism completely. Instead, he consciously cultivates a new method of rendering his poetry intense in its complex allusions: he retains unique symbols, but he repeats them so frequently, in poem after poem, that they acquire a life of their own that goes far beyond the bounds of any one particular lyric. Their occurrence in any one stanza, therefore, implies a wider reference, a deeper significance, than their local habitation could possibly give them, much as four plays of Shakespeare gain weight by the repeated introduction of Falstaff, or as novels by Balzac or

Thackeray merge into a larger scheme because characters from earlier novels reappear in later ones. Yeats has made repetitions so much a part of his technique of symbolism that to trace the uses and significance of recurring symbols through all his poems would require a volume longer than the collected poems themselves.

Yeats's *A Vision*, that remarkable book of patterned philosophy spun out of lonely introspection, is perhaps the most important prose gloss that a poet has ever designed in order to make his difficult or obscure or speculative art more comprehensible. All its ramifications and its rigidity, its mysticism and mechanism, its humor and dogma, its sweep of world history and its delicate individual psychological speculations, combine to show again, when their light is thrown upon Yeats's poems, that a poem is at once unified and complex. Next to reading Shakespeare, no better way of realizing the complexity of poetry—and the coherence and subtlety of Yeats's thought— may be found than a close reading of all of Yeats's poems coupled with *A Vision*. Yeats is primarily a lyric poet. He has, however, perfected his own method of infusing into his poems intensity and complexity by repetition of symbols. The insistent and consistent use of symbols, exploited systematically only late in his life, has made Yeats a major poet. And his effects in short poems are comparable to those achieved by poets who work in larger forms. His lyrics, though they may stand by themselves, carry implications far beyond themselves; they belong to a great family; their interaction increases the power of each one, and makes the collected lyrics of Yeats comparable in scope and scale and effect to an epic or a great tragedy.

All this talk as to how Yeats secures effects of complexity has been general and fragmentary. It must remain so, for an artist's lifetime of pioneering cannot be reduced to a few pages. Nevertheless, a stanza might be singled out with a few suggestions as to its connections with other poems. These are the closing lines of possibly his greatest poem, "Byzantium":

> Astraddle on the dolphin's mire and blood,
>   Spirit after spirit! The smithies break the flood,
>   The golden smithies of the Emperor!
>   Marbles of the dancing floor
> Break bitter furies of complexity,
>       Those images that yet
>       Fresh images beget,
> That dolphin-torn, that gong-tormented sea.

Byzantium itself, in his many writings, Yeats has taken as a symbol not only for old age but for the old age of a civilization in the repetitive cycles of history. It also represents permanence as opposed to transience, art opposed to impulse, intellect opposed to animal existence. As a city, flowering between 500 and 1500, it embodies concretely and specifically the contemplative, critical life in diametrical antithesis to the active, instinctive vitalism expressed in the thousand years that center on the birth and life of Christ, or, two thousand years before Christ (to adopt Yeats's chronology), on Dionysus. These various dichotomies Yeats has already presented more formally in the simpler and clearer poem "Sailing to Byzantium," which, brutally paraphrased, might be called "Accepting Old Age," or "Resolving upon Dedication to Art," or "Foregoing Sensual Music for the Singing School of the Soul." Now all these ideas are simultaneously present in the one symbol of the city of Byzantium. What is almost as important in Yeats's theory as well as in his practice, a clear awareness of any element calls up its opposite: a profound awareness of sensuality, for instance, generates a knowledge of spirituality; old age—"a tattered coat upon a stick"—only makes the poet more poignantly sensitive to the shattering, dizzying pulsation of youth and passion.

For Yeats, in brief, a symbol may have multivalent references; it will suggest strongly its "masks," that is, its opposites; and it will evoke many associated symbols that have been repeated throughout his other poems. Thus he has always represented physical life by "fish, flesh, or fowl"—by the dolphin, the salmon, the mackerel, and the fish that run in schools. The sea, or water, for Yeats as for T. S. Eliot, is a natural symbol for physical life; so is blood, which he also associates with clay or mire; and tangles them all together with intense adjectives— bitter, furious, tormented, frenzied, screaming. The ecstasy of the moment, of the transient, he suggests repeatedly by a reference to something which shatters a calm: birds break the silence with their cries, or, as here in the last line, the sea's surface is *torn* by the dolphins' curvetting; the silent seas are *tormented* and broken by a gong. Opposed to the fury of the moment and of unthinking existence is the quiescence of unchanging thought and art, which he evokes by such symbols as the stone, the rock, the tower, gold, a mummy, a mosaic. These symbols persist through his poems. In "Sailing to Byzantium," for instance, the artist's passion for giving permanence to his art is expressed in a welded and wedded image that is merely suggested in the stanza quoted above from "Byzantium":

> such a form as Grecian goldsmiths make
> Of hammered gold and gold enamelling
> To keep a drowsy Emperor awake;
> Or set upon a golden bough to sing.

Sometimes his symbols will in one word combine opposite ideas, of transience and permanence, action and contemplation, life and art. Yeats makes such enormously suggestive symbols particularly out of the tree, the flame, the wind, and the dance.

These remarks, rising as they do from the last stanza of "Byzantium," have of necessity generalized about Yeats's practice. Any one of them could be illustrated at length. Yet if they are assumed to be true, it becomes evident that hardly a word in the stanza quoted lacks its complex connections and oppositions and associations and memories. Gradually we come to realize that Yeats speaks only after long thought and far travel. We can follow his method and note his results, as we have

done above, just so far; beyond that, the effects of poetry resist analysis. But the effects are there. Many a reader has felt
the explosive force, the fascinating rightness, of

> That dolphin-torn, that gong-tormented sea

without any capacity to explain how the line gains its power.
For if poetry is at once complex and unified—if it is living—
then no analysis is its equivalent. The more deeply we experience poetry, the more we may come to agree with T. S. Eliot
that poetry may be enjoyed, valued, and sensed as poetry long
before it is fully comprehensible. And the very complexity of
poetry deeply felt may force us to adopt Yeats's position that
memory and knowledge may be evoked by symbols, that
images may beget fresh images, and that attempting to separate
the concept from its embodiment, the "meaning" from its metaphorical vehicle, is as murderous to the whole poem as trying
to separate in a human being soul from body.

Poetry has its own dignity and mode of existence. The principle of complexity, rightly understood, implies that the study
of poetry cannot be a science; and any attempt to reduce it
*completely* to the terms of the intellect or of common sense is
as ridiculous as would be, inversely, an attempt to make the
quantum theory or the national budget into a poem. If a poem
may be compared to a human body, then the volume you hold
in your hand might be likened to a textbook on anatomy. The
medical student may pore over diagrams and plates and skele-
tons and dissected members; his knowledge of anatomy, however, can be of value only after countless schematized drawings
have helped him better to understand actual living bodies.

If we acknowledge, then, that criticism is not the equivalent
of the art criticized, we may safely proceed to a few more diagrams of complexity achieved by other means than direct and
simple allegory.

A poet should be able to present complex thought *always
within the limits of a story*, rather than by translating concepts

into a fable mechanically. Browning possessed such ability in good measure. Now and then, of course, he looks like a plain allegorist: his "Childe Roland to the Dark Tower Came" may be seen fairly simply as the triumph of courage over the most sinister and sordid circumstances. Yet this is merely a personal interpretation, and according to the well-known story, a clergyman was bold enough to ask Browning what he meant by the poem, and Browning himself was puzzled enough, or poet enough, to give an indefinite reply. But such characteristic poems as "My Last Duchess," "Porphyria's Lover," and "The Bishop Orders His Tomb" are more than character sketches in dramatic form. The approach to each subject is poetic: judgment is withheld; or more exactly, conflicting judgments are implied in such profusion that the scales are kept in motion or balanced delicately. The Duke of Ferrara may not be all bad even though he seems to have had his last wife murdered; and his Duchess may not be all saint, even though she smiled sweetly at everyone. Porphyria's lover may know why "God has not said a word" during the long night after the strangling of Porphyria, but the reader is left wondering whether he has listened to a speaker from a madhouse cell, or whether God has turned away his face from the lover, or whether God (or Browning's God) approves of this moment of ecstatic decision and murderous action. And Browning's bishop alternately shocks and delights, in a poem which is neither an indictment of the Italian Renaissance nor a panegyric. No single cue is completely satisfying to an alert reader. The full, complex satisfaction of poetry comes from the coexistence of varied, even of incompatible, ideas.

This awareness of the complexity of actual experience, of its dynamic rather than static nature, is the quality which Keats admired in Shakespeare and found to be the mark of a poet's nature. He gave it the name of "negative capability"—the capacity to accept the indeterminate, the conflicting or incompatible hypotheses. "I mean *Negative Capability*, that is, when a man is capable of being in uncertainties, mysteries, doubts, without any irritable reaching after fact and reason." The crude statement of final opinions has little place in poetry, for it destroys those delicate, infinitely branching trees of the poet's mind that Keats mentions in "Sleep and Poetry" and the "Ode to Psyche." A poem holds in solution many different and often unrelated elements; it is not necessary to precipitate these elements in poetry, as it is, for instance, in commercial chemistry.

The inevitable complexity in a great work of art leads I. A. Richards to say that irony, which destroys inferior works, is never far distant from the highest art, for irony "consists in the bringing in of the opposite, the complementary impulses," and implies, therefore, a more complete comprehension of whatever subject it plays upon. Thus the great artist sees life in the round, as it were. And to see it in the round he must see it from two positions or more at the same time. One might venture to connect this argument with T. S. Eliot's belief in the objectivity of the artist and his statement that poetry is not an expression of personality but an escape from personality. If "personality" is taken to mean passionate simple conviction, as it commonly is, then the great artist will not limit himself to such partial truth. His vision and his judgment will be multiple. He will lower his face in sorrow, like Dante, over lovers *justly* condemned to hell; his delighted spirit will be bathed, like Spenser's, in the loveliness of a Bower of Bliss that must righteously be destroyed; he will plead the cause of Satan, like Milton, so eloquently that the devil may appear to be the hero of a poem justifying God's ways to men. To the rational mind of comedy, Monsieur Jourdain's remark to partisan speakers, "Vous avez raison tous deux," may appear ridiculous. But in tragedy and serious poetry, opposed forces may both be right, and indeed the simple conflict between good and evil is not tragic. The poet's conception of life is not monolithic. "The web of our life is of a mingled yarn, good and ill together: our virtues would be proud, if our faults whipped them not; and our crimes would despair, if they were not cherished by our virtues."

Browning's "A Toccata of Galuppi's," one of his best poems, gains its effects through the multiplicity of attitudes it presents. The eighteenth-century Italian organist Galuppi is creaky and dust-covered, a ghostly cricket. The dead Venice he stands for is frivolous and immoral; but it is also gay. The judgment on Venice, then, is double, though it is more subtly expressed than a similar judgment at the end of another of Browning's poems, "Confessions":

> How sad and bad and mad it was—
> But then, how it was sweet!

The listener to Galuppi's old organ music—Browning or some other mid-Victorian—lives, on the other hand, in an age of scientific advancement and high moral seriousness. He is ironically aware of his own virtues, and also aware that to be aware of one's virtue is close to a weakness. He is dimly conscious of dissatisfaction and hollowness in this modern world of progress. The judgment on nineteenth-century England, therefore, is also double. The poem, then, yokes the two contrasting civilizations; choosing between them is choosing between the lady and the tiger. Browning awards no palms or medals; he passes no sentences; he ends the poem with a question and a regretful look across the abyss of the years as the speaker thinks of the Venetian ladies:

> Dear dead women, with such hair, too—what's become
> of all the gold
> Used to hang and brush their bosoms? I feel chilly
> and grown old.

The poet's conception of a complex universe is formalized in the structure of Browning's *The Ring and the Book*. Here the same series of happenings is reviewed over and over again by different people; every interpretation and hypothesis is advanced to explain events and judge character. In theory, at least,

Browning held that in the fusion of this mass of conflicting opinions and testimony the slag of lies would be melted away, leaving only the pure golden ring of truth. Actually, the poem gets its effect as a whole—and how infinitely nobler it is than his early "Pippa Passes"!—from the gradual, wavering, and only partial emergence of love and self-sacrifice out of the drifting mists of error. *The Ring and the Book* is the epic of the relativity of truth. G. K. Chesterton's remark on Browning, that he was a kind of cosmic detective that penetrated into the foulest of thieves' kitchens and publicly accused men of virtue, may be an epigrammatic overstatement, but it touches upon one way in which a poet may work. And conversely, the poet may penetrate into paradise and publicly applaud saints for their vices.

Pompilia's trustful love after her exhausting loneliness and torture, Caponsacchi's spontaneous self-sacrifice, could not come out so forcefully without the preparation and setting of a long poem. Critics of poetry have paid too little attention to the relations of length, complexity, and greatness in a work of art. Ordinarily, the greatness of a poem varies directly with its complexity and comprehensiveness. And further, the general rule may be laid down that a single line of poetry or any individual passage has more chance of being great if it occurs in a long poem than in a short poem. Any reader can establish this for himself by turning over in his mind his own favorite lines and passages and appraising them with regard to "greatness" as poetry. The larger the context, the more exact, intense, and significant may be the effect of any particular word, line, or passage. It stands to reason that complexity is achieved with difficulty in limited space. In considering so many short lyric poems, therefore, this chapter has deliberately taken much recalcitrant material to build up the argument for the complexity of poetry. Complexity in longer poems is more immediately obvious. Not only is the effect of a long poem as a whole felt to be complex, but the individual sections assume increased

complexity of meaning and suggestion because of their relation to the whole.

Perhaps the effect of the length of a poem upon its parts may
be shown most easily by considering some of the lines which
Matthew Arnold chose as touchstones or yardsticks for determining the worth of a poet in his essay "The Study of Poetry." Dante's

> *E 'n la sua volontate è nostra pace*

> And in His will is our peace

has been mentioned in the preceding chapter. It requires little
effort of the imagination to see what this line has gained from
being imbedded in the *Divine Comedy*, surrounded by hundreds of examples of those who have lost peace, or who are
striving for it, or who have found it in God's will forever.
Considered apart from the "Inferno," the "Purgatorio," and the
"Paradiso," the line stiffens into the rigidity of an apophthegm,
and loses its poetic freshness as quickly as a cut flower.
Yet our imaginations are fortunately so constituted that this
line may be considered "poetically"—that is, one may concentrate on it as an individual line and still preserve in memory the
vast and shadowy background of the whole poem, much as one
may listen to a phrase in a symphony and still be aware of the
phrase in the whole movement and the place of the movement
in the symphony. The sense of complexity must be maintained
to get the true *poetic* sensation from any collection of words.
The last line of the "Inferno" is:

> *E quindi uscimmo a riveder le stelle.*

> Thence we came forth, to see again the stars.

The idea of "seeing again," ordinary enough in itself, here intensely conveys a sense of liberation and relief after the long,
dark, and painful sojourn in the caves of the earth. The brilliance of the stars as Dante pictures them throughout his poem
increases the effectiveness of the line, and indeed this line takes

on increased significance after one has read the "Paradiso" and witnessed the ardent patterns and choruses of the stars. What poetic delight is added to this one line from the realization that each of the three great sections of the *Divine Comedy*, with all its fixity and fire, ends with the word *stelle!*

One of the lines which Arnold chooses to illustrate Shakespeare's greatness is Hamlet's injunction to Horatio:

> Absent thee from felicity awhile.

Obviously this line cannot stand by itself (Arnold first quotes it in a slightly expanded context), except as pleasing to the ear. Even from the point of view of technique, if we do not know that Hamlet is wounded and dying, we lose much of the effect of those light vowels and whispered sibilants. In its place at the end of the play, the line is great because it touches so many of the deepest issues of the tragedy. In its context, we know that "felicity" means death. Two of Hamlet's four great soliloquies have centered on speculations about death and possible life after death. How has he achieved the peace and certainty that flow through this line? Partly from completing, after so many accidental judgments and casual slaughters, the solemn, but to him torturing, task laid upon him by his father. Partly from seeing his haven in sight, the consummation for which he had wished so devoutly. The very contrast between death and the brutal, restless world comes out in the succeeding line of rough monosyllables:

> And in this harsh world draw thy breath in pain.

But we cannot pluck out the heart of Hamlet's mystery. Is, then, the final felicity to be insentient repose: "to die, to sleep. No more"? Hamlet's last words, "The rest is silence," offer no single answer. The overtone suggests that the rest is rest. But they may mean simply that Hamlet can speak no more; they may mean that death is a perpetual sleep and silence; they may mean that so far as mortals are concerned, only silence follows their questions about a future life. Despite Shakespeare's "negative capability" to leave questions unanswered because he can imagine so many possible answers, the line Arnold has chosen pulses with confidence and calm, with a sense of triumph not fully explicable, a sense of pity that can come only from the weight of all the preceding action, a feeling of resignation but not of the resignation of values, a reaffirmation and a sense of prayer:

After life's fitful fever he sleeps well.

Drama is a higher form of literature than the epic, Aristotle decided, because, of the elements of plot, moral judgment, intellectual fiber, fitting language, music, and spectacle, drama contains all six whereas the epic utilizes only the first four. Although the standard here is quantitative and somewhat mechanical, such a judgment does maintain that poetry must be complex. Aristotle's opinion still holds; the greatest poetry remains dramatic and epic. If the greatest poets of the last hundred years or so have written their best work in lyric forms, it is only because the epic and the poetic drama have become less appropriate to modern conditions. Modern poets have explored new means—Yeats through repeated symbols, Eliot through literary allusions—for achieving unusual complexity even in brief lyric forms. Since we have been unable fully to exhaust or explain the complexities of a short lyric, it would be emptying the sea with a sieve to try analyzing adequately any poetic drama or epic. We shall merely glance at these two forms of poetry, therefore, not to cover their complexity, but to reaffirm the position that a poem read simply or on a single level loses much of its poetry—that the poetry comes *through* the words and does not reside in mechanical counters culled from a dictionary, and once again, that poetry liberates the imagination instead of chaining it, that poetry suggests far more than it states.

Shakespeare's great tragedies, for example, have principal

figures that represent complex human beings. The relations between such main characters give the tragedies themselves an
even greater complexity. Shakespeare's *methods* of gaining
such complexity through the interplay between characters are
in themselves complex and varied: he repeats, or varies, or contrasts ideas, or key phrases, or actions, or successive scenes and
situations. Nor need this be a balance of scene against scene, or
character against character. An action may balance a speech, as
Bradley has pointed out:

ALBANY. The gods defend her! . . .
[Enter Lear, with Cordelia dead in his arms.]

Pity and fear here touch hands. In the light of the whole play,
even this melodramatic contrast is not simple or decisive, and
Shakespeare is saying far more than that the President of the Immortals had at last finished his sport with Cordelia. Not only
the appeal on various levels and to all the parts of human consciousness, but the simultaneous presentation of conflicting
emotions on the same level, may give that sense of being alive
which is essential to poetry. Greatness springs from comprehensiveness, from complexity. In the geometry of the mind, it
is open to question whether a narrow idea can ever be profound.

A large book could be devoted to analyzing the complexities in the one play *Antony and Cleopatra*. Although Shakespeare holds simple, unwavering ideas of Cleopatra's two traits
of underlying love and surface variability, he develops these
qualities in his heroine by oblique and extremely complex
means. In a one-act playlet, or in a lyric poem, they could not
possibly have been brought before us so convincingly. No isolated sonnet has that power to move complex emotions in a few
short words which belongs to Cleopatra's

. Not know me yet?

in its context, after the defeated Antony's hysterical cursing of
Cleopatra as a half-blasted boggler, and filth, and a cold morsel

upon dead Caesar's plate. Wherever we turn in the play—if we
consider closely the effect *as poetry* of Antony's every action,
of the drunken Lepidus, of the marriage of state with Octavia,
of the moonlit death of Enobarbus, of music departing under
the earth, of a clown with a basket of figs—wherever we turn
we find borne out again the rule that the relation of various
elements of the play to any single passage increases its complexity. The more extensive a work of art, the greater the
chance that any part of it will create *qualitative* effects of complexity, significance, and intensity. When a work of art is small
in compass, like a brief lyric, the creative artist must cast about
for devices to extend its suggestiveness. A poem, someone has
said, is like a seacoast with a vast unexplored hinterland. The
area of this hinterland becomes greater as the seacoast length-
ens. Although the view immediately before us at any one moment and in any one passage is as limited in a tragedy as in a
lyric, our imaginations let us know whether our landfall is
Zanzibar or the whole continent of Africa.

Shakespeare, as his good friend Ben Jonson deplored, lacked
the classic disciplines. Milton, on the other hand, was conscious
of the forms of art, and had set himself to school under the
Greeks. Does his sense of order and form and clarity preclude
complexity? By no means. It merely makes the characteristically Miltonic complexity different from the Shakespearean.
His vocabulary, syntax, and punctuation at times fall into purposeful ambiguity, with the result that a word or phrase will
work in two directions, flavor or unite two ideas. The successful dramatic elements in *Paradise Lost* inevitably make it complex, for opposing ideas, dramatically presented, must be
accorded free and independent expression. Thus, in a poem designed to justify God, the fallen angels must be allowed to
curse him in poetry which to some—when they forget the
whole structure—has the ring of final truth. Here complexity
results from conflict between dramatic and didactic purposes.

Complexity also arises from the clash between Milton's individual or instinctive beliefs and the Christian system which he
is defending; or between parts of his own nature, as scholar,
artist, political theorist, and theologian. The poem, in spite of
Milton's supreme sense of ordered composition, is complex
enough to permit new interpretations that satisfy each age and
person—from Dryden to Bentley to Pope to Johnson to Blake
to Shelley to Tennyson to Francis Thompson to the hosts of
modern attackers or defenders that wage battle around Milton's
proud towers.

But Milton's most characteristic complexity makes itself evident in his conveying, consciously and even rationally, the sense
of the relationship of the whole to any part. Milton's invocation to light at the beginning of Book III, which appears in
anthologies as a lyric about the poet himself, gains from its
place in the poem, with the long dark sojourn in hell behind it,
dim chaos immediately at hand, and sun-bathed Eden and the
white floors of heaven ahead. Or again, when at the end of
Book V, the angel Abdiel refuses to follow Lucifer and his
hosts, his action (made more complex by thinly veiled allusions
to Milton's lonely predicament at the time of the Restoration)
does not stand by itself, but takes on import in the light of
Lucifer's previous revolt, and is thereby transformed into a
rebellion against rebellion. Because it is more highly organized
than any other work in English poetry, no part of *Paradise
Lost* can be fully sensed unless the whole poem is kept in solution in the reader's imagination while the particular line or paragraph is read. Consider the line that Arnold singles out as the
touchstone of Milton's greatness:

> And what is else not to be overcome.

This appears as the climax of Satan's first speech in Hell, infusing courage into the prostrate Beëlzebub:

> If thou beest he; But O how fall'n! how chang'd! . . .

> . . . What though the field be lost?
> All is not lost; the unconquerable Will,
> And study of revenge, immortal hate,
> And courage never to submit or yield:
> And what is else not to be overcome?

A glorious presentation of resolved independence and indomitable spirit. Yet even within the speech itself, the words "hate" and "revenge" might warn the wary against unqualified admiration. Dramatically, these ideas are Satan's, not Milton's. This passage should not be considered as a purely lyrical outburst of passionate conviction on Milton's part. The deliberate lifework of a great poet will hardly be a pastiche of unrelated impulses. As Milton conceived him, this is the angel who a little later three times burst into tears before he could speak; who promised to his followers, and to Sin and Death, and to Chaos, his conquests in the world; the angel distorted by destroying emotions on Mount Niphates; this is the sly liar beneath the branches of the Tree of Life; this the vulture, the cormorant, the creeping mist, the lion, the wolf, the tiger, the toad, the great serpent, limbs and countenance constricted and vanishing, prone on his belly. To forget all this is to assume that Milton was not writing an epic but rather, shall we say, a sort of sonnet non-sequence, a collection of fine lyrical fragments. We cannot fully appreciate Lucifer's utterances in Book I without remembering Adam's in Book XII. It is well to set against the

> . . . study of revenge, immortal hate

Adam's line:

> Henceforth I learne, that to obey is best.

And we should weigh Lucifer's scornful courage against, later,

> The better fortitude
> Of patience and heroic martyrdom

and

> Be strong, live happie, and love, but first of all
> Him whom to love is to obey, and keep
> His great command.

Through his genius for organizing, Milton has given to each part of his poem a tension and a nobility that comes from the weight of the complex whole.

An accidental but nevertheless actual complexity resides in great poetry simply because it has been there so long. Critics encrust it with comments; later poets play variations upon it. The modern reader inevitably finds in the *Iliad* what Homer could not have put there. Perhaps he remembered Plato's and Aristotle's observations; he senses the *Aeneid* and *Paradise Lost*; he is more or less aware of innumerable allusions made long after Homer was in his unknown grave. Arnold's line from Milton cannot but recall to a reader moderately acquainted with English poetry—perhaps it explains Arnold's choice—the close of Tennyson's "Ulysses":

> One equal temper of heroic hearts,
> Made weak by time and fate, but strong in will
> To strive, to seek, to find, and not to yield.

Though such complexity arises accidentally, it need not be deplored. As long as memory and the power of association persist, the past will influence the present and the present will influence our interpretation of the past. In looking at the intensity of poetry, we have already considered the device of quotation and paraphrase and allusion to other poems as a means for securing compression and complexity in a fresh work of art. Any poem written in an acknowledged tradition or an accepted form gains some of its dignity from the shadows of its great ancestors. And if Shakespeare and a popular rhyme and Arnaut Daniel and Dante and an unknown late Latin poet and Swinburne and Gérard de Nerval and Thomas Kyd and the Upanishads can all contribute in a few lines, less than a sonnet's space, to the complex finale of Eliot's *The Waste Land*, why should not Eliot's work in turn change our estimation of what his predecessors have done? I know of one man who became a Wagnerite because of *The Waste Land*, and there can be little doubt that in his case *Tristan und Isolde* and *Die Götterdämmerung* flicker with the flames of "The Fire Sermon." Another man has told me that since reading the opening of "The Fire Sermon," with its sordid picture of the Thames and its repetition of the refrain

> Sweet Thames, run softly till I end my song,

he can never reread Spenser's "Prothalamion" as a conventional Elizabethan marriage song. When Eliot introduces Spenser into his verse, he enters himself into Spenser's. We create the past in our own image. More than that, so long as the present is conscious of the past, the past is neither dead nor fixed, but shifts and moves and breathes, a most contemporaneous ghost, in the complex enigma that is time. Age itself, therefore, in a work of art as in a human being, inevitably adds to complexity.

# CHAPTER SIX

# POETRY
# IS RHYTHMICAL

Art requires a medium. The medium of poetry is language, which must be handled with precision in order to express the mind of the poet. Moreover, since poetry deals in images, the language used must be concrete. The two principles of exactness and concreteness therefore govern in part the use of the poetic medium—language. The principles of intensity, significance, and complexity focus on poetic qualities achieved within the medium of language.

Yet prose may use language exactly and concretely in order to produce effects that are at once intense, complex, and significant. Consider *Gulliver's Travels* and *Wuthering Heights; Urn Burial* and *Marius the Epicurean;* Ecclesiastes and Hamlet's "What a piece of work is a man!" If we stop with the argument advanced in this book so far, these prose monuments and all their like should indeed be considered as poetry. Sidney's conception of poetry was not indefinite, though it was comprehensive, when he classed Xenophon as a poet. We might even go beyond the medium of language and ask, What *qualities* are poetic, no matter in what medium they find expression? Shelley was thinking solely of poetic qualities when he wrote that the poetry of Rome was to be found in her institutions.

Keats for the moment was thinking of poetry in a very broad sense when he began a sonnet, "On the Grasshopper and Cricket," with

The poetry of earth is never dead.

All of the arts, to greater or less degree, share the poetic qualities. Music and painting, sculpture and architecture, the opera, the movies, and the dance, may be simultaneously intense, complex, and significant. To one who believes that poetry consists in a certain mood or approach, or that it is sufficiently defined by its effect, the medium in which such moods or effects are produced becomes unimportant, adventitious, a matter for the cataloguers. If Saint-Gaudens' "Grief" and the Taj Mahal and a Tchaikovsky symphony and Pavlova's "Dying Swan" and Puccini's *La Bohême* and Tennyson's "Tithonus" all generate poignant and subtle effects of sorrow, then they are all poetry.

There is no cause for quarreling here. It is enough if we realize to what extent our definitions are partial, and for what particular purposes they are designed. A thing may be described by *qualities*—"Man is a torturing animal"—or by *structure*—"Man is a two-legged creature without feathers"—or by *function*—"Man adapts his environment to himself, not himself to his environment"—or by any other means. These statements are not contradictory because they do not coincide; they are simply partial. Much of the bewilderment as to what constitutes poetry rises from accepting a limited critical statement as the only truth or the whole truth. We might, therefore, agree that the basic way to consider poetry is in its qualitative essences—its intensity, its complexity, its significance, its sense of the real world discovered through individual eyes. Nevertheless, practically considered, it is at least of some value to limit the conception to the expression of such qualities by means of language. Most of us feel more at ease when we are told that Thucydides or Bacon is a poet than when we learn that a

Roman senator and a chirping cricket are poets too. Poetry and literary language are naturally associated. The further limitation, that poetry must be rhythmical, is also in accord with the common belief and practice of men in all times and places. That poetry should be rhythmical is a practical rule of thumb; meter can do much to make a poem. It contributes even to those qualitative effects which are the essence of poetry.

We may, then, disregard Wordsworth's celebrated footnote:

Much confusion has been introduced into criticism by this contradistinction of Poetry and Prose, instead of the more philosophical one of Poetry and Matter of Fact, or Science. The only strict antithesis to Prose is Metre. . . .

We may disregard it partly because the earlier chapters have already considered the "more philosophical" distinction between poetry and matter of fact. And we may also disregard it because Wordsworth himself assumes for convenience that poetry is metrical, "though." he writes, "against my own judgment." The two words "poetry" and "prose" have served useful purposes for a long time, although no definite boundary, acceptable to everyone, can be drawn between them.

The essence of the poet, according to the best critics of antiquity, of the Renaissance, and of the second Renaissance among the Romantics, is his creative power. The poet is the maker, the creator, the priest and prophet. He sees that which is not and brings it into being. He forms a little cosmos of his own; he is spirit, "that which moves" and shapes; he partakes of the nature of God.

But how is the poet to create? He not only creates; he also constructs. He constructs in time—that is, in words written, and read, during a period of time—rather than in space. To make his temporal structure apparent, rhythm is necessary. The word derives from the Greek verb *rhein*, which means "to flow"; the poet is the man who can make words flow through time. To achieve this flow, rhythm is the sole force. If proof were needed, the close connection, in early or primitive societies, of poetry and music and the dance should suffice. The powerful and mesmeric effect of rhythm is the most direct way to bring into complete being those other unvarying qualities which are poetic.

Consider a single stanza:

> Break, break, break
>  On thy cold gray stones, O Sea!
> And I would that my tongue could utter
>  The thoughts that arise in me.

Why does this affect us as it does? How does it manage to arouse in us a receptivity so different from that aroused by prose? To say, "Ocean, break on your rocks! And I wish I could say what I am thinking," is to enter a different world. Partial causes of the difference in effect lie in the diction and the sound. But almost all of the difference may be attributed directly to the rhythm found in the verse and lacking in the paraphrase. It exerts a spell, as genuine, though not so insistent, as the spell of the rhythm that hypnotizes African dancers, marches soldiers into danger, or gains converts at revival meetings.

Effective rhythm in poetry rouses our spirits and then dominates and soothes them, holding us as if we were in a trance of heightened awareness. Some of Wordsworth's most original thought (and here he is a pioneer in a field where speculation is difficult) is devoted to analysis of the purpose and effects of meter:

The end of Poetry is to produce excitement in co-existence with an overbalance of pleasure. . . . Now the co-presence of something regular, something to which the mind has been accustomed in various moods and in a less excited state, cannot but have great efficacy in tempering and restraining the passion by an intertexture of ordinary feeling, and of feeling not strictly and necessarily connected with the passion.

This is to argue that the controlled beat of meter acts as a continual reminder that the pain and ecstasy, the pity and fear, the love and anger in a poem are not directly and immediately experienced; that the meter constantly strengthens in us the consciousness of esthetic contemplation. We do not act or suffer: we behold. In Coleridge's conception of poetry, "a more than usual state of emotion" balanced or reconciled with "more than usual order," rhythm is an important and certainly the most continually present manifestation of the sense of order. The sense of control and of mastery, which the regularity of rhythm suggests so indirectly yet so effectively, explains, in Wordsworth's theory, our enjoyment of poetic tragedy in spite of its painful subject matter. In prose, without a formal rhythm, the same subject matter, he maintains, cannot easily be endured. Wordsworth rereads the distressing passages in *Clarissa Harlowe* or *The Gamester* with reluctance; he reads Shakespeare's most pathetic scenes over and over again with enjoyment—"an effect which, in a much greater degree than might at first be imagined, is to be ascribed to small, but continual and regular impulses of pleasurable surprise from the metrical arrangement."

One might argue, with Wordsworth as a guide, that the pleasurable effect of rhythm is triple: intellectual, esthetic, and physiological. Intellectually it pleases by its continuous although not obtrusive assurance that order, control, purposefulness are at work. Esthetically, its artificiality and formality hold us steadily; it leads us pleasurably into the mood of imaginative contemplation, out of the real world of action and utility, "from the tendency of metre to divest language, in a certain degree, of its reality, and thus to throw a sort of half-consciousness of unsubstantial existence over the whole composition." Physiologically, little more can be said with certainty than that men naturally delight in rhythm. In basic theory, therefore, perhaps this chapter can go little further than Wordsworth's simple statement:

All that it is *necessary* to say, however, upon this subject, may be effected by affirming, what few persons will deny, that of two descriptions, either of passions, manners, or characters, each of them equally well executed, the one in prose and the other in verse, the verse will be read a hundred times where the prose is read once.

Yet a paragraph of hypothesis might be pardoned. This love of rhythm, and its particular embodiment in poetry, may be connected with physiological processes. Our living is rhythmical—waking and sleeping, inhaling and exhaling, contracting and expanding the heart. Connections probably exist—if for no other reason than that one must occasionally inhale while reading a poem aloud—between the length of a breath and the length of the most widely used rhythmical units, such as the classical hexameter, the French alexandrine, or the English blank verse line and heroic couplet. With regard to the simplest and shortest rhythmical unit, the foot, modern methods of scientific measurement have determined—what the Greeks had assumed in their verse-making—that a long or accented syllable is equivalent in time to two short or unaccented syllables. The average unaccented syllable, in all kinds of poetry (though it is longer in lyric poems, shorter in narrative or dramatic), has a time length of about a fifth of a second; the average accented syllable, it has been proved, takes two-fifths of a second to pronounce. That means that about a hundred two-syllable feet may be read in a minute, and about seventy-five three-syllable feet. I find, for instance, that read at the tempo I like best, the first sentence of *Paradise Lost* takes exactly one minute. Sixteen lines long: eighty feet to a minute. The average human pulse beat is not far from that. Is it too much to believe that the exhilarating effect of poetry, Aristotle's and Horace's and Sidney's and Wordsworth's sense of delight, may come from the fact that the rhythm of poetic feet is usually slightly faster than the rhythm of the pulses? If this were so, then indeed poetry would be the language of the heart. It would be written in blood. Delight in it would spring from an instinctive pulsation beyond the usual conscious or intellectual considerations of criticism. And even more clearly, ruling out recurring rhythms from poetry would be depriving it of its life. Only the analysis of his own experience will enable a reader to accept or reject this physiological theory of the rhythm of poetry. And whatever his conclusion, "all that it is *necessary* to say may be effected by affirming that the verse will be read a hundred times where the prose is read once."

For the purposes of this chapter, rhythm may be defined as the more or less regular recurrence of any pattern detectable in time. In this sense, it is meaningless to speak of a Greek temple or a Raphael fresco as rhythmical, for their organization is not organization which depends upon intervals of *time*. Furthermore, the course of a drop of water over a series of natural cascades, though it takes place in time, is not rhythmical, for the steps in its flowing descent do not recur *regularly* enough to establish a detectable pattern. But the breaking of waves upon a beach is rhythmical. So is breathing. And a marching army. And a poem.

It will be noticed that this definition of rhythm depends upon the elastic phrase, "more or less regular recurrence." Rhythm is a broader term than meter. Anything metrical is rhythmical, but not all rhythms may be successfully reduced to meter. This chapter does not maintain that "Poetry is metrical," for that would imply too limited and mechanically regular a pattern. Insistence upon meter, though it would apply to most poems, would exclude many pieces of writing which are obviously poems but not obviously shaped in rigid metrical molds. Yet such pieces are "rhythmical" because they set up an expectation of a recurring time pattern and gratify this expectation, "more or less," as they proceed.

The great question is the question of regularity in rhythm. How regular should a rhythm be? How mechanically precise should be the repetitions that mark it? One might sensibly conclude that this is a matter of tastes, which are supposed to be beyond dispute; but tastes in rhythm have been debated for so long a time that we also must enter the argument.

Let us begin by looking for some regular lines. And let us look for them in the commonest of English feet, the iamb ( ˘ ´ ), and the commonest iambic pattern, the pentameter or five-foot line. So often has it been the medium for poetry since the time of Chaucer that English verse should abound with perfect lines of

$$\breve{\phantom{x}} \acute{\phantom{x}} \, \breve{\phantom{x}} \, \acute{\phantom{x}} \, \breve{\phantom{x}} \, \acute{\phantom{x}} \, \breve{\phantom{x}} \, \acute{\phantom{x}} \, \breve{\phantom{x}} \, \acute{\phantom{x}}$$

where ˘ marks an unaccented syllable and ´ marks an accented syllable. Yet perfect lines are not common. Sometimes a syllable that should be heavy cannot support as strong a beat as the other accented syllables; sometimes a syllable which in the pattern should be weak will actually take a heavy accent or require a longer time to pronounce than the strict pattern allows; sometimes an extra light or slurred syllable will be inserted in the pattern. If we select some iambic pentameter lines and italicize every departure from the metrical pattern, it will be evident that even in smooth and regular and correct versifiers a mechanically perfect line is a great rarity. This, then, from Marlowe's *Hero and Leander:*

> And there, for honey, bees have sought in vain,
> *And*, beat from thence, have lighted there again.
> About her neck *hung* chains of pebble-stone,
> *Which*, lightened *by* her neck, like diamonds shone.
> She ware *no* gloves, for neither sun nor wind
> Would burn or parch her hands, but *to* her mind;
> Or warm or cool them, *for* they took delight
> To play up*on those* hands, they *were so* white.

Five of these eight lines force accents upon prepositions, conjunctions, and the colorless verb *to be*. It is a structural peculiarity of the English language that its prepositions, as well as its Latin suffixes, make the writing of perfect iambs for any length of lines almost impossible. Moreover, even this simple

passage makes it evident that pure accentual rhythm cannot be
determined and marked apart from the sense. For, in the last
three lines, compensation for the four dropped accents comes
from the preceding pauses and from the sense of the sentence,
so that the reader must make an effort to realize that any irregularity in the actual rhythm exists. The interplay between sense,
pauses, the sounds of words, and the formal accentual pattern
cannot be reduced to rule; nor will prosodic critics ever be
able to fix a rate of exchange between such elements. But in
practice, the poets are so sensitive both to their art and to their
experience that they are able to strike exquisite balances, with
ever new combinations and ever new delight.

More easily than any of the great English poets, Spenser
moves in the pentameter line with a fluid but unvarying regularity. His verses avoid monotony through harmonious variations in their combinations of vowels rather than through
changes in the light ripples of the rhythm:

> And more, to lulle him *in* his slumber soft,
> A trickling streame from high *rocke* tumbling downe
> And ever-drizling raine upon the loft,
> *Mixt with* a mur*muring* winde, *much* like the sowne
> Of swarming Bees, did cast him *in* a swowne:
> *No oth*er noyse, nor peoples troublous cryes,
> As still are wont *t' an*noy the wallèd towne,
> Might there be heard: but carelesse Quiet lyes,
> *Wrapt in* eternall silence farre from ene*myes.*

In this magnificent stanza, the accentual variations are reduced
to a minimum. True, Spenser here desires to lull us into an
enchanted sleep; but this stanza merely accentuates his characteristic movement. In this passage also, variations spring
mainly from the weakness of prepositions. There are three
variations, in the form of inverted feet, at the beginnings of
lines—a favorite device of English poets, marking the larger
rhythm of the line by some slight shift in accent. In fact, such
inversion of a foot at the beginning of a line, or after a pause

within the line, is the commonest of all variations from the
regular pattern of the pentameter.

The great age of the correct pentameter runs from the
Restoration through the eighteenth century. Yet its masters
do not achieve, or aim at, absolute regularity. "Waller was
smooth," writes Pope, yet Edmund Waller at his smoothest
allows departures, or seems to build a completely regular line
only as preparation for a subsequent subtle rhythmical variation. If, as extended examples could demonstrate easily, the
most energetic and meaningful lines are those in which there
are variations, then it may be that in the hands of an artist the
rhythm itself may underline the poetic meaning, may parallel
a movement of mind by some suggestive rhythmical movement, and may therefore by technical means add to the accuracy, completeness, and complexity which prose, lacking a
formal pattern, cannot achieve.

Dryden takes Waller's smoothness and gives it unsurpassable
force. His heavy syllables are certain; the verse moves rapidly;
the parts of the line and of the couplet are so balanced that he
has made the heroic couplet itself into a splendid vehicle for
argumentation and exposition. Much of this power and clarity
comes from the slight variations he makes from his strongly
marked pattern of accents:

> *What can*not praise effect in mighty minds,
> When flatt*ery* soothes, and *when* ambition blinds!
> Desire of pow'r, on earth a vicious weed,
> *Yet,* sprung from high, is *of* celestial seed:
> In God 'tis glory; *and* when men aspire,
> 'Tis *but* a spark *too* much of heav*enly* fire.

Three times in three couplets a pause compensates for a dropped
or slighted accent. The effect of this variant is to divide the
second and fifth, and possibly the fourth, lines into balanced
halves.

Similarly, the intellectual sinews of Alexander Pope's argument are brought into relief by the departures from expected accents and by the pauses that the pattern cannot formally demand:

> *Those* rules of old discover'd, not devis'd,
> Are Nature still, but Nature methodis'd;
> *Nature*, like liber*ty*, is *but* restrain'd
> By *the same* laws which first herself ordain'd.

Here, in the last line, impetuous conviction of thought is suggested by the rhythmical change, or syncopation, of the expected ˘ ′ ˘ ′ into ˘ ˘ ′ ′. Pope, indeed, who strives to be the most correct of poets, does not equate correctness with complete regularity. He even formulates rules governing the use of pauses to keep them from falling repeatedly in the same place in succeeding lines.

The relatively infrequent variations which Thomas Gray introduces into the "Elegy in a Country Churchyard" usually contribute by their very change of rhythm to the image or thought they are conveying. The unusual basic regularity itself helps to create a meditative and relaxed solemnity for the whole.

The most conservative of our poets, therefore—Waller, Dryden, Pope, Gray—cannot, or will not, conform to strict patterns in pentameters. The difficulty of writing perfectly regular lines has already been mentioned: grammar and sentence structure and the peculiarities of the English language get in the way. Furthermore, the meaning of any sentence throws emphasis upon some words and makes others weak, so that it is foolish to expect that of the ten syllables of a line, five will be equally heavy, and five equally light.

If this is true for the commonest meter in English poetry, how much more true must it be of more complicated meters! Swinburne achieved a fluency of his own with the three-syllable foot:

> / Out of the / golden re/*mote wild* / west where the / sea
> without / shore is,

/ Full of the / sunset, and / sad, if at / all, with the
 / fullness of / joy,
As a / *wind sets* / in with the / autumn that / blows
 from the / region of / stories,
/ Blows with a / perfume of / songs and of / memories
 be/loved from a / boy.

Rhythmically this is pretty bad—perhaps just because *metrically* it is nearly perfect. The English language evidently does not adapt itself naturally to three-syllable feet. Unless a reader can persuade himself that the essence of poetry lies in nouns strung together by "with the," "in the," and "of the," regular dactyls [´ ˘ ˘] or anapests [˘ ˘ ´] are hard to take. And Swinburne's departures from this meter of the metronome do not serve any purpose here, unless it be to show that he is conscious that a long syllable such as "wild" or "sets" has the time equivalent of two short syllables, as in classical prosody. Swinburne can, at times, be much better. In the following four lines, his substitutions of pauses (marked below as ^) for unaccented syllables, and of two-syllable feet for the expected three-syllable norm, contribute rhythmically to the thought and emotion:

I have lived long enough, having seen *one thing*, ^ that
 love hath an end; ^ ^
Goddess and maiden and queen ^ ^, be near me now and
 befriend.
Thou art more than the day or the morrow, the seasons
 that laugh or that weep; ^
For these *give joy and sorrow;* but thou, ^ Proserpina,
 sleep.

And the last line of this same "Hymn to Proserpine" is a powerful expression of Swinburne's thought because it is an exquisite and purposeful modulation of the rhythmical pattern

˘ ˘ ´ ˘ ˘ ´ ˘ ˘ ´ ˘ ˘ ´ ˘ ˘ ´ ˘ ˘ ´ :

For there is *no God found stron*ger than death; ^ and
 death is a sleep.

Yet Swinburne is not one of the great masters of English poetic rhythm. It is true that the oral reading of his verses has a powerful mesmeric effect, like the beating of tomtoms. But this lulling into quiescence of the rational faculties is only the preparation for poetry, and no poetry follows. Mr. Eliot has said that Swinburne is interested only in the word; even this may be an overstatement. He is not interested in the full poetic possibilities of a word; his interest is narrowed to verbal effects of melody and metrics, and even in these effects Swinburne is superficial. The rhythmical skill of a poet should serve to bring out his thoughts in the same way that the manual dexterity of a violinist may increase the pathos or joy of a Beethoven concerto, or that roadwork and rope-jumping may help a boxer to knock out an opponent. As ends in themselves, these skills are of little interest or importance. And Swinburne's technical experiments are too much ends in themselves. Comparing his verse to brilliant set pieces rolled off on a player piano may be unfair to his skill; but the comparison would not arise if he had welded more completely his technique to significant emotion.

The most complex metrical pattern is simple in comparison with the actual rhythms of great poetry. For no matter how complex, a "correct" meter exists by itself in its own singleness. In great poetry, the syncopation of emotion or thought against the formal pattern continually recurs; there is always the harmony, the tension, or the conflict between the control exercised by the formal abstract rhythm and the immediate intense particularity of what is being expressed in that rhythm. Swinburne's technical experiments, therefore, often seem superficial and unimportant because they exist in and for themselves; the flow of the verse has little connection, usually, with the passions and ideas to which it is accidentally linked.

We may advance, then, to the position that extreme regularity in rhythm is almost impossible, and when, infrequently, it is achieved, it proves displeasing. Poetry may be considered as a vine growing on a trellis. The rhythm furnishes the trellised support and pattern which the poem needs for its growth and shapeliness. But each individual poem uses its arbitrary rhythmical scheme merely as a directing and sustaining framework; it departs and varies from the rigid pattern upon which it grows. A poem that adhered perfectly to a pre-established meter, if such a poem could be created, would be as unnatural and unattractive as a vine made out of laths, building blocks, and T-squares. The law of rhythm in poetry, therefore, cannot accept the extreme tyranny of the metronome.

At the opposite pole, the principle of poetic rhythm cannot proceed on the assumption which many critics have maintained, that all language is rhythmical. Aristotle observed long ago that ordinary speech falls into iambic rhythm. Greek orators and rhetoricians worked out elaborate theories of prose cadences. Robert Louis Stevenson labored as hard to get the blank verse out of his prose (as if it had crept into the first drafts in spite of him) as Dickens may have worked to produce the regular rhythms of his climaxes. And there are books and articles on the rhythm of prose and the rhythms of prose writers. They are not pertinent to this chapter. As we have defined rhythm—the more or less regular recurrence of a temporal pattern—the rhythm of prose is slight. There have been writers, like Sir Thomas Browne and Thomas De Quincey and Gertrude Stein and James Joyce, so sensitive to the poetic uses of language that it is difficult to consider their writings either purely as prose or as poetry. Their experiments in rhythm are subtle. But even these authors, and all inferior craftsmen who fail to distinguish between the right uses of prose and poetry, become at times wanderers between two worlds, leaving their readers uneasily trying to find the proper mood in which to approach their amphibious productions.

At its best, elaborately stylized prose is wasteful. Beautiful as any individual movement of words may be, it cannot gain cumulative power through repetition without becoming, formally, a poem. The cadences of prose are born without ancestors and die without direct issue. And even at its best, mannered prose must front a dilemma: if "prosaic" ideas of no particular tension or complex immediacy are to be presented, then suggestions of formal rhythm are distracting; if, on the other hand, complex emotions are to be tellingly conveyed, the full resources of a definite rhythm to foster and maintain such complex emotions are not being utilized. In theory, poetic prose has little to recommend it, being neither fish nor fowl. In practice, it is used by those authors who wish to create in their work the qualitative effects of poetry. In most prose writers, moreover, it is generally true that intensity of emotion, thought, conviction, or imagery is paralleled by a tendency toward increasingly definite rhythms.

The writers of poetic prose have as brothers those professed poets whose works the lay reader can identify as poetry only by the typography.

> But mere indentations
> And Capitalizations
> or lack of capitalizations
> And all the tricks of ingenious printers
> And, in addition,
> The matter and the mood of poetry,
> Cannot make such a sentence
> As this
> Into a poem
> > without
> RHYTHM.

Professor Lowes in *Convention and Revolt in Poetry* and Robert Bridges in *Humdrum and Harum Scarum* have opposed free verse so tellingly that little need be done here except to call attention again to some of their arguments. In liberating verse from the tyranny of a pattern, experimenters do not so much give their product freedom and power as they destroy its opportunities to show its own freedom and power by rebellion *within* a fixed pattern. They seek liberty and achieve license. The organizing "unit" of free verse is the line. If lines are determined by divisions of thought, then they function merely as marks of punctuation; if they do not strictly follow logical divisions, then what keeps the division by lines from being mere whimsy? A poem written in any regular meter and set up as prose may be reset as verse by any amateur. But a free-verse poem set up as prose would be recast as verse in ten different ways by ten people. If free verse had form in any real sense, its form would be detectable. Far from securing freedom and variety for verse through arbitrarily irregular lines, free verse produces an effect of monotony. In assassinating its rhythmical governors, free verse has become so free that it is aimless; it has lost the exciting opportunity to upset, at a significant time, an established order. The unreality of the "cadence" as a formal organizer of poetry is perhaps seen best in the development of Amy Lowell, who passed from confident though vague definitions and conceptions of free verse to the discovery of "polyphonic prose," which utilizes all the devices of poetry except formal rhythmical organization. Some three hundred years before, Lyly and Sidney and Sir Thomas Browne had made similar experiments. The theorists of the twentieth century have only succeeded in arriving at the position of Byron's poetaster:

> Who both by precept and example shows
> That prose is verse, and verse is merely prose.

The formless monotony of free verse can best be realized by imagining what a long poem—the *Iliad, Paradise Lost, Lear*—would be like if deprived of the support of its metrical pattern. Nor is it sufficient defense of free verse in general to point out individual successes by Walt Whitman or W. E. Henley or D. H. Lawrence or Amy Lowell. Concerning any fine piece of work written in loose, amorphous word movements, one should ask these questions seriously: Would the product have been inferior if the writer had possessed and exercised a mastery over rhythm? Does the rhythmical formlessness contribute positively to the effect of the poem? In most instances, the answers to both questions will be No. Whitman's attempts in regular rhythms are for the most part grotesque; perhaps he did well to leave the sprawling giants of his thoughts in their loose lines. But only for writers akin to Whitman and Lawrence, who seem deliberately trying to give effects of groping toward a new world or a new mode of existence, does free verse serve an artistic technical end in making confusion more clearly confounded.

The vers librists belong to the first third of our century. These strictures upon them might seem like beating a dead horse if the influence of free verse, though variously modified, were not present in so many contemporary poets, where it often betokens the author's technical incompetence and arouses the reader's boredom. The great argument of the free-verse proponents is that the rhythms of traditional poetry are too rigid, artificial, and dulled by constant use to permit effective expression: each individual thought must now find its own unique, individual word movement. The argument will lose its weight if it can be shown that the presence of an underlying rhythmical pattern contributes to, instead of detracting from, the exact and intense expression of significant experience. To that end the rest of this chapter will be dedicated.

The defense of rhythm in this chapter is really a defense of the mean. Absolute metrical regularity is impossible and undesirable. Complete irregularity, though all too possible, is undesirable. Great poems display a tension between an arbitrary abstract rhythmical pattern and its particular concrete embodiment. The various conflicts between fixed rhythm and fluid thought, between grammatical divisions and line or stanza divisions, between metrics and rhetoric, with all the resultant adjustments and compromises, the satisfying or disappointing of expectations for rhythmical recurrences—all these concords and discords between technique and spirit give to a poem part of its essential life.

In considering how the seventeenth and eighteenth centuries handled five-beat lines, we have already noticed that slight variations from the established meter may be eloquent in expressing the thought. When Cowper writes

> Give me the line that plows its stately course
> Like a proud swan, conquering the stream by force,

the rhythm is an echo of the sense. Impetuosity and force take the place of placid regularity in the second line, by means of two hurried light syllables followed by two strong ones, then a pause, then a foot with accent inverted. Instead of ˘ ´/ ˘ ´/ ˘ ´ we have ˘ ˘ / ´ · // ´ ˘ ˘, where // represents a decided pause in the sense. Perhaps it is not carrying impressionistic criticism too far to say that the dactyl ( ´ ˘ ˘ ) of "conquering" (or slurred dactyl: "conqu'ring") serves very well to suggest both the image of the swan as it takes a stroke and the thought of powerful verse. Departure from a pattern, particularly when the pattern has been well established, can produce exciting effects of rightness which are impossible both in verse completely free and in verse completely regular.

Suppose we dare set a passage of Milton as free verse:
> Him
> The almighty power
> Hurled
>         headlong
>            flaming
>                 from the ethereal sky
> With hideous ruin and combustion
>     Down
> To bottomless perdition
> There to dwell
> In adamantine chains and penal fire
> Who durst defy the omnipotent
>     To arms.

And suppose also we sacrifice the splendor of its diction for the sake of an exact pattern:

> Then Almighty God
> Did hurl him headlong flaming from the sky
> In frightful ruin, dire combustion down
> To dark and deep perdition, there to dwell
> In adamantine chains and penal fire
> Who durst defy the potent God to arms.

In contrast to both of these, Milton's actual passage gains its heady magnificence from the clash between pattern and irregularity, between convention and revolt in rhythm:

> Him the Almighty Power
> Hurld headlong flaming from th' Ethereal Skie
> With hideous ruine and combustion down
> To bottomless perdition, there to dwell
> In Adamantine Chains and penal Fire,
> Who durst defie th' Omnipotent to Arms.

There is a tremor in the redundant swift or almost elided syllables of "the Almighty," "th' Ethereal," "hideous," and "th' Omnipotent," which, *through rhythm*, gives to Milton's Messiah the electric energy of Michelangelo's Creator of Adam on the Sistine ceiling. The "Hurld headlong" line intensifies this shattering power through its shattered iambs. The pattern

$$/ \; \smile \; , \; / \; \smile \; , \; / \; \smile \; , \; / \; \smile \; , \; / \; \smile \; , \; /$$

here becomes:

$$/ \; , \; / \; , \; / \; , \; \smile \; / \; , \; \smile \; \smile \; \smile \; \smile \; / \; , \; \smile \; \smile \; / \; , \; /$$

and the falling rhythms give us Lucifer, a comet with a train, falling through space. The rush of the opening, with its immediate powerful beats and sequent weak syllables, carries without pause to the pause after "perdition"—carries, one might say, until Lucifer hits bottom. After this rushing descent, Lucifer is held there by the powerful rhythm of "there to dwell" [ $/ \; \smile \; /$ ]. And in both paraphrases

In adamantine chains and penal fire

is the one line that was not changed, for it forms a unit of
thought and is completely regular, so that in Milton's version
its *contrasting* mechanical regularity may suggest the long
monotony of Satan's doom.

For some readers, this impressionistic analysis may seem
fanciful. But wherever our common sense calls a halt to such
interpretation, the interplay between order and freedom remains a powerfully expressive instrument. It constitutes the
real rhythm of poetry. Its effects are lost under either the dictatorship of mechanical correctness or the anarchy of free
verse.

Milton, with his fine musical ear, carries variations from a
pattern as far as they can be carried without losing the pattern entirely. Yet in *Paradise Lost* his astonishing innovations
and inventions are achieved within a framework of rules from
which he rarely departs. Verse of true musical delight, he himself writes, must have "apt numbers, fit quantity of syllables,
and the sense variously drawn out from one verse into another." This last requirement shows Milton aware that monotony may be avoided by contrast between a line of fixed
length, and thought structures of varying length. He demands
"fit quantity of syllables," and rarely permits himself even the
extra unaccented syllable at the end of the line which by his
time had become a convention. Within the line his extra syllables may either be easily elided, as when a vowel follows a
vowel ("hid*eous*," "*the Al*mighty"), or else they occur in words
such as "spirit" or "heaven" which his contemporaries accepted
as monosyllables. Hardly a line can be found in *Paradise Lost*
which, granted Milton's rules, does not contain exactly ten
active syllables. But in spite of this fixed quantity, as the few
lines quoted above show, Milton's "numbers"—that is, his
rhythms—could hardly be more "apt" for the expression of
his thought. The numbers have gained their aptness because of
metrical variations; but these would not have been detectable

if the quantity of syllables and the pattern of expected accents had not been fixed.

In Milton's development as a poet, his rhythms become more and more complex. In his early poems "L'Allegro" and "Il Penseroso," the vacillation between the usual iambs ($\smile$ $'$) and the dancing trochees ($'$ $\smile$) keeps monotony out of the simple meter, but such variations are themselves relatively simple and obvious. The "Hymn on the Morning of Christ's Nativity," similarly, has a complex stanza form, but the rhythmical variations within the stanza are not particularly effective. At the other end of Milton's life, in contrast, the choruses of *Samson Agonistes* are so complex in rhythm that they have been misunderstood and condemned by some, read with instinctive delight by many, and fully analyzed by no one. What is true of Milton's technical development is generally true of all poets and even of schools of poetry: a poet begins with simple rhythms, masters them, and proceeds to variations.

> True ease in writing comes from art, not chance,
> As those move easiest who have *learned* to dance.

It may be more than accidental that both Chaucer and Milton won their first major victories—"The Boke of the Duchesse" and "L'Allegro"—in the four-beat line, but later abandoned it for the five-beat line. The tetrameter line does not contain enough possibilities for variation. Like the hexameter, it splits too easily into halves. But how can five beats in ten syllables be divided into two equal parts? The pentameter line has become the favorite vehicle for English poetry because it has no rivals in rhythm: its pattern is fixed and well known, but the variations within that pattern are inexhaustible. Chaucer and Spenser, initiating two great ages of poetry, use the pentameter with relatively few variations; they are conquering new territory; they learn to move within its bounds. In comparison with the pioneers Chaucer and Spenser, Shakespeare and Milton make the pentameter supple, syncopated, and elastic. Mil-

ton, the last of a great lineage, uses it with an unmatched sinu-
ous skill.

Within his own verse Shakespeare passed through the transition from regularity, the prim consciousness of feet and lines,
to a virtuosity in which syncopation almost destroys the pattern. His early *Love's Labour's Lost*, with its many experiments
in other forms of verse than the pentameter, shows Shakespeare
conscious of the delights of rhythm. But he has not yet learned
to dance well; he is watching his feet. The rhythm is a little
monotonous, a little clumsy:

> A lover's eyes will gaze an eagle blind;
> A lover's ear will hear the lowest sound,
> When the suspicious head of theft is stopp'd:
> Love's feeling is more soft and sensible
> Than are the tender horns of cockled snails;
> Love's tongue proves dainty Bacchus gross in taste:
> For valour, is not Love a Hercules,
> Still climbing trees in the Hesperides?

Years of practice and of listening to actors speak enable him,
by the turn of the century, to fit the rhythm like a glove to
the thought. Halfway through his career, in *Measure for Measure*, he voices Isabella's passionate realization of man's petty
pride in resilient, syncopated verse:

> *Merci*ful heaven,
> Thou rather with thy sharp and sulph*urous* bolt
> *Splitt'st the unwedgeable* and gnarlèd oak
> *Than the soft myrtle;* but man, *proud man,*
> *Dress'd in* a little brief authori*ty* . . .

In the next-to-last line, only one foot in five is regular,
and the pattern

$$/ \smallsmile \ '/\smallsmile \ '/\smallsmile \ '/\smallsmile \ '/\smallsmile \ ' \ /$$

has become

$$/ \smallsmile \smallsmile \ / \ ' \ ' \ / \smallsmile \ \wedge/\!/ \smallsmile \ ' \ / \ '' \ /.$$

The falling of the third beat on a rest—on a syllable that isn't there—is a rhythmically effective device to prepare for the rush of bitter contrasting thought in the powerful three last syllables.

Such extreme liberties with a pattern can be taken only if the pattern is thoroughly established. This in itself would be an argument for maintaining a single meter through a long poem, for the longer a meter is carried on, the more striking are any deliberate departures from its insistent subconscious beat.

By the end of his career, blank verse had pulsed so long in Shakespeare's veins that his principal interest as dramatic poet might be said to be technical. His experiments would seem formless were it not that the five-beat line is deeply incised in the minds of author and audience alike. This from *The Winter's Tale:*

> When you do dance, I wish you
> A wave o' the sea, that you might ever do
> Nothing but that; move still, still so,
> And own no other function.

Here the variations cannot be precisely graphed. How impossible it is to reduce to a conventional prosodic system those words "move still, still so," where four heavy and equal beats are syncopated against an expected three feet of six syllables! And yet where, if we are looking for sheer delight in verbal rhythms, can we find any English poetry comparable in breathtaking boldness and subtlety to Shakespeare's last plays?

These plays of Shakespeare—*Antony and Cleopatra, Coriolanus, Pericles, Cymbeline, The Winter's Tale, The Tempest* —as well as Milton's *Paradise Lost, Paradise Regained* and *Samson Agonistes*, authenticate the rule of rhythm for the greatest poetry: establish firmly the great line of a consistent rhythm, and then depart from it deliberately. The reader's awareness of fixed pattern intensifies his awareness of purposeful occasional freedoms. The most careless rapture in poetry, analyzed, is found usually to derive its carelessness and rapture from careful plotting.

If it were not for the great tradition of five-beat iambs, the liberty of such lines as these from Eliot's "A Song for Simeon" would look like looseness:

> Lord, the Roman hyacinths are blooming in bowls and
> The winter sun creeps by the snow hills;
> The stubborn season has made stand.
> My life is light, waiting for the death wind,
> Like a feather on the back of my hand.
> Dust in sunlight and memory in corners
> Wait for the wind that chills towards the dead land.

Similarly, if it were not for the long history of pentameters in English and hexameters in classical poetry, the wavering and billowing irregular lines of Bridges' *Testament of Beauty* might appear as free verse. Bridges is already assuming the reader's long familiarity with pentameters when he writes, much earlier, in "London Snow":

> And all woke earlier for the unaccustomed brightness
> Of the winter dawning, the strange unheavenly glare:
> The eye marveled—marveled at the dazzling whiteness;
>
> The daily thoughts of labor and sorrow slumber
> At the sight of the beauty that greets them, for the
>     charm they have broken.

Obviously, the growing liberties with rhythm taken by poets with such delicate ears as Eliot and Bridges indicate no lack of care or of skill, but rather depend upon tradition and take for granted on the part of their readers a knowledge of, and sensitivity to, the rich rhythmical heritage of English poetry during the last five hundred years.

The stronger the sense of fixed rhythm and the longer it is maintained, the stronger the effect of spontaneity, intensity, lyricism, in departures from it. A sonnet, for instance, is so

short that its rhythm is hardly established fully before its four-
teen lines are finished. Variations, therefore, should be spar-
ingly introduced, and not too early in the sonnet. Once Keats's
sonnet is well known, the opening line

> Bright star! would I were steadfast as thou art!

parallels rhythmically the burst of feeling. It does little, however, to establish at the start the pattern for succeeding lines,
and taken by itself, few readers would accent the last word
of the line heavily enough to suggest its importance to the
rhyme scheme. In the same fashion, the opening of one of
John Donne's most famous poems, "A Valediction Forbidding
Mourning," is faulty in that it does not indicate the norm for
the stanza:

> As virtuous men passe mildly away.

How should that be read? Has it eight or ten active syllables?
Where do the accents fall? The second line sets us straight:

> And whisper to their souls, to go.

Now we can elide in the first line and read it:

> As vírtuous mén pass míldly awáy.

But it is a safe rule in poetry not to depart from a rhythm before it is clearly established. Where Donne's variation in the
*first* line is of doubtful value, Keats's variation in the *fourth*
line of "La Belle Dame Sans Merci," after creating the expectation of regular tetrameters in the first three lines, is a
discovery:

> Oh what can ail thee, knight at arms,
>> Alone and palely loitering?
> The sedge is withered from the lake
>> And no birds sing.

The sense of slowness, heaviness, of something incomplete or
questioning, is brought out rhythmically by the surprise of
the cadence

◡ ╱ ╱ ╱

in place of the expected

◡ / ◡ / ◡ / ◡ /

> (And nightingales no longer sing).

This variation in Keats's fourth lines is extremely artful and successful. In the regular ballad stanza a simpler change probably explains why such an old form does not seem monotonous. This usual variation is the alternation of four-beat lines with three-beat:

> There lived a wife at Usher's well,
> And a wealthy wife was she;
> She had three stout and stalwart sons,
> And sent them o'er the sea.

True, pauses after the second and fourth lines of the ballad stanza usually fill up the lines to the same actual duration as those with more syllables and beats; nevertheless, the slight shift to a dropped beat, though regularly introduced, gives variety to the uniform pattern.

The nineteenth century practiced many cunning variations on the ballad stanza. It also explored fully, in such poets as Thomas Moore, Browning, Swinburne, and Kipling, the possibilities of three-syllable feet in English. And it developed, in Coleridge, Hopkins, Kipling, and Meredith, the idea that although the number of syllables in a line may vary, the number of beats and their timing should be fixed. This principle, native to Old English verse, had long been neglected in practice. When such organizing rhythmical principles become well known through frequent use, variations upon them, or combinations, will not destroy the reader's perception of rhythm. An individual may be unmistakably himself, and yet the characteristics of his ancestors may be visible in his face.

The title of such a freely rhythmical poem as Walter de la Mare's "The Ghost" might be considered as aptly describing its rhythmical technique. Its lyrical, singing quality would not have been appreciated, say, in the eighteenth century, when more obvious patterns were the rule. Yet in this poem, the rhythmical *revenants* of the ballad, of the three-syllable foot, and of the elastic line with fixed number of beats combine to give it an ancestry. One may be conscious of a pattern even when that pattern is departed from, or another pattern is superposed. The sense of 4/4 time, for instance, that underlies such a syncopated ragtime phrase as

produces an entirely different effect from the same notes, in the same time, without the syncopation of three against four:

Similarly, in de la Mare's poem, the pattern, difficult as it is to graph, and even allowing for different possible readings, blends simpler patterns; the strangeness and freshness of a brave new poem spring from the wedding of more conventional rhythmical forms:

> "Who knocks?" "I, who was beautiful,
> Beyond all dreams to restore,
> I, from the roots of the dark thorn am hither,
>   And knock on the door."
>
>    "Who speaks?" "I—once was my speech
>    Sweet as the bird's on the air.
>    When echo lurks by the waters to heed;
>      'Tis I speak thee fair."
>
> "Dark is the hour!" "Aye, and cold."
> "Lone is my house." "Ah, but mine?"
> "Sight, touch, lips, eyes yearned in vain."
>   "Long dead these to thine. . . ."

> Silence. Still faint on the porch
> Brake the flame of the stars.
> In gloom groped a hope-wearied hand
>     Over keys, bolts, and bars.

> A face peered. All the grey night
> In chaos of vacancy shone;
> Nought but vast sorrow was there—
>     The sweet cheat gone.

What is the normal rhythm here? Can a pattern stanza be determined when no two stanzas are exactly alike? The beautiful third lines of the stanzas are set definitely as four-beat elastic lines in the first two stanzas

> I, from the roots of the dark thorn am hither

and

> When echo lurks by the waters to heed.

The irregularity of the other third lines becomes fascinating simply because it is in conflict with this established rhythm:

> Sight, touch, lips, eyes yearned in vain

> In gloom groped a hope-wearied hand

> Nought but vast sorrow was there—

How the next to the last stanza will be read depends upon which principle has won domination in this silent struggle. Again, either furnishes a beautiful reading; although the preference might be given to the three-syllable reading as more smoothly rhythmical, it might with equal justification be given to the ballad reading as more psychologically apt in expressing the mood of mystery and waiting:

> Sílence. Still fáint on the pórch
> Brake the flámes of the stárs.
> In glóom groped a hópe-wearied hánd
>     Óver kéys, bolts, and bárs.

versus:

> Sílence. Stíll fáint on the pórch
> Bráke the flámes of the stárs.
> In glóom gróped a hópe-wearied hánd
> Over kéys, bólts, and bárs.

The poem gains much of its energy and establishes its mood of excitement and uncertainty and half-presences *rhythmically*, through conflicts between different organizing principles. Two, possibly three, differing metrical schemes, then, may serve simultaneously in organizing a poem.

Usually, however, the conflict or the harmony comes between a formal metrical pattern and the sense of what is being said. The most effective variations are introduced in order to reinforce, through some rhythmical device, a turn in thought. Housman is a master at such subtle suggestion. In "When Smoke Stood up from Ludlow," he tells the story of the young plowman who kills a blackbird because it sings of death, only to realize in his soul that death is unescapable. The poem unrolls in six stanzas of straightforward narration; there are almost no metrical substitutions; the verbs of action have been connected *at the beginnings of the iambic lines* seven times by a Biblical "and" before the end of the fourth stanza, which is here quoted:

> I heard the tune he sang me,
> And spied his yellow bill;
> I picked a stone and aimed it
> And threw it with a will:
> Then the bird was still.

So regularly have the stanzas been developed that the omission in the last line of one unaccented syllable, that one colorless little word "and," acutely reinforces the shock of death. The only other departure in the whole thirty-line poem from an iambic opening for each line comes at the start of the following stanza, where the realization of death and its resolute accept-

ance—the change to a different world, not so blithe and full
of whistling—are underlined rhythmically by the same device
of omission:

> *Then* my soul within me
>  Took up the blackbird's strain,
> And still beside the horses
>  Along the dewy lane
>  It sang the song again.

Indeed, in any complete study of poetic rhythm, a skillful
use of omission might almost be used as the mark of a poet.
Many of the finest effects come from omitted syllables—sometimes even from omitted feet, like rests in music. The good
poet, by manipulating his formal pattern, can compel such
pauses. Without the metrical pattern, his only devices would
be punctuation and the arbitrary terminations of lines, both of
which are about as crude and blunt as inserting the word
STOP in a telegram. For delicacy and breathlessness of rhythm,
gained largely by omitting syllables after firmly establishing a
pattern that requires them, the last poem in *Last Poems* is un-
surpassed. The seventh line of each stanza is especially interesting because in each of the five stanzas it wavers between
two and three beats. Here is the first stanza:

> When lads were home from labour
>  At Abdon under Clee,
> A man would call his neighbour
>  And both would send for me.
> And where the light in lances
>  Across the mead was laid,
> Thére tó the dánces
>  I fétched my flúte and pláyed.

By the time Housman arrives at the last four lines of the final
stanza, he may maintain the pattern while omitting expected
syllables:

> To-morrow, more's the pity,
> Away we both must hie,
> To air the ditty,
> And to earth I.

In the final line, the conflict between sense and meter is apparent. The pattern demands six syllables and three beats; Housman supplies four syllables which would ordinarily require only two beats with a pause between them (⌣ ⌣ ╱ ⌢ ╱). In the reading, a beat must somehow be suggested on the "and" ( ⌣̇ ⌣ ╱ ⌢ ╱). And the effect of this balancing between metrical and logical elements is actually to enhance the total sense the passage conveys—in a dissolving, whispering, fading close.

These "hovering rhythms," caused by the clash between the pattern and the sense, immeasurably increase the complexity and richness possible to poetry. A poem is kept nervously alive by tensions between these two independent principles. At times they exactly coincide, to produce a powerful effect of inevitability; as in Cowper's

> But Í benéath a róugher séa
> And whélmed in déeper gúlfs than hé

or Wordsworth's

> And néver lífted úp a síngle stóne.

The metrical pattern may be used to throw accents on words so that we seem to hear the inflections of a living voice. Often, however, sense and meter are at variance. A whole theory has been successfully advanced that the vitality and drive of Donne's verse come from his acute awareness of the struggle between his rhetorical and his metrical patterns. If we indicate the sense accent by x and the metrically required accent by ´, the following eight lines from "The Ecstasy" will show how the nervous energy of Donne's poetry derives from shifting conflicts and coincidences in the two organizing principles:

    x ⁄   x ⁄    x ⁄     x ⁄
But oh, alas, so long, so far
    x ⁄     x ⁄      ⁄    x ⁄
Our bodies why do we forbear?
    x ⁄          x ⁄      x ⁄   x ⁄
They are ours, though they are not we; we are
   x ⁄   ⁄     x ⁄    x ⁄
The intelligences, they the sphere.
   ⁄       x ⁄     x ⁄       x ⁄
We owe them thanks, because they thus
   x ⁄   x ⁄    ⁄      ⁄
Did us to us at first convey,
   x   ⁄    x   x ⁄     x ⁄      x ⁄
Yielded their forces, sense, to us,
    ⁄      x    ⁄      ⁄    x ⁄
Nor are dross to us, but allay. [= alloy]

The greatest conflict in these lines comes from the hovering final foot of the third line—"we are"—where the opposing demands of meter and sense result in about equal accents upon the two words. Through most of the lines, meter and sense reinforce each other. The actual rhythm may even make the sense plainer, the living accent easier to hear, as in

    They're *ours*, though *they*'re not *we*.

Conversely, the sense (not to mention the normal pronunciation) makes us quick to catch the rhythmical variations in a line, as opposed to its mechanical reading:

    Yielded their forces, sense, to us
    ⁄ ◡ ◡ / ⁄ ◡ ∧ / ⁄ ∧ / ◡ ⁄

instead of:

    ◡ ⁄ / ◡ ⁄ / ◡ ⁄ / ◡ ⁄ .

The variations in this line are great, but they are not so great as in the next line, where only one of the four required accents falls where it should:

    Nor are dross to us, but allay.

The scansion ◡ ◡ ⁄ / ⁄ ◡ / ∧ ∧ / ◡ ◡ ⁄ is the closest I can come to it, and few people would read this line naturally without falling into syncopation which all the prosodists in the world could not analyze satisfactorily.

And yet it is obvious that the line has two *principal* accents. One of the open secrets of poetry lies in this simple truth of a larger rhythm. The lines from Donne have a more beautiful rhythm if they are read with two principal and two secondary beats in each verse, the incidence of these two main beats shifting from one verse to the next. The real rhythm of poetry is lost if we consider mechanically its smallest units. We know the rhythm is there; we sense it and delight in it; but it vanishes if we try to force it through the fine wire mesh of iambs and trochees and spondees and anapests and dactyls. The minute rhythms are present in an unimportant sense; but the organizing rhythm is a larger movement.

In English dramatic and narrative verse, the rhythmical unit is the line, not the foot. Possibly the five-beat line has become the norm instead of the four- or six-beat precisely because the number five minimizes the emphasis upon the little unit of the foot. Any musician knows how difficult it is to beat time accurately in a 5/4 measure, whereas 4/4 or 6/8 sets up an easy monotony which whole notes and sixteenth notes and all the resources of syncopation in music can hardly hide. The five beats of the pentameter, then, provide an organizing principle without glaring insistence upon a singsong pattern. In good verse, the grammatical structures and normal pronunciations, coupled with the sense of what is being said, will introduce endless variations, so that between heavy beats, half-beats, and no beats, the lines will vary from 3 to 3½ to 4 to 4½ to 5 and even to more than five beats:

3   He enter'd, but he enter'd full of wrath;

4½  His flaming robes stream'd out beyond his heels,

4   And gave a roar, as if of earthly fire,

3¾  That scar'd away the meek ethereal Hours

4½  And made their dove-wings tremble. On he flared,

5     From stately nave to nave, from vault to vault,

4     Through bowers of fragrant and enwreathed light,

5     And diamond-paved lustrous long arcades,

4½    Until he reach'd the great main cupola.

A spatial pattern for the accents in this passage from Keats's *Hyperion* might look something like this:

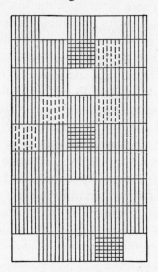

The nine lines have seven different movements in accents represented by different types of shading. A third of the pauses in sense and cadence do not coincide with the formal pauses at the ends of lines. There are at least four different types of feet, not to mention probable anapests ( ᵕ ᵕ ˊ) not marked in the diagram. And the feet themselves do not all take exactly the same time to pronounce. Light feet such as "as if" or "-ola" are read more rapidly than dragging feet such as "wings trem-" or "main cŭp-." Such actual variations in the duration of feet not only are pleasing, but also frequently pass unnoticed.

The human ear is not skilled to detect slight differences in duration with nearly the same accuracy that the eye can detect differences in size. Succeeding feet radically unequal in duration may be accepted as equal. The significance may act as governor, so that since the swift line

He enter'd, but he enter'd full of wrath

fittingly expresses rushing speed, and the slow and powerful line

From stately nave to nave, from vault to vault

fittingly expresses stateliness, the tailoring of technique to thought is accepted, without examination, as an exact equivalence in duration. And finally, by a kind of poetic attraction, a slow or heavily accented foot may absorb some of the unused temporal and accentual elements from surrounding weaker feet; or one or two light, swift feet may build up a reserve of accents and duration which a later foot spends. "Main cupola" is so heavy on the first two syllables that the last two, though they constitute technically a foot, may pass almost without accent. And in the phrase "And made their dove-wings tremble," the first three syllables are so fast and light that they can afford to pass on to the next three syllables three heavy accents that schematically should have been scattered in alternation.

Thus the lines of English pentameter verse—and the passage here quoted is more regular than the average, rather than less so—are as unstable yet as rhythmical as the waves of the ocean. Each may have its individual ripples, a higher crest here may cause a lower trough there, but the general rhythm of the whole is unbroken. A great long poem, in its minute rhythmical units, shimmers and shifts like the northern lights; and, like the northern lights, it changes without losing unity and identity. Or to take a final image, one line of blank verse differs from another as successive stills of a candle flame taken by a moving-picture camera; each picture may be different, as the flame sways and diminishes and flickers and swells again. But just as the flame endures as a flame and keeps its entity through time, so the pentameter line, despite innumerable changes, retains its persistent rhythm.

The smaller foot units of the pentameter, then, shift irregularly within the regular larger organizing unit of the line. In lines other than the pentameter, however, lines which of necessity break into halves and fourths, the usual larger rhythm comes from doubling the small foot units. A moment's consideration is enough to convince most readers that in a long balanced line all accents are not given equal weight. Only a bad reading of Tennyson's "Locksley Hall" would assume that justice is done to its rhythm in:

Saw the Vision of the world, and all the wonders that would be.

Most of us would compound these eight small feet into four larger ones:

Saw the Vision of the world, and all the wonders that would be.

And as we read the whole poem, the lines may even tend to compound the compound feet, so that we are left with two principal and two secondary accents, marked (´):

Saw the Vision of the world, and all the wonders that would be.

Many common stanzaic forms have such larger rhythms. Actually, the ballad stanza becomes most effective rhythmically with two principal beats to a line:

The many men, so beautiful!
And they all dead did lie:
And a thousand thousand slimy things
Lived on; and so did I.

I moved my lips—the Pilot shrieked

And fell down in a fit;

The holy Hermit raised his eyes,

And prayed where he did sit.

Even the limerick is best grasped as a rhythmical whole if it is considered as really a four-line stanza, with two enormous compound feet to a line, the third line having internal rhyme and the other three lines filled out to their full length by pauses at the end:

There was an Old Man who said, "How

Shall I flee from this horrible Cow?

I will sit on this stile, and continue to smile,

Which may soften the heart of that Cow."

And many of the most fascinating rhythms in modern verse —the epilogue to Browning's "Fifine at the Fair," Meredith's "Love in the Valley," Kipling's "The Last Chantey"—owe their resilience to a definite, an invariable, underpattern which may be called eight small feet (often present only as rests or single syllables), or four larger feet, or two superfeet. Read against a quick-ticking metronome, Masefield's "Cargoes" would run:

Dirty British coaster with a salt-caked smoke stack.

As a four-beat line of complex or compounded feet, it becomes:

Dirty British coaster with a salt-caked smoke stack.

And in its largest rhythm it is seen to be, much like the limerick, a five-line stanza only in appearance, actually a four-line stanza with two principal beats to a line:

Dirty British coaster with a salt-caked smoke stack,

Butting through the Channel in the mad March days,

    With a cargo of Tyne coal,

    Road-rails, pig-lead,

Firewood, iron-ware, and cheap tin trays.

The sinuosity and springiness of Meredith's "Love in the Valley" could never be achieved except against the rigid underlying pattern. And again, reading by compound feet increases the rhythmical beauty of the poem:

/Hither   she / comes;   she / comes to me; she / lingers,

/Deepens her brown / eyebrows, / while in new sur/prise

/High rise the / lashes   in / wonder of a / stranger;

/Yet am I   the / light   and / living of her / eyes.

/Something friends have / told her / fills her heart to / brim-

    ming,

/Nets her in her / blushes,   and / wounds her,   and / tames.

/Sure of her / haven,   O / like a dove a/lighting,

/Arms up, she / dropp'd:   our / souls were in our / names.

For a satisfactory metrical analysis of this stanza, and of any lyrical and singing poem, some form of musical notation is necessary. The rhythms of poetry are indeed comparable to the rhythms of music. And perhaps there is no better way to end this chapter than to suggest that the complex effects which music may secure as it writes its arabesque on moving time—the great gap between a whole note and a grace note, the powerful emotions aroused by a change in tempo, a rubato, a ritardando, or an accelerando passage—all these are possible because of the rigid formality of the bar and the time signature. Without an established pattern, variety cannot be detected; it becomes, in fact, a monotony that cannot vary from its own perpetual formlessness. Apart, then, from arousing the expectation of a patterned return in time, and from satisfying *in some manner* that expectation, no combination of words is rhythmical. And no combination of words is a poem, realizing the poetic potentialities of language to the full, unless it is rhythmical.

# CHAPTER SEVEN

# POETRY
# IS FORMAL

AFTER the first five chapters, which were concerned with the arrangement of thought in poetry, the sixth chapter turned to the arrangement of words. The words themselves must so fall as to give the reader a sense of a pattern in time. If the pattern of rhythm contributes something essential to a poem, then the element of *pattern*, however manifested, may be considered as furnishing the last of the essential qualities of poetry. The principle of rhythm, in fact, is merely one aspect of the general principle of form. In the nature of poetry as it flows through time, rhythm is so ever-present and yet so protean in its changes that it has demanded separate scrutiny. Yet the preceding chapter is merely a prologue, a vestibule, to this section, in which the principle of formal organization must be extended to the poem as a whole.

The application of the law of rhythm has shown, I hope, that such a governing principle may rule without ruling arbitrarily. No critic of poetry can afford to be a fanatical Robespierre, destroying everything that does not fit his burning and narrow convictions. He has seen too many Robespierres among the creating poets themselves, and has felt that in some measure each of these destroyers and preservers has seized truth. The laws of poetry are not the laws of the Medes and the Persians; they are the laws of a democracy rather than of a dictatorship, for poems make the laws—the laws do not arbitrarily and in advance determine the poems. A poem has been defined as rhythmical if it arouses an expectation of the return of a temporal pattern and in some manner satisfies that expectation. Such a regulating principle is neither rigid, like a steel cylinder, nor amorphous, like mud; it is structurally organic, like a man. A poem may move and still have a backbone and a skeleton. If the verse of Eliot and Bridges, the lyrics of de la Mare and Yeats—even the choruses of Milton, the freely moving experiments of Arnold, and the poems of D. H. Lawrence and Hart Crane—are seen to be rhythmical under our definition, then the law of rhythm will hardly be taken to mean that the poet must gallop on a rocking horse.

Establishing the conception of organic rhythm is a necessary prelude for this basic law of form. For the general conception of form also is no bed of Procrustes, which poems must be stretched or hacked in order to fit. Saying that a good poem must be formal is not the same as saying that it must be "correct" and rigid; or that it must fit into some long-established category of sonnet or elegy or ballad; or that form must be a quality recognizable only by the intellect. The principle of form in poetry does point out, however, that one of a poet's chief interests is the shape, the shaping, of his materials.

Poetry is a way of speaking. That statement is ambiguous and it should be taken in all its senses. If an inquirer had asked how Charles Lamb talked, one of his friends might have said, "He speaks wittily," and another, "He stutters." Both would have been right, but the first would have been thinking of Lamb's approach to his material, the second, of his way of presenting it. A third might have said, "He is partial to puns." Such a judgment would have suggested both the whimsical complexity of his thought and the form in which his humor found expression. The first chapters on the nature of poetry dealt with a poet's way of speaking considered qualitatively. The poet speaks personally and intensely and in figures; he thinks he has something to say and he wishes to communicate it; but he naturally appeals to all parts of consciousness, so that a whole person is expressed, and not just a brain or tears or the images on a pair of eyeballs. The poet's way of speaking, then, is partly determined by his way of looking at life. But speaking is something that must be learned; it is a craft, an art. The poet will take advantage of all the possibilities of language to express his complex awareness of the world. He will use it as an instrument with all the attention to practical ends of a lawyer drawing up a will or a businessman writing a letter or a statesman composing a treaty. His ends, of course, are different, and his use of language will in consequence be different. But he will never cease to use words *as instruments* to achieve his purpose, to reveal his complex vision. He will feel, for instance, that a rhythm is good if it helps to express his thought.

Yet there is something more here. To a poet, language is not only an instrument, but an end in itself. No one can read Spenser or Milton or Pope or Swinburne or Kipling without feeling that these poets took delight in rhythm apart from, or in addition to, its powers to express their thoughts. Their words must be related to each other so that the very relation creates a feeling of pleasure, a sense of harmony which we call beauty. This contemplative delight in the ordering of words— entirely apart from anything their ordering may accomplish— is accidental in the lawyer, the wholesaler, and the treaty maker; it is essential in the poet. He manipulates words as if they were meant to be not only useful but beautiful.

The poet, then, has certain ways of speaking which come from his approach to experience; he has certain other ways of speaking which come from his approach to his medium. Januslike, he looks at both life and art. He is at once receptive of experience and creative in art. He is both passive and active. And he cannot be completely described except in terms of his dual nature. When Shelley gives a *functional* definition of a poet as the unacknowledged legislator of the world, we ask: "But *how* should the legislator proceed?" When Coleridge gives a *technical* definition of poetry as "the best words in their best order," we are left with the question: "And *why?* For what purpose are these words ordered?" Wordsworth, classifying his verse as "Poems founded on the affections," "Poems of the fancy," "Poems of the imagination," "Poems of sentiment and reflection," is considering psychological elements in poetry. D. H. Lawrence, dividing his collected verse into a volume called "Rhymed Poems" and another called "Unrhymed Poems," is viewing poetry in one of its formal aspects. Neither a functional nor a technical definition of poetry is complete; both are necessary. A poem is the objectification of an intuition. There is such a thing as a poetic intuition, and such a thing as a presentation of it in poetic language. Not until one is added to the other is there such a thing as a poem.

"The best words in their best order." Rhythm may order a poem. But there are other principles of organization. And there is the complex ordering that results when two or more principles work together.

The most usual and understandable order is that of the deliberate intellect. And, since Matthew Arnold clearly saw the need for organization in poetry and consistently interpreted that organization in limited intellectual terms, certain of his poems should serve as excellent introductions to the principle of form.

Consider a single, haunting line:

        The unplumb'd, salt, estranging sea.

As it stands, the phrase is emotional, rhythmical, intelligible, vivid, and comprehensive. The two-, one-, and three-syllable adjectives play against the regular iambic rhythm and contribute cumulatively and exactly to the final noun. They are "the best words in their best order," but the words are few. As the climax of the whole poem, "Isolation," they become unforgettable very largely because Arnold has prepared for them by crystal-clear balances and oppositions in thought:

> Yes: in the sea of life enisl'd,
> With echoing straits between us thrown,
> Dotting the shoreless watery wild,
> We mortal millions live *alone*.
> The islands feel the enclasping flow,
> And then their endless bounds they know.
>
> But when the moon their hollows lights
> And they are swept by balms of spring,
> And in their glens, on starry nights,
> The nightingales divinely sing;
> And lovely notes, from shore to shore,
> Across the sounds and channels pour;
>
> Oh then a longing like despair
> Is to their farthest caverns sent;
> For surely once, they feel, we were
> Parts of a single continent.
> Now round us spreads the watery plain—
> Oh might our marges meet again!
>
> Who order'd, that their longing's fire
> Should be, as soon as kindled, cool'd?
> Who renders vain their deep desire?—
> A God, a God their severance rul'd;
> And bade betwixt their shores to be
> The unplumb'd, salt, estranging sea.

The marked use of alliteration and of assonance aids, by technical means, in creating a feeling that the thought, too, must be coherent. The rhyme scheme of the stanza, a quatrain followed by a couplet, is formed to hold together the thought in the first four lines and bring it to a point in the last two. Except in the last stanza, Arnold uses this rhyme scheme to clarify the thought scheme. In stanza one, the couplet summarizes a resultant feeling after a description of the mortal state; in stanza two the couplet comes as a final third which combines the images of the first lines; in stanza three, the couplet is used for antithesis—the "now" balanced against the earlier "once." The quatrain in this stanza also is built as a contrast between two moments: "then" and "once"; and the couplet now repeats, with a variation, the balanced contrast: a present longing has been followed by a statement about the past; now a statement about the present is followed by a longing for the past. In the final stanza, the thought overrides the rhyme division of four against two lines; with something of the feeling of the sestet of a sonnet, the thought movement splits into two equal halves, so that in the larger rhythm of the complete thought, the whole last stanza acts as a kind of concluding "couplet." In each stanza, then, the smaller units of thought build up to a conclusion.

The thought of the whole poem is similarly organized. The first stanza presents the human lot of isolation; the next two stanzas, grammatically related by "But when" and "Oh then," contrast our customary inescapable isolation with moments of intense longing for union. The final stanza, more rapid in its movement of thought, asks why such a contrast should exist between destiny and desire; and answers with an acceptance of universal law which transcends human wishes.

This brief description has moved very largely within the bounds of the intellectual argument; but the apportionment of the parallel moods or emotions, and of their contrasts, is equally clear and would run something like this:

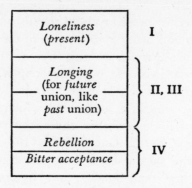

Nor have we yet exhausted the formal organization. There is, throughout, a contrast between various *moments* in time—the usual state of existence in stanza one versus the poignant moments of realization in stanza two; the shifting tenses of the last stanza; and particularly the quadruple shift in time during the third stanza—from present to past to present to future.

The imagery throughout is consistently controlled. Indeed, the most usual sign of organization in a poem is the consistent carrying through and developing of a complex image. There is little likelihood of mistaking the symbols in Arnold's poem. The "islands" are human individuals; their "farthest caverns" are their hearts; the "moon," the "spring," and the "night-ingales" are the beauties of nature (and possibly the beauties of art); the "sea" is life, existence in this material world; the sunken "continent" is our common humanity, now lost in iso-lation—or *insula*tion. Sharp desire frustrated by dull existence is translated into an implied metaphor of fire cooled and quenched by the sea water. And the imagery in general corre-sponds so exactly with the thought that such a word as "end-less" in stanza one seems a defect in artistry, since Arnold or-dinarily avoids such poetic ambiguities as endless-infinite versus endless-everlasting. There is a kind of balance, also, between the dominance of imagery of the first two stanzas and the dominance of comment of the last two. The strikingly successful technical trick of beginning the poem with the one word "Yes" increases the unity of emotion and thought, as if life and its meaning were seen clearly and immediately, even if this flash of intuition must be developed in its parts by the succeeding argument. And the form of the whole poem is given the perfection of a circle by a return at the end to the image of the beginning—a progress that is no progress, but a meditation—from the "sea of life" to the "unplumbed, salt, estranging sea."

Arnold's poem is so clear and direct that much of our analysis here may have appeared too elaborate or too obvious. Yet it has been necessary. If the principle of form is not established in poems where the organization of material is incontrovertible, it will hardly be accepted or even recognized when that organization becomes hidden and subtle. And the law of form must be realized as essential. Too many readers are still unaware that brainwork, intense and unremitting, is part of the creation of poetry; too many people accept unquestioningly as a poem some effusion that is as formless as a decaying jellyfish.

Arnold's sonnet on the "Austerity of Poetry" tells in the first eleven lines that the bride of an early Italian poet, dying, was found to wear sackcloth beneath her beautiful garments and her sparkling jewels; the last three lines are:

> Such, poets, is your bride, the Muse! young, gay,
> Radiant, adorn'd outside; a hidden ground
> Of thought and of austerity within.

Perhaps Arnold does not sufficiently hide the ground of thought and austerity in his verse. The fable and the moral, as in this sonnet, are too easily detachable; so that his poems frequently are synthetic rather than organic. The best of intentions and the clearest of intellects and the finest of poetic theories will not necessarily produce verses that have *poetic* unity. But Arnold's conception of poetry is permanently true. And although his "hidden ground of thought" was probably moral, such austere thought is no less necessary in the artistic formulation of almost any distinguished poem. There is much of the discipline of sackcloth under the jewels and silks that a poet bestows upon his muse.

Both of these poems by Arnold show one type of formal building in a poem, one principle of organization: the equating of complex conceptions with complex images. This commonest device of poetic organization we accept without question whenever we pick up such long poems as "The Parliament of Fowls," or "The Hind and the Panther," or "Prometheus Unbound," or "Manfred," or "The House of Life."

Almost as frequent as the *equating* of one dominating thought with its embodiment in one dominating image is the organization of a poem by *contrasting* two thoughts, or by presenting successive stages in an idea, or by suddenly reversing the expected development of an argument. Arnold, we have seen, uses such oppositions and partitions in the poem "Isolation." It is the usual movement of thought in a sonnet, frequently following the rhyming division into octave and sestet; or, in the Shakespearean sonnet, delaying until the last two lines for the reversal or opposition or new idea. Rossetti lays down formal rules for the ideal sonnet, and exemplifies them in one of the most perfectly constructed, compact, and balanced sonnets in English:

> A sonnet is a moment's monument,
> Memorial from the soul's eternity
> To one dead deathless hour. Look that it be,
> Whether for lustral rite or dire portent,
> Of its own arduous fulness reverent.
> Carve it in ivory or in ebony
> As day or night may rule; and let Time see
> Its flowering crest impearled and orient.
>
> A sonnet is a coin; its face reveals
> The soul, its converse to what Power 'tis due:

Whether for tribute to the august appeals
Of Life, or dower in Love's high retinue
It serve, or 'mid the dark wharf's cavernous breath
In Charon's palm it pay the toll to Death.

This extraordinarily complex yet formal sonnet might be analyzed at as great length as was devoted to Arnold's "Isolation." But here, I shall only point out certain major oppositions and parallels: (1) the formal relationship between ideas and images in all parts of the sonnet; (2) the contrast between the moment and eternity in the octave; (3) the contrast, in lines 6–8, between joy and fear, ivory and ebony, day and night, art and Time; (4) the change from the image of the monument to the image of the coin precisely at the start of the sestet; (5) the conception of the sonnet as being divided in the thought movement into two parts, like the sides of a coin; (6) the suggestion that these two parts are (*a*) a presentation of a moment, and (*b*) an interpretation of the significance of that moment; and (7) the triple parallel between three fitting sonnet themes and three uses of money. If we can generalize from the theory and the practice of this one sonnet, a conscious formality in structure, a building by opposed halves, is one of the surest ways of attaining the "arduous fulness" of poetry.

Form achieved through such oppositions between two thoughts may vary from the tiny tick-tock of thought in Pope's couplets or even within his single lines, up to the grand shaping conceptions of tragedy, with its conflicts between love and honor, pity and fear, good and evil in some particular manifestation, free will and destiny.

Arnold affords a good example of the deliberate attempt to create poetry. He knew what it should and should not be. For one thing it should have form. But the most painstaking intellectual organization, evident alike in his short lyric "Requiescat" and his classical drama *Merope*, does not always rouse that pleasure which a less easily analyzable poetic form might give. Arnold's sense of rhythm was never very acute; in the short lyric, particularly if it has an extreme formality in thought structure, a sure yet resilient rhythm is necessary to awake a sense of organic unity. If we turn back to de la Mare's "The Ghost," on page 215, we find under the elastic and living rhythm a thought pattern as formal in its movement as a minuet:

| | | |
|---|---|---|
| I | Question | |
| | | Answer |
| II | Question | |
| | | Answer |
| | Comment | Reply |
| III | Comment | Question |
| | Comment | |
| | Reply | |
| IV | Description | |
| | Narration | |
| V | Description—Narration | |
| | Significant conclusion | |

Dialogue (brackets stanzas I–III)
Reflection (brackets stanzas IV–V)

The first three stanzas of dialogue are rounded out by the two final meditative stanzas. The division in the first stanza—a question half a line long against an answer in three and a half lines—is repeated like an echo in the second stanza. And the third stanza has three sets of replies exactly balanced against three short speeches.

Many of de la Mare's subjects are so tenuous that they require such formal support to keep them from vanishing, and de la Mare has the tact of an artist in supplying these structures. In the following poem, the triple illustration of a theme, which is such a common device of organization, is so perfectly used that it needs no comment. But the off-center balance of one against seven, of a statement in one line and its embroidery in the seven that follow, is unusual and effective. "All That's

Past" seems to flow through the first two long stanza-sentences, to pause, and fall into silence in the third.

> Very old are the woods;
>     And the buds that break
> Out of the brier's boughs,
>     When March winds wake,
> So old with their beauty are—
>     Oh, no man knows
> Through what wild centuries
>     Roves back the rose.
>
> Very old are the brooks;
>     And the rills that rise
> Where snow sleeps cold beneath
>     The azure skies
> Sing such a history
>     Of come and gone,
> Their every drop is as wise
>     As Solomon.
>
> Very old are we men;
>     Our dreams are tales
> Told in dim Eden
>     By Eve's nightingales;
> We wake and whisper awhile,
>     But, the day gone by,
> Silence and sleep like fields
>     Of Amaranth lie.

This pattern de la Mare follows exactly in another poem called "Music Unheard," a companion piece. Indeed, de la Mare rings many changes upon structure through triple division. His lyrics "Autumn," "Alone," "Clear Eyes," and "April Moon," for example, afford good evidence of the extent to which poetic delight may spring from awareness of form.

The three-stanza division, with its possibilities for pointing and counterpointing the thought, was used with involutions and variations by the Elizabethan song writers, the Cavaliers, and the Metaphysicals, in the great days of the English lyric. John Donne can use it formally to parallel his thought, as he does in "The Good-morrow" or "Go and Catch a Falling Star." More characteristic of his peculiar way of weaving a poem is "Lovers' Infiniteness," which must be reproduced in full as a further illustration that although poems may be as individual and delicately patterned as the shells of the sea, their similar structures and organization will often indicate their ancestors and their species:

> If yet I have not all thy love,
> Deare, I shall never have it all,
> I cannot breath one other sigh, to move;
> Nor can intreat one other teare to fall.
> And all my treasure, which should purchase thee,
> Sighs, teares, and oathes, and letters I have spent,
> Yet no more can be due to mee,
> Then at the bargaine made was ment,
> If then thy gift of love were partiall,
> That some to me, some should to others fall,
>    Deare, I shall never have Thee All.
>
> Or if then thou gavest mee all,
> All was but All, which thou hadst then,
> But if in thy heart, since, there be or shall,
> New love created bee, by other men,
> Which have their stocks intire, and can in tears,
> In sighs, in oathes, and letters outbid mee,
> This new love may beget new feares,
> For, this love was not vowed by thee.
> And yet it was, thy gift being generall,
> The ground, thy heart is mine, what ever shall
>    Grow there, deare, I should have it all.
>
> Yet I would not have all yet,
> He that hath all can have no more,

And since my love doth every day admit
New growth, thou shouldst have new rewards in store;
Thou canst not every day give me thy heart,
If thou canst give it, then thou never gavest it:
Loves riddles are, that though thy heart depart,
It stayes at home, and thou with losing savest it:
But we will have a way more liberall,
Then changing hearts, to joyne them, so wee shall
    Be one, and one anothers all.

The poem has many obvious balances: the complicated stanza is exactly repeated; the important ideas "partiall," "generall," and "liberall," fall in the same place in the stanza; each stanza has "all" in the first line, and each ends with "all." In fact, the meditation on the infinity of love is technically controlled by the constant recurrence of that word "all." Obviously, also, the poem builds by *contrasts* (the "yets" and "buts" show that), by *arguments* (a "so" and a "since," and many "therefores" and "becauses" in the thought), and by *hypotheses* (there are five "ifs" in the poem). "Loves riddles" are to be presented by a logical prestidigitator. Yet in spite of his sinewy logic, Donne avoids the rigid formality of Arnold. The shifting facets of his thought, like those of a cut diamond turning in the sun, do not exactly coincide with the stanza structure.

Donne's method of building a poem, then, allows the summer lightnings of his speculations to play around a theme, his questions and suppositions to lead him toward an overwhelming answer. The energy and number of his meditations tend to set value on the emotions he is contemplating; and the successive propositions, a mosaic of thoughts chipped and fitted to each other by the cutting tools of logic, convey a single sincere mood or emotion. Sometimes the form is obvious, as in *La Corona*, which is a succession of paradoxes, "murdering impossibilities," set in an endless crown of seven sonnets, the last line of each forming the first line of the next, designed to develop the feeling of awe before the mysteries of the Christian faith.

But usually, as in "Lovers' Infiniteness" and "The Dream" and "The Ecstasy" and "The Funeral" and "A Nocturnal upon Saint Lucy's Day," Donne's disparate hypotheses are thrown together with seemingly careless energy; a hiatus in the thought or a veiled, sophistical premise is quickly passed over; a single effect is produced as if by accident; and one must look close to see the design in the argument.

Sooner or later every poet, though he may not be as careless and confident as Donne, takes the great simple forms, the dual or triple or quadruple divisions, and shapes them for himself. When Burns, for instance, whistles the rest of his troubles away, his irony and his realistic humor produce an entirely different effect, in his building by contrasts, from that of Arnold's intellectual antitheses. I have italicized most of the words and phrases that suggest either balances or contrasts:

> *First*, when Maggie was my care,
> *Heav'n*, I thought was in her air;
> *Now* we're married—spier nae mair—
>     *But*—whistle o'er the lave o't!
> Meg was *meek*, and Meg was *mild*,
> *Sweet* and *harmless* as a child:
> Wiser men than me's *beguil'd*—
>     *Whistle o'er the lave o't!*
>
> *How we live*, my Meg and me,
> *How we love*, and *how we gree*,
> I care na by how few may see—
>     Whistle o'er the lave o't!
> Wha I wish were maggots' meat,
> Dish'd up in her winding-sheet,
> I could write (*but* Meg wad see't)—
>     Whistle o'er the lave o't!

Four times the thought breaks, always just before the shoulder shrug of the refrain. A reversal of thought or mood occurs twice in the first stanza, and again and best of all, in the next to the last line of the second stanza. Contrasts and parallels in grammar and thought organize the whole poem; but the principal contrast, of course, is that between romantic young lover and cynical husband; the two stanzas as wholes balance the two roles. There is also a steady progress, or descent, from "heaven" at the start to the humorous and macabre close.

A running analysis of Yeats's "Sailing to Byzantium" may show how much its beauty depends upon formal elements, how our delight in it as poetry could not have been aroused apart from pure architectonics. It is already acknowledged to be one of the fine poems of the twentieth century; such easy acceptance does not result so much from appreciation of its original and complex thought as from the obvious harmony and perfection of its form. Yeats writes it in four stanzas of *ottava rima*, holding his thought closely parallel to the *a b a b a b c c* rhyme scheme in the first two stanzas, counterpointing his sense rhythms and pauses against the rhyme pattern more freely in the last two. The first stanza represents the transient sensual existence of youth; the second, the intellectual or spiritual life of old age; the third identifies art with this unchanging wisdom of old age; the fourth fuses the permanence of art with the transient energy of its raw material, human life.

None of this is stated baldly, but through images, of which the principal is Byzantium itself, simultaneously a symbol of art, intellect, and age. The contrasting themes of permanence and transience are set against each other by many cunning devices; and each stanza ends with the idea of the everlasting —"unageing," "Byzantium," "artifice of eternity," and "what is past, or passing, or to come."

I

That is no country for old men. The young
In one another's arms, birds in the trees,
—Those dying generations—at their song,
The salmon-falls, the mackerel-crowded seas,

Fish, flesh, or fowl, commend all summer long
Whatever is begotten, born, and dies.
Caught in that sensual music all neglect
Monuments of unageing intellect.

Formally, in the light of the whole poem, the abrupt opening
sentence increases the sense of passion; rhythmically, grammatically, it is designed to create an impression of the spontaneous, the unthinking. And the initial word—"That" instead
of "This"—places the writer in time and space. The first short
sentence sets the poem as a debate between youth and age.
Then follow the four symbols of life; and the water, with its
imagery of fluidity; the formal alliterative compression into
"Fish, flesh, or fowl"; the more generalized triple summary of
all mortal life, "Whatever is begotten, born, and dies"; and
the increasingly clear significance of all these images in the
phrase "that sensual music" with its opposition to "Monuments of unageing intellect." The themes of fluidity, of life,
of music, are opposed in this stanza only by those stony monuments.

The second stanza catches up these images of sea, of music,
and of stone. It is shaped by contrasting old age with "the
young" of the first stanza:

II

An aged man is but a paltry thing,
A tattered coat upon a stick, unless
Soul clap its hands and sing, and louder sing
For every tatter in its mortal dress,
Nor is there singing school but studying
Monuments of its own magnificence;
And therefore I have sailed the seas and come
To the holy city of Byzantium.

The third stanza intensifies the contrast between soul and
body—fire and gold as opposed to water—as it turns more and
more to the unchanging "monuments" of intellect and art, in

imagery which suggests Sancta Sophia and Byzantine mosaics. It comes, too, almost as a formal incantation, an invocation to the sages, after Yeats's resolved acceptance at the end of the second stanza—or, to hold to the image, after he has sailed the seas and come to Byzantium:

### III

> O sages standing in God's holy fire
> As in the gold mosaic of a wall,
> Come from the holy fire, perne in a gyre,
> And be the singing-masters of my soul.
> Consume my heart away; sick with desire
> And fastened to a dying animal
> It knows not what it is; and gather me
> Into the artifice of eternity.

After such a prayer, which is not achieved by an easy renunciation of the "sensual music," nor by a denial of its values and its reality, the fusion of life and art in the image of the golden nightingale in the fourth stanza comes with a sense of resolution, of completeness, of rest. Almost every word and phrase in this final stanza calls up similar or contrasting ideas and images from preceding stanzas: "nature" as opposed to the holiness of God; the hammered form upon its "golden bough" as opposed to those earlier "natural things," the "birds in the trees"; the two contrasted songs—the artistic contemplation "Of what is past, or passing, or to come" versus that first instinctive, unthinking commendation of "Whatever is begotten, born, and dies."

### IV

> Once out of nature I shall never take
> My bodily form from any natural thing,
> But such a form as Grecian goldsmiths make
> Of hammered gold and gold enamelling
> To keep a drowsy Emperor awake;

Or set upon a golden bough to sing
To lords and ladies of Byzantium
Of what is past, or passing, or to come.

Yeats is himself a great goldsmith. In this poem itself he has made a golden bird which, we may easily believe, will sing forever, because it has been taken "out of nature" and given "such a form as Grecian goldsmiths make." The dyingness and the desire, expressed through controlled form in the first three stanzas, are now over; tension has given way to fusion, expressed also through controlled form; and we have been gathered into the eternity of artifice.

Yeats has the stamp of a classic, because back of each poem we feel his unremitting care, his lonely and independent and coherent and continued thought, his burning reverence for the craft of poetry. Yeats worshiped shapeliness; he never felt that a poem could be either accidental or unimportant.

John Keats resembles Yeats in his conviction that art is lasting. The "Ode on a Grecian Urn" and the "Ode to a Nightingale" are similar in thought to "Sailing to Byzantium." Their forms, however, which we considered in the chapter on concreteness in poetry, are different. Keats teases himself out of thought gradually, progressively; but usually he begins and ends *within* thought, that is, in a fairly relaxed and prosaic mood. The organization of these two odes is largely a progression from one imaginative state to another, a slow increasing in imaginative identification with the subject, and a swifter return to the everyday world at the end.

Such progress along a curve of changing emotional and imaginative intensities shows Keats's most characteristic mastery of form. He can build in other patterns. The "Ode on Melancholy" and the "Ode to Autumn," which were considered in the chapter on intensity, belong equally in this chapter on form. Keats shapes them by the simplest of all harmonizing devices: the gathering of numerous illustrations and suggestions around a central argument or a central theme. Thus,

the "Ode on Melancholy" presents through grouped poetic
images this argument:

I.   Do not seek sorrow in conventional, unrelieved gloom.
II.  Seek it rather in the fair beauties of an hour.
III. For true sorrow springs from the realization of the
     mortality of beauty and joy.

And in the three stanzas of the "Ode to Autumn" illustrations
cluster around sensuous motifs:

I.   Autumn is mellow, *ripe,* mature, in numerous manifes-
     tations.
II.  Autumn, if *visible* [here again, in the middle stanza,
     Keats allows the fancy to cheat us out of actuality
     in a way that he does not permit in the beginning and
     ending stanzas], might appear to us as this figure, or
     this, or this, or this.
III. Autumn, as well as Spring, has her *songs*—and five are
     mentioned.

Shelley, also, can build as formally as he does in the "Ode
to the West Wind." But the typical form of a long Shelleyan
lyric is a train of associated thoughts gradually leading to a
climax of such intensity that the poem is shattered, and thus
through the form itself impresses the reader with Shelley's belief that the most glorious poetry "is probably a feeble shadow
of the original conceptions of the poet."

Almost every poet expresses himself through his own forms,
the new shapes that old patterns assume when he uses them.
We come to sense the rocket flights of Shelley; the gently
molded curves, the delicate imaginative gradations, of Keats;
the intellectual jugglery of Donne; the tight, pure, classical
form of de la Mare with its myriad minute variations; the control over structure, themes, and diction, of Yeats, with his
aristocratic, almost arrogant, sureness of touch. Characteristic
form may depend upon thought, or technique, or both. Gerard
Manley Hopkins gets his effects of intensity mainly by tech-

nical means—compression and ellipsis, piled up adjectival mod-
ifiers, inversions, powerful "sprung rhythms." George Herbert, on the other hand, establishes his signature through his
thought; his medium is the complicated, rather precious stanza,
a new one for each poem, of any of the seventeenth-century
lyricists; but his highly personalized Christian beliefs are expressed through some incident or object in everyday life or
in the Bible, conceived consistently as a symbol. And Blake
combines thought and technique in building his poems out of
a schematized, extremely individual symbolism and singing,
simple stanzas that defy scansion.

The argument up to this point in the chapter might be condensed to two propositions: that the law of form applies primarily not to parts of a poem but to the poem as a whole;
and that form must be conceived not as mechanical but as organic. These two conceptions are so important, yet so open
to misunderstanding, that they need further illustration. Let
us consider, then, the difference between poetic unity and
formalized rules by looking at some of the practices and
theories of the last two centuries.

The nineteenth century revolted against the poetry of Dryden and Pope very largely because the neoclassic writers accepted rules governing "correct" versification and "correct"
patterns in which poems should be written. The Augustan
poets, Keats writes,

> were closely wed
> To musty laws lined out with wretched rule
> And compass vile: so that ye taught a school
> Of dolts to smooth, inlay, and clip, and fit,
> Till, like the certain wands of Jacob's wit,
> Their verses tallied. . . .
> they went about,
> Holding a poor, decrepit standard out
> Mark'd with most flimsy mottos, and in large
> The name of one Boileau!

Poetic diction, the heroic couplet, the prescribed forms of elegy, pastoral, epistle, or satire, the rules of decorum and elegance—these were the fixed stars of the neoclassicists. Keats, of course, is too indignant in the lines quoted above. Nevertheless, it is true that rules cannot produce form in the sense of organic unity. Perhaps the English neoclassical poets are more open to attack because essentially they are not formal enough. Is it not usually the case in the poems of both Pope and Dryden that one cannot see the whole because of the parts? Both men were conscious of the "form" of the heroic couplet, and each achieved complete mastery within its bounds. But that is to regard each heroic couplet as a poem in itself. How can the larger unity of a long poem in couplets be achieved? Neither Dryden nor Pope gives a very good answer. They build by accretion around a topic, like bees adding cell to cell. But although each couplet may have form in itself and fit neatly against its neighbor, the whole poem has about as much form as a honeycomb in a hollow tree. One cannot get from Pope or Dryden, as one gets from de la Mare or Yeats or Donne or Shakespeare or Milton, the sheer delight in contemplating a form that seems inevitable. There is nothing inescapably right and pleasing about the "design" of *Absalom and Achitophel* or *The Hind and the Panther*, *An Essay on Man* or *The Dunciad*. Topics are announced and illustrated and followed by other topics; intellectual frameworks are mechanically superposed; but the elements of the poems do not fuse to produce perfect works of art. Pope, accepting the universe, writes:

All are but parts of one stupendous whole.

The trouble with his couplets is that *they* are not. And Dryden's spacious and powerful but commonplace mind felt form only superficially. Rules to him were enough. If the couplet's regularity cramped him, he did not introduce occasional minor variants, but constructed new rules: a hexameter would be allowable, or an extra rhymed half-line, or a triplet. Nothing else. If these irregularities in accord with the new rules of the game were not enough, then irregularity itself must be set to rule, as in "Alexander's Feast" or "Mistress Anne Killigrew"; and Dryden's respect for mechanical form and precedent must be eased by calling the results Pindarics.

The principle of form in poetry, like all the others, cannot be rigidly applied. It resolves into the recognition that more form is better than less form. And it does not mean that Dryden and Pope in such typical pieces as "Mac Flecknoe" and the "Elegy to the Memory of an Unfortunate Lady" did not produce poems; it means that those poems would have been better if they had possessed a greater sense of form, which the two poets did at times achieve, as in *All for Love* and *The Rape of the Lock*.

Yet if the eighteenth century erred in an acceptance of rules and categories as the equivalents of genuine structure, the nineteenth century went even further astray by abandoning architectonics altogether. They destroyed mechanical form without discovering a substitute. Their typical long poems become the promenades of solitary dreamers; their shorter lyrics are still too long and too loose. Arnold, perhaps rightly, felt he was doing Wordsworth and Byron a service when he sought to give their works more form by selections and excerpts. The great poetic fragments that strew the century show that however rich the Romantic and Victorian temperaments were in the other qualities of poetry, they were deficient in a sense of form, in the ability to see the whole and to subordinate details, however beautiful in themselves, to a complete pattern. *Don Juan* and *Hyperion* and "Christabel" and "Kubla Khan" are obviously unfinished. It is not enough to say that Byron did not live long enough to finish *Don Juan*; Methuselah could not have finished it. The end of a poem should come into being at the same time as the beginning. Even the Romantic poems that are ostensibly concluded, or that end, at any rate, with a slight settling of the thought, are not demonstrably complete. What is to keep *Childe Harold* or *The Excursion* from going on? Certainly no sense of related parts or rounded form or finality. Would we know that the poem was incomplete if the fourth and final act of *Prometheus Unbound* disappeared, or a lyric were dropped from *Maud*, or a section omitted from *The Ring and the Book?* Nineteenth-century poets may have felt "a more than usual state of emotion"; they failed to display "more than usual order."

Arnold, as usual, was right in praising the fine lines of his contemporaries and immediate predecessors, and in censuring them for carelessness with regard to total structure. Very often they found the "best words" that constitute poetry; too seldom did they discover the "best order" in relating the parts of their conceptions. A ceramist, given the shards of an Indian pot or Greek vase, can fit them together and restore the original, because the original had shape. The poems that have been reproduced and analyzed in this chapter could be easily reconstructed if they existed only in separate unsorted stanzas, for they too have form. But if ten people were given the jumbled stanzas of Shelley's "Adonais" or of Tennyson's "Mariana" or the separate sections of *In Memoriam* and told to set them in order, we may safely assume that ten different products would result. This comes close to being a dangerously effective argument that the fault of such poems lies in an inherent lack of form. The order of Shakespeare's sonnets in their first publication suggests a progress from mood to mood as effectively as the order of the 132 sections of Tennyson's *In Memoriam*. The unity of this collection of 132 individual lyrics comes solely from a common inspiration and a common metrical form; the relations among the separate lyrics, in most instances, are shadowy.

Something is wrong with the poetic spirit of a century in which two of Coleridge's three most famous poems are unfinished; in which Byron introduces digressions as a satiric joke and ends by making them the essence of his best and longest poems; in which Wordsworth's greatest poem, though in many ways genuinely organized, is rarely read as a whole and remains a prelude to something that never got itself written; in which Tennyson, approaching epic material, produces little stories and pictures; and Morris writes verse, as Trollope wrote novels, by the piece, by the hour, by the yard. The great fault lay in a general failure to realize, or to create, that sense of form which demands constant awareness of the whole design, of the relations between parts, and of the steady progression from one part to another. With regard to form, the poets of the amorphous nineteenth century are inferior to those of the mechanical eighteenth century; and both are inferior to the poets of the Elizabethan period and the seventeenth century.

Perhaps the greatest formal merit in the poetry of the present century might be called the sense of musical organization—the repetition with variations of dominating images, characters, events, words, or phrases; much as motifs are repeated and varied to give structure to a movement in a symphony; and the relating of such repeated themes to each other, as movements in music are carefully built to reinforce or contrast with or supplement each other. Such "musical form" is, of course, no modern discovery. Dante, Spenser, and Shakespeare used it with a skill almost beyond analysis. It is best illustrated in modern poetry, fully developed, in William Butler Yeats or T. S. Eliot.

In the partial analyses that have been made in these chapters of a few poems by Yeats, it has been impossible to avoid some consideration of his returning and contrasting symbols. He chants and rhymes his readers into increased awareness; he evokes emotions by the clashing of symbols, and dominates them by means of a controlling pattern. Eliot also builds musically. *The Waste Land* has fathered so many critiques and commentaries and analyses that it suffices here to point out that the structure of Eliot's poem is strong enough, stable enough, yet complex and subtly interwoven enough, to warrant such analyses.

We may hope that this century will make its contribution to English poetry by reasserting the importance of organic form. If we look at stanzas as outward and visible signs of an inward desire for the patterns and the unity of art, then the law of form seems to be in the ascendant. Yeats, Eliot, and Auden, as their work progresses, all tend toward the traditional forms—the *ottava rima*, the pentameter line, the Chaucerian stanza—as if they could express themselves freely and completely enough in variations within such established patterns. Anarchy is not the only possible state in which individuality is conceivable. The whole resurgence of the Metaphysical School among modern poets suggests that an interest in brainwork, in the organization of the total poem, is again dominant.

What of organization in long poems? We are limited in our discussion here, since it is difficult to talk of form without exact illustrations, and although a complete lyric may be reproduced, it is hardly practicable to hold up for exhibit an entire poetic drama or epic. The demand for form, of course, goes beyond such mechanical rules as that an epic begins *in medias res* or that a play should have five acts and should or should not conform to the three unities. Briefly, therefore, let us look again at two such well-known works as *Antony and Cleopatra* and *Paradise Lost*, and let us consider some of their formal elements.

Shakespeare's profound sense of organic form comes out most clearly when he is compared with Dryden. Dryden must have felt that Shakespeare was deficient in formality, in rigid correctness of outline. If he had not felt so, he would hardly have dared the inevitable comparison between himself and Shakespeare which would result from using Shakespeare's materials in his own play, *All for Love*. What are the *formal* merits of Dryden's version of the story of Antony and Cleopatra? Clarity and balance. Dryden liked rules and precepts;

he could follow but one at a time. His play, therefore, is a succession of clarities and simplicities. Structure for him rests not
upon conviction but upon ceremony. The turns in his plot are
plainly charted; we walk by straight paths through a formal
garden. Everyone openly declares his or her thoughts; arguments and actions are both given forms of balanced clarity;
perspicuous generalizations abound. The explicit and the direct
conquer the ironical. Dryden's form appeals almost wholly to
the rational mind, which tends to believe that whatever is not
clear, and immediately clear, lacks form.

Shakespeare's conception of form was different. Dryden,
with his taste for simple symmetry, may have considered
Shakespeare's art unbalanced. Nevertheless, we may hold that
there is method in Shakespeare's madness. He has, for instance,
managed to suggest *indirectly* and powerfully Antony's profound love *by formal means:* by contrasting Antony's torrent
of curses flung at Cleopatra with the two small words, "Dead,
then?" when he hears of her supposed death. And so throughout. If we acknowledge that there exists an *ars celare artem*, we
are simply admitting that one principle of form is superposed
upon another principle, and that the highest art may consist
in hiding the original necessary but mechanical frame, the
brainwork that must precede a finished masterpiece. Such art
Shakespeare acquired. That he could practice and value a more
ceremonious symmetry is evident in such an early play as
*Love's Labour's Lost* or such a late comedy as *The Tempest*,
in which form and formality are not far apart. The structure
of *Antony and Cleopatra* is not so clearly manifest. An essay,
or a volume, might be devoted to an analysis of the form of
this one work, which is so often dismissed as an overgrown and
rather shapeless chronicle play inferior to his great tragedies in
structural achievement.

Shakespeare makes it into his greatest tribute to love—
through formal means, yet never in such long asseverations as
Dryden puts into the mouth of Antony. "There's beggary in

the love that can be reckon'd," says Shakespeare's Antony, and
Shakespeare rarely tries to achieve his effects by direct reck-
oning. Many of the underlying principles, however, that build
up this love may be discovered. The central governing hypothesis in constructing the play might be phrased: The greatness of this love for which Antony and Cleopatra sacrifice
everything may be demonstrated only by showing the greatness
of everything that is sacrificed. This argument would seem too
obvious for statement; but Dryden practically disregards it.
*All* for love, Dryden professes to consider. But that "all" consists of Antony's sense of duty, honor, leadership, and the
affection for him felt by a soldier, a friend, a wife, and two
children. Dryden's version becomes a kind of domestic drama
presenting in its successive acts five cases of individual conscience. Shakespeare does not forget such motifs; but he goes
further. He makes us *feel* that Antony is a great leader and
soldier, and has been a greater. The repeated flashbacks to his
early career, the long reminiscences by Octavius and Antony
of the man he was, the appraisals *and the actions* of Scarus and
Enobarbus and Eros and his other followers, Cleopatra's mocking adoration of his soldiership—each attests in its own way
his greatness as a man. And all this is accomplished naturally,
indirectly, almost unnoticeably, in the establishment of a deliberate thesis. Shakespeare is persistent though uninsistent.
His fastidious nature will not allow him, in important matters,
to protest too much.

Antony, moreover, is an influential and practiced statesman.
The scenes of his marriage bargain with Caesar and of the
*Pax Romana* on board Pompey's galley demonstrate this more
convincingly than any number of formal statements could. He
is also a triple pillar of the world. It is more important to the
organic form of the work that we know Antony's world stature
than that the unity of place be observed. Shakespeare knew that
"the mind is its own place." The scenes, therefore, shift from
Egypt to Rome to Sicily to Athens to a plain in Syria. Such

scenes are relevant to the form and are deliberately calculated.

But side by side with the world hero, the figure of the great lover is created. Instead of Dryden's great oscillations, a formal building of one aspect of his nature followed by a formal tearing down, Shakespeare has lover and leader coexistent, fighting their bitter war in Antony's tremendous bursts of fury and despair. Again, Shakespeare's Antony does not publish abroad how great his passion is, how great his pride; he displays them in his irrational actions and psychological agonizings. For Shakespeare's theory of art is that it holds a mirror up to *nature:* since it is not natural for man to analyze himself correctly before others, he rarely permits his characters such public self-criticisms. The business of the *artist* is to understand clearly and to evaluate; in Shakespeare's practice, it is no less his business *as artist* to give his judgments *indirectly* in the form of the actions and speech of natural men.

Cleopatra's underlying constancy to Antony and her surface variability—both formalizing conceptions—run unwaveringly through the play. Shakespeare, whose mature taste favored asymmetry in structure rather than formal balance, did not feel it necessary to show that Cleopatra as well as Antony sacrificed a world for love. He contrasts her complete absorption in love with Antony's divided nature. The action of the play, indeed, has the simple lines of a battle between Octavius Caesar and Cleopatra for the possession of Antony.

Selection or invention of details depends upon the underlying form. The invented death of Enobarbus, from heartbreak or suicide, elevates Antony's stature, which the play builds up in every conceivable fashion. Dryden had introduced with hesitation Octavia and her children by Antony, and came to consider their presence an artistic fault, since "the compassion she moved to herself and children was destructive to that which I reserved for Antony and Cleopatra." Shakespeare must have made some such artistic criticism before, instead of after, writing the play. We do not learn from him that

Antony had children by Fulvia and Octavia and Cleopatra. The children would have confused the issue.

With such selection and suppression and invention, the play moves to a climax. The cards have been stacked. History has been imperceptibly shaped in order to make love transcendent and glowing, though reached by the hero only after sacrifice and torture. Again and again, in short scenes, Antony passes through shifting, painful moods to arrive finally at love of and trust in Cleopatra. The whole fourth act takes up this structural motif of a changing hero, and repeats it on a large scale through fifteen scenes. Dissolution slowly becomes resolution, as Antony's character wavers through bravado, sentimentality, god-likeness, bravery, generosity, soldierly action, triumph, nobility, defeat, and vile debasing rage, to a final mood of contemplation. Again, Shakespeare's sense of form sums up in an image what he has exemplified in action through the preceding thirteen scenes:

ANT. Sometime we see a cloud that's dragonish;
A vapour sometime like a bear or lion,
A tower'd citadel, a pendent rock,
A forked mountain, or blue promontory
With trees upon't, that nod unto the world,
And mock our eyes with air: thou hast seen these signs;
They are black vesper's pageants.
EROS. Ay, my lord.
ANT. That which is now a horse, even with a thought
The rack dislimns, and makes it indistinct,
As water is in water.
EROS. It does, my lord.
ANT. My good knave Eros, now thy captain is
Even such a body.

And after this one rare mood of contemplation comes the final flare-up against Cleopatra, and the immediate contrasting return to her, dying, for the last scene of love, and faith, and thought for her welfare, and death.

This clears the whole fifth act for Cleopatra's leave-taking. Antony's struggle is over; and the act is less a finale to a tragedy than a lyric poem in praise of surpassing love. Shakespeare, who always works structurally through contrast, builds the high pinnacle of Cleopatra's death on the broad base of empire; treaties are broached, kingdoms traded, and Caesar coolly manipulates the world; and all these to Cleopatra are words that keep her from nobility to herself. Everything contributes to the magnitude of two figures and their love. One more follower, Dercetas, announces Antony's death and laments him; his enemies—Maecenas, Agrippa, and Caesar—mourn his greatness almost in a formal dirge; Cleopatra in her dream of Antony builds up the most towering and opulent full-length figure in the play, and by her great sorrow wins one more Roman, Dolabella, as her servant in the cause of death. The worlds of emperor and of clown intrude for two brief actions, as if to give a standard of the commonplace against which to measure Cleopatra. But the surge of her passion closes in more compellingly around these little islands of worldliness; the theme of darkness and death is repeated, antiphonally, musically, formally, after the long, bright day; the early memories of the first meeting now return—"I am again for Cydnus, To meet Mark Antony"—; and the dream of reunion after death, which Shakespeare rigorously excludes from his other tragedies, colors Cleopatra's images as it had colored Antony's:

> Stay for me:
> Where souls do couch on flowers, we'll hand in hand,
> And with our sprightly port make the ghosts gaze:
> Dido and her Aeneas shall want troops,
> And all the haunt be ours.

Shakespeare deliberately creates Elysium, not because he believes in it, but because he believes in its imaginative effectiveness in his portrayal of the triumph of love. All the structural resources of poetry—retrospect and prophecy, changing

rhythmical movements, refrains, repetitions of motifs with
variations, deliberate contrasts of moods as well as of ideas,
a profuse but selected imagery that does not bewilder but intensifies and enriches, echoes and recurrences and returns—
are in the closing scenes magnificently in play. Even Shakespeare himself wrote no greater poetry than the last acts of
*Antony and Cleopatra*. And its greatness depends upon, is inextricably a part of, the formal structure which is so deliberately
conceived and skillfully concealed.

The form of *Paradise Lost* is no less wonderful than that of
a Shakespearean tragedy. To many, it appears as an even greater
edifice, since they can more certainly detect its more rational
and more conventional principles of organization. *Paradise
Lost* follows the rules for an epic in its division into twelve
books; and Milton is fully aware that twelve may be divided
by two, three, four, and six. In its great outlines, the poem splits
into thirds related to the contrasting themes of the fall of man
and his salvation. Thus, the first four books proceed in a straight
line to the first temptation of man, which is thwarted at the
end of Book IV, the completion of the first third of the poem.
The second third is Raphael's revelation to Adam of past events
and causes, showing him how he is responsible and how he may
live in harmony with God; the eighth book closes with admoni-
tions and hopeful precepts. The last third of the poem repeats
these two themes or actions, condensed and intensified. The
theme of the fall returns with terrible force in Books IX and
X, and this time it is not thwarted. The last two books are again
angelic revelation, and balancing Adam's and Eve's heart-
breaking despair in Book X is Adam's joyful acceptance of
God's plan in Book XII, so that he says:

> O goodness infinite, goodness immense!
> That all this good of evil shall produce,
> And evil turn to good; more wonderful
> Than that which by creation first brought forth
> Light out of darkness!

This shaping of the fable by formally apportioning it within the book divisions is the most obvious organizing principle. Many other principles are at work. Milton gives spatial structure as well to his narrative. The action shifts back and forth on the three great planes of hell, heaven, and the world. Book III, for instance, has scenes simultaneously occurring in the realms of heaven, chaos, and the world, as Satan journeys on his mission. Exactly balancing it, in the mathematical proportions, Book X also roves through all space—the earth, heaven, chaos, hell—as Satan returns after his victorious attempt. The first third of the poem is principally devoted to scenes and actions in hell; the second third to scenes and actions in heaven; the third remains almost entirely on the earth itself. The earth, indeed, is the focal point for the whole poem, the battleground in this warfare between the two mighty opposites, the Messiah and Lucifer, for the possession of man's soul. In order to concentrate on human moral values, Milton deliberately chooses the Ptolemaic rather than the Copernican cosmology because it places the world at the center of things *spatially*, as Milton wished to do *formally*. And again, by spatial means, he focuses intently upon Paradise. The World, a great sphere cut from Chaos by the golden compasses of the Messiah, hangs between the vast regions of heaven and hell. Through the concentric spheres, Satan descends from "the bare convex of this World's outermost Orb" until he lights on the central sphere, the Earth. Best of the Earth is Eden; best of Eden is the Garden of Eden, the mount of Paradise; central in the Garden is the Tree of Life. Milton lives so naturally in his inner eye that he even catches up his spatial images and repeats them as if they were themes: the four rivers of hell are paralleled by the four rivers of Paradise; the Tree of Life has its ashen, ironic ghost in hell.

Most important to the organic unity of a poem, Milton marshals his material thematically. Something of this we have discussed in the chapter on complexity. Lucifer rebels against God, Abdiel against Lucifer, Death against Satan; Eve rebels

against Adam and listens to the rebel Satan; and Adam, beholding the rebellious Eve, rebels against God. Pride and obedience,
passion and reason, selfishness and sacrifice, liberty and law,
justice and mercy, willfulness and free will, are set against each
other and played over and over again in new harmonies and
discords and variations. The fall of man is prepared for by a
similar action on a grand scale, the fall of the angels sweepingly
described in Books V and VI. The art of poetry is the art of
preparation: by the time Milton reaches the actual fall of man
in Book IX, every significant action, every fatal trait of his
characters, has been in some form already suggested. Eve's
susceptibility to flattery and her pique at Adam's superiority,
her desire for mastery, Adam's inability to resist her beauty,
Eve's weakness without Adam and Adam's weakness with Eve,
rebellion against God's power, speculation as to how knowledge can possibly destroy, the deadly sins and the protecting
virtues, the blindness of evil and its slow blackening of the soul
—all have been sketched in thematically in earlier books.

Subtlest and most unmatchable of all means for giving formal
unity to the poem is Milton's use of his medium: the spacious
and resilient rhythms, and the diction so carefully chosen and
consistently maintained that the poem is held throughout on
its high plane, unworldly and timeless. Milton had a sense of
what was fitting and harmonious. He is the great English master of decorum.

That these different principles of organization, and others
besides, were present in Milton's own mind is evident in the
various invocations that begin Books I, III, VII, and IX. The
first invocation serves primarily to organize the poem *intellectually:* the theme is man's first disobedience; the natural
question is, What caused that disobedience? The invocation
preceding the third book—"Hail, holy Light!"—depends upon
a *sensuous* contrast between light and dark as symbols of good
and evil, a contrast which persists through the whole poem as
a principle of organization-through-imagery. In Book VII, Mil-

ton is principally aware of *spatial* organization: he descends from heaven "to my native element"

> Within the visible diurnal sphere;
> Standing on Earth, not rapt above the pole.

And Book IX—"I now must change Those notes to tragic" —shows Milton conscious of *the component forms*—such as tragedy, epic, history, hymn, idyl, apocalyptic vision, prayer —that enter in as elements of his larger design.

Whether the compass be great or small, therefore, no piece of writing constitutes a poem if it lacks formal organization. Form makes it memorable, makes it pleasurable, makes it art. This chapter has argued that the principle of form is not something dead or superficial. Relatively little attention has been paid here to the organizing potentialities of rhymes, of stanzas, and of divisions by sections or books. The poetic power of such technical devices is obvious and needs little discussion. Anyone who doubts it would feel no loss in reading Homer or Ariosto or Goethe in prose translation, would see no great difference between Charles and Mary Lamb's *Tales from Shakespeare* and Shakespeare himself.

On the other hand, a technical pattern is no guarantee that a work possesses form. Rhythmical and stanzaic structures contribute, of course, to a larger form, and are usually a sign that some controlling principle is at work. But considered as one of the essentials of poetry, the law of form is a law of organic form. Form in *The Canterbury Tales*, to take an example, comes less from the repeated pentameter couplet than from such an invention as the "Marriage Group" of tales, in which various pilgrims present diverse views of marriage that lead to a suggested judgment. Form in Shakespeare lies not in the five-act division, to which in fact he pays little attention as far as significant structure is concerned, but in his comprehensive reconciliation of the good and the true. Form in Spenser is less to be found in the long undulations of his liquid stanzas than in his musical repetition of motifs, in the harmonies of his shifting panoramas, and in the contrast between his conscious moralizings and his instincts, between his Christian faith and his pagan worship of beauty, between "rule" and "flow."

Form is the soul of a poem. It generates at once a sense of poetic unity and of poetic complexity. Many of the illustrations of the law of complexity might be used as aptly to develop the law of form; and most of the examples quoted in this chapter would aid in demonstrating at greater length the law of complexity. The first five principles governed the poetic spirit; the last two govern its objectification in a poem. And just as a controlled rhythm may accent certain words and bring out thought, so a controlling form may increase the complexity of poetic thought, setting form against freedom, second thoughts against first raptures, control against impulse. The principles of poetry are not separate; they overlap; they play into and depend upon each other.

In any ultimate sense, then, the seven laws of poetry do not exist. "Poetry" does not exist. Poems exist. All the rest is generalization parasitically sustained by the actual things that are poems—mistletoe of the mind growing on the tree of art. But such hypothetical laws afford the means of contemplating, for a moment, the beauty and the delight that poems afford. The laws are the tributes of criticism to the art that impels it; they may lead us back to the poems themselves with their revelation of what is permanent and important, of the universal values beyond the compulsions and the strident insistence of the gliding present moment. And this book has tried to demonstrate that such universal values need not be cold and impersonal and abstract, but personal and intense in their significance, concrete, complex, and singing in their form. The values of poetry are as warm and precious as life itself, since they exist and persist only in that living, complex, and unified organism— that *form*—which we call a poem.

As we experience these poems immediately and reflect upon

their qualities at leisure, slowly they create for us a world which is more spacious and more lasting and better built than our day-to-day world of thoughtlessness, compromise, and improvisation. To read poetry is not to escape from life. It is a strenuous conquering, that gives us the energy, grace, and exaltation to lead life more fully and surely. In the last event, then, we find that the world we live in, expressed as completely as it can be expressed in human terms, is revealed to us by poetry. We may best approach the realm of poetry if we assume that it is neither to be glimpsed casually nor passed over as incomprehensible. We do not travel into its domain to escape from life, but to understand life. And there, for moments at least, we discover human experience expressed at its fullest, noblest, and best. For such is the nature of poetry.

# NOTES

THESE NOTES are not necessary for an understanding of the text. They are addressed solely to curious or thorough readers. Most of them are placed here to keep the text from heaviness. They locate principal quotations which are not sufficiently identified in the book itself; the leisurely reader with a fair library may be able to view the illustrations more exactly by setting the short quotations in their larger contexts. All titles are italicized, except in the cases of poems usually known by their first lines.

The longer notes amplify arguments made in the body of the book. They rarely introduce any new points, but add examples for the sake of those who resent being hurried to a conclusion.

*Prologue*

p. 11   Keats: In the sonnet, *On First Looking into Chapman's Homer*.

p. 12   Chaucer: See his descriptions of the Miller and the Cook in the Prologue to the *Canterbury Tales*. Eliot: See his poem *Triumphal March*.

p. 14   John Crowe Ransom: *The New Criticism*.

p. 16   "The curfew tolls the knell": Gray, *Elegy in a Country Churchyard*.

p. 16   "For God's sake, hold your tongue": John Donne, *The Canonization*.

p. 16   "Ruin seize thee, ruthless King!": Gray, *The Bard*.

p. 16    "I must confess it could not choose but be": Donne, *The Dreame*.

p. 22    "Soule is forme": Spenser, *An Hymne in Honour of Beautie*, 133.

p. 22    "Transported with celestiall desyre": Spenser, *An Hymne of Heavenly Beautie*, 18–19.

p. 22    "Into my heart an air that kills": A. E. Housman, *A Shropshire Lad*, No. XL.

**Chapter 1**

p. 31    "The red-breast": Thomson, *The Seasons*, Winter, lines 246–64.

p. 33    "O, wert thou in the cauld blast": Burns's lyric is usually identified by this first line.

p. 33    "Had we never lov'd sae kindly": Burns, "Ae Fond Kiss, and Then We Sever."

p. 34    "I am nae poet": Burns, *Epistle to John Lapraik*, stanzas 9–10.

p. 35    "While I am lying on the grass": Wordsworth, *To the Cuckoo*.

p. 35    "One drew a sharp knife": Tennyson, *A Dream of Fair Women*.

p. 36    "I put my hat upon my head": Wordsworth uses this quotation effectively in his preface to *Lyrical Ballads*.

pp. 35–36  Tennyson: As one further example of the search for exactness, consider the 1833 and the 1842 drafts of Tennyson's *Mariana in the South*. Here he is trying to contrast a girl's lonely grief and the immense, silent universe. First version:

> . . . large Hesper overshone  
> The mourning gulf, and on her soul  
> Poured divine solace, or the rise  
> Of moonlight from the margin gleamed,  
> Volcano-like, afar . . .

Second version:

> Large Hesper glitter'd on her tears,
> And deepening thro' the silent spheres,
> Heaven over Heaven rose the night.

p. 39    "Fierce noises of the fiery nightingales": Swinburne, *Anactoria*.

p. 42    "The sound must seem an echo to the sense": Pope, *Essay on Criticism*, line 365.

p. 43    "Rocks, caves, lakes, fens": Milton, *Paradise Lost*, II, 621.

p. 43    "Mosaic; underfoot the violet": Milton, *Paradise Lost*, IV, 700.

p. 43    "The importance of the right rhythmical choice": Compare, for instance, the stanzaic *préciosité* of Milton's *Ode on the Morning of Christ's Nativity* with his treatment of the same subject in *Paradise Lost*, XII, 360–71, in a meter which better fits the mood of exalted solemnity.

p. 46    Quotations are from the openings of Chaucer's *Nun's Priest's Tale* and Dryden's *The Cock and the Fox*.

p. 48    "If thou beest he": Milton, *Paradise Lost*, I, 84 ff. For later quotations in this paragraph, see *Paradise Lost*, I, 242 ff., and Dryden's *State of Innocence, or the Fall of Man*, I, i, 13–14; I, i, 1–4; and I, i, 5–6.

p. 49    "Dryden's best efforts, therefore, cannot duplicate Chaucer's eye and heart": To Chaucer and Milton, we might also add Shakespeare, considering Dryden's adaptation of Shakespeare's *Antony and Cleopatra* in his own play, *All for Love*. Here he reduces Shakespeare's imaginative excrescences to logical and grammatical order. Shakespeare's subtly passionate simplicity becomes generalized clarity; Shakespeare's nobility is transformed into a more relaxed and sane series of ethical pronouncements. In another connection, Dryden's and Shakespeare's two dramas are compared in Chapter VII in some detail.

p. 49    "What Dryden aimed at": Bonamy Dobrée, *Poems of John Dryden*, Introduction, p. xi.

p. 51 "While they ring round the same unvaried chimes": Pope, *Essay on Criticism*, lines 348–53. The two following quotations from Pope are lines 297 and 300 in the same poem.

p. 51 "The language of the age is never the language of poetry": Thomas Gray, in a letter to Richard West, April, 1742.

p. 53 A. E. Housman: *The Name and Nature of Poetry.*

p. 54 "The languid strings": Blake, *To the Muses.*

p. 54 "So sung a little clod of clay": Blake, *The Clod and the Pebble.*

p. 55 "The eternal gates' terrific porter": Blake, end of *The Book of Thel.*

p. 55 "Why an ear, a whirlpool fierce": Blake, end of *The Book of Thel.*

p. 55 "the power of exciting sympathy": Coleridge, *Biographia Literaria*, ch. xiv.

p. 56 Robert Bridges: "Poetic Diction in English" in *Collected Essays*, III (1928).

p. 56 "wreathed his lithe proboscis": Milton, *Paradise Lost*, IV, 346–47; "No fear lest dinner cool": *Paradise Lost*, V, 396. The bad puns are in *Paradise Lost*, VI, 558–67, and 609–27.

p. 58 "Four ducks on a pond": William Allingham, in *Day and Night Songs* under "Spring."

Chapter II

p. 62 "Nay, but beneath this rock": Theocritus, Idyl VIII; translation by Andrew Lang.

p. 62 "Medieval and Renaissance poets": See the medieval legendaries in English verse; Lydgate's *Fall of Princes;* the *Mirror for Magistrates* in its many Elizabethan editions. Ovid's *Metamorphoses* had shown that men and gods change; Chaucer's Monk tells seventeen out of his threatened hundred tales to demonstrate that even the great must die. These themes are all arguments. An argument should progress from point to point; when it has been clinched, there is no need to repeat it. Each of the above poems is in constant danger of sounding like a broken phonograph record, and in consequence, not one of them, considered as a whole, has the intensity of the best poetry. Chaucer's pilgrims, in their impatience, break off the Monk's tale in the middle of one of his stories.

p. 63  "at length she found the troden gras": Spenser, *Faerie Queene*, I, iii, 10.

p. 65  "Far in a western brookland": Housman, *A Shropshire Lad*, No. LII.

p. 66  "The least that I could say": de Musset, *La Nuit de Mai*.

p. 66  "I stood tip-toe upon a little hill": Keats, the first line of the first of his *Poems*, 1817.

p. 66  "I shrieked, and clasped my hands in ecstasy": Shelley, *Hymn to Intellectual Beauty*.

p. 66  "The red fool-fury of the Seine": Tennyson, *In Memoriam*, Sec. *CXXVII*.

p. 67  "Ah, quanto a dir": Dante, *Inferno*, I, 4.

p. 67  "The simple and direct statement of an emotion, therefore, is in itself seldom poetic": The Elizabethans, however, often resort to direct hyperbole. Their favorite device for intensification is to compare a subject to a superlative, which the subject paradoxically surpasses. Thus Marlowe's Doctor Faustus, in caressing Helen's beauty, finds her fairer, brighter, lovelier, than the fairest, brightest, loveliest of sights—the starlit sky, the lightning, sunlight on water.

> O thou art fairer than the evening air,
> Clad in the beauty of a thousand stars,
> Brighter art thou than flaming Jupiter,
> When he appear'd to hapless Semele,

> More lovely than the monarch of the sky
> In wanton Arethusa's azur'd arms.

The game of capping superlatives, which they practiced with such delight, has in the hands of the Elizabethans a kind of naïve and fresh charm. It shows clearly the constant drive of the poet toward intensity of expression.

p. 71    "Thick as . . . scatter'd sedge": Milton, *Paradise Lost*, I, 302 ff.

p. 73    "All whom the Flood": Donne, *Holy Sonnets*, VII.

p. 73    "Fall'n Cherub": Milton, *Paradise Lost*, I, 157–58.

p. 73    "What if this present, were the world's last, night?": This, and the following five quotations from John Donne, are taken in order from *Holy Sonnets* XIII, XVIII, III, *La Corona* 5th sonnet, *Holy Sonnets* VII, and XIV.

p. 74    "And, eyes, heart, what looks, what lips": Hopkins, *Hurrahing in Harvest*. The poems by Hopkins successively quoted are *The Windhover*, *The Bugler's First Communion* (three times), and *The Windhover* again.

p. 75    "In groups forgetting the gun in the drawer": W. H. Auden, Ode III of "Six Odes" in *The Orators*.

p. 76    "A bugler boy": Hopkins, *The Bugler's First Communion*.

p. 76    "No, I'll not, carrion comfort": Hopkins, *Carrion Comfort*.

p. 78    "I am not Prince Hamlet": Eliot, *The Love Song of J. Alfred Prufrock*.

p. 79    "by the barbarous king": Eliot, *The Waste Land*, which is paraphrased throughout the sentence.

p. 80    "My mistress' eyes": Shakespeare, Sonnet CXXX.

p. 80    "Get with child a mandrake root": Donne, *Song*, "Go and catch a falling star."

p. 80    "Garlic and sapphires in the mud": Eliot, *Burnt Norton*.

p. 110   "our sage and serious poet Spenser": Milton, *Areopagitica*.

p. 111   "Milton's Devil as a moral being": Shelley, *A Defence of Poetry*.

p. 114   *Lycidas* is Milton's; *The Cry of the Children* is Elizabeth Barrett Browning's.

p. 115   Donne, *The Flea;* Burns, *To a Louse. The Flea* is quoted in full on pp. 151–52.

p. 116   "I am aware of the damp souls of housemaids": Eliot, *Morning at the Window.*

p. 118   John Livingston Lowes: *The Road to Xanadu.*

p. 119   "of the gigantic shadows which futurity casts upon the present": Shelley, *A Defence of Poetry.*

*Chapter IV*

p. 120   "Poetry is the art of uniting pleasure with truth": Johnson, the life of Milton, in *Lives of the English Poets.*

p. 123   "Thou still unravish'd bride of quietness": Keats, *Ode on a Grecian Urn,* which is paraphrased throughout this paragraph.

p. 126   *"fabulator maximus":* Milton, *De Idea Platonica quemadmodum Aristoteles Intellexit,* a Latin poem.

p. 126   "Lewed peple loven tales olde": Chaucer, Pardoner's Prologue in the *Canterbury Tales,* lines 437–38.

p. 127   "to teach and delight": Sidney, *An Apologie for Poetrie,* from which succeeding quotations are also drawn.

p. 129   Alexander Pope: His tendency to illustrate a statement *after* making it comes out in his romantic narrative, *Eloïsa to Abelard,* as well as in his didactic poems.

p. 130   *Religio Laici* is by John Dryden; *The Seasons* by James Thomson; *The Grave* by Robert Blair.

p. 131   "Wordsworth begins with the world of eye and ear; he ends in thought": His poem *To my Sister* furnishes an excellent further example: he begins with a redbreast singing in a larch tree, and progresses to "the blessed power that rolls / About, below, above"; he moves from "the bare trees" to "a universal birth." Even in a relatively late poem such as *Laodamia*, the crystallized thought seems to spring from prolonged contemplation of the particular story, clothed in space and action.

p. 132 "Keats . . . tends to begin and end poems with something very like a prose statement": Compare also his *Ode on a Grecian Urn* and the song of the Indian maid in his *Endymion*, Book IV.

p. 133 "the mind in creation": Shelley, *A Defence of Poetry*.

p. 134 "Les sanglots longs": Verlaine, *Chanson d'Automne*.

p. 135 "him whose strenuous tongue": Keats, *Ode on Melancholy*.

p. 135 "Batter my heart": Donne, *Holy Sonnets*, XIV.

p. 136 "The imponderable fragrance": Bridges, *The Testament of Beauty*, Book IV, 466–503.

p. 138 "by indirections find directions out": Shakespeare, *Hamlet*, II, i, 66.

p. 139 "At the round earths imagin'd corners": Donne, *Holy Sonnets*, VII.

p. 147 "Time hath, my lord": Shakespeare, *Troilus and Cressida*, III, iii, 145–70.

p. 149 "Villon": Swinburne, *A Ballad of François Villon*.

p. 151 Dryden on Donne is quoted from Herbert J. C. Grierson's excellent introduction to *Metaphysical Lyrics and Poems of the Seventeenth Century*.

p. 153 "outward soul": Donne, *The Funeral*. Compare Andrew Marvell's *Definition of Love*, which heightens personal emotion by means of theology, philosophy, paradox, and even geometrical propositions.

p. 153  "E 'n la sua volontate è nostra pace": Dante, *Paradiso*, III, 85–86.

**Chapter V**

p. 155  poetry is "simple, sensuous, and passionate": Milton, *Of Education*.

p. 155  "The high forms of literature": Allen Tate develops this position in various sections of his *Reason in Madness* and his *Reactionary Essays*.

p. 156  Dante's *Convivio*, Book II, ch. i.

p. 156  "Into my heart an air that kills": Housman, *A Shropshire Lad*, No. XL.

p. 156  "in harmony with nature": From Arnold's sonnet, *To an Independent Preacher*.

p. 157  "It is so many years": Yeats, *Reveries over Childhood and Youth*.

p. 158  "four types of meaning": I. A. Richards, *Practical Criticism*.

p. 159  "blackguard": See Housman's *Last Poems*, No. IX, beginning "The chestnut casts his flambeaux."

p. 162  "No longer mourn for me": Shakespeare, Sonnet LXXI.

p. 163  "Shakespeare's daffodils": *The Winter's Tale*, IV, iv, 118–20.

p. 165  "That a sorrow's crown of sorrow": Tennyson, *Locksley Hall*.

p. 168  Yeats's poems are quoted from the *Collected Poems*, Macmillan Co., 1933 ed. The prose quotations are drawn from his essays, in *Ideas of Good and Evil*, p. 227, p. 176, and p. 64.

p. 176  "Negative Capability": Keats, letter to George and Thomas Keats, dated Dec. 22, 1817.

p. 177  irony "consists in the bringing in of the opposite . . . impulses": I. A. Richards, *Principles of Literary Criticism*.

p. 177    "Vous avez raison tous deux": Molière, *Le Bourgeois Gentilhomme*, I, ii.

p. 177    "The web of our life is of a mingled yarn": Shakespeare, *All's Well that Ends Well*, IV, iii, 83–87.

p. 179    G. K. Chesterton, *Robert Browning*, p. 52.

p. 180    "E 'n la sua volontate": Dante, *Paradiso*, III, 85.

p. 181    "Absent thee from felicity awhile": *Hamlet*, V, ii, 358.

p. 182    "After life's fitful fever he sleeps well": *Macbeth*, III, ii, 23.

p. 183    "The gods defend her!": *Lear*, V, iii, 256.

p. 183    "the President of the Immortals": A paraphrase of Hardy's paraphrase of Aeschylus, at the close of Hardy's *Tess of the D'Urbervilles*.

p. 183    "Not know me yet?": *Antony and Cleopatra*, III, xiii, 158.

p. 185    "If thou beest he": *Paradise Lost*, I, 84, 105–9. The later quotations from *Paradise Lost* may be found in Book XII, 560; IX, 31–32; and VIII, 633–35.

**Chapter VI**

p. 189    Shelley: In *A Defence of Poetry*.

p. 191    "Much confusion has been introduced": Wordsworth, Preface to *Lyrical Ballads*.

p. 192    "Break, break, break": Tennyson's poem is usually identified by this first line.

p. 192    "The end of Poetry": Wordsworth, Preface to *Lyrical Ballads*. The following Wordsworth quotations and paraphrases are from the same source.

p. 193    "a more than usual state of emotion": Coleridge, *Biographia Literaria*, ch. xiv.

p. 196    "And there, for honey": Marlowe, *Hero and Leander*, I, 23–30.

p. 197    "'And more, to lulle him'": Spenser, *Faerie Queene*, I, i, 41.

p. 198    "Waller was smooth": Pope, *Imitations of Horace*, Book II, Epistle I, 267.

p. 198    "The most energetic and meaningful lines are those in which there are variations": Compare as an example the variations italicized in the following lines from Waller's *Poems*, "Of the last verses in the book" (1686):

When we for age could neither read nor write
The subject made us able *to* indite;
The soul, with nobler *re*solutions decked,
The body stooping, *does* herself erect.
*No* mortal parts are requi*site* to raise
*Her that*, unbodied, *can* her Maker praise.
The seas are quiet *when* the winds give o'er;
*So*, calm are we when passions *are* no more.
For then we know how vain it was to boast
Of fleeting things, so certain *to* be lost.
*Clouds of* affection *from* our younger eyes
Conceal *that* empti*ness* which age descries.
The soul's *dark* cottage, battered *and* decayed,
*Lets in new* light through chinks that time has made.

Here the unexpected weak syllables coincide with unimportant connections between thoughts; the unexpected strong syllables with strong thoughts; and the inverted feet with the most powerful emotional thought.

p. 198    "What cannot praise effect": Dryden, *Absalom and Achitophel*, I, 303–8.

p. 199    "Those rules of old discover'd": Pope, *Essay on Criticism*, I, 88–91.

p. 199    "He even formulates rules": Pope, letter to Cromwell, dated Nov. 25, 1710: "Every nice ear must, I believe, have observed that in any smooth English verse of ten syllables, there is naturally a pause either at the fourth, fifth, or sixth syllables. . . . Now I fancy that, to preserve an exact harmony and variety, none of these pauses should be continued above three lines together, without the interposition of another; else it will be apt to weary the ear with one continued tone—at least it does mine."

p. 199  "Out of the golden remote wild west": Swinburne, *Hesperia*, 1–4.

p. 204  "Who both by precept and example shows": Byron, *English Bards and Scotch Reviewers*, writing of Wordsworth.

p. 206  "Give me the line that plows its stately course": Cowper, *Table Talk*, 522–23.

p. 207  "Him the Almighty Power": Milton, *Paradise Lost*, I, 44–49.

p. 208  "apt numbers": Milton's prose introduction to *Paradise Lost*, entitled "The Verse."

p. 209  "True ease in writing": Pope, *Essay on Criticism*, 362–63.

p. 210  "A lover's eyes": Shakespeare, *Love's Labour's Lost*, IV, iii, 334–41.

p. 210  "Merciful heaven": Shakespeare, *Measure for Measure*, II, ii, 114–18.

p. 211  "When you do dance": Shakespeare, *The Winter's Tale*, IV, iv, 140–43.

p. 214  "There lived a wife": *The Wife of Usher's Well.*

p. 217  "When Smoke Stood up from Ludlow": Housman, *A Shropshire Lad*, No. VII.

p. 219  "But I beneath a rougher sea": William Cowper, *The Castaway.*

p. 219  "And never lifted up a single stone": Wordsworth, *Michael*, 466.

p. 219  "The metrical pattern may be used to throw accents on words so that we seem to hear the inflections of a living voice": Compare Donne's *The Flea*, quoted on pp. 151–52, particularly the second stanza. Conflict is here present too. The balanced sense in the first line, "*three lives* in *one flea*," is thrown off balance by the meter, "three *lives* in *one* flea." So in the last line, sense is syncopated against rhythm; the argument asks us to read: "*three* sins in killing *three*," and the meter insists upon: "three *sins* in *kill*ing *three*."

p. 220    "the opposing demands of meter and sense": Compare, as a fine example of hovering accent, the word *absence* in this passage from Donne's *Valediction Forbidding Mourning*:

> Dull sublunary lovers' love,
>    Whose soul is sense, cannot admit
> Absence, because it doth remove
>    Those things which elemented it.

Both syllables must be accented equally for the sake of meaning, in order to bring out the etymological pun upon which his argument depends; the rhythm of speech demands ábsence, and the rhythm of the verse demands absénce, so that on all counts the two syllables are left perfectly balanced.

p. 221    "He enter'd": Keats, *Hyperion, A Fragment,* I, 213–21.

p. 224    "The many men": Coleridge, *Rime of the Ancient Mariner.*

p. 225    "There was an Old Man": Edward Lear, *The Book of Nonsense.*

*Chapter VII*

p. 231    "the unacknowledged legislator": Shelley, *A Defence of Poetry.*

p. 231    "the best words in their best order": Coleridge, *Table Talk.*

p. 236    "This commonest device of poetic organization": The poems mentioned here are by Chaucer, Dryden, Shelley, Byron, and Dante Gabriel Rossetti. An excellent further example of the device is Arnold's *The Future*, in which time is a river and man is a wanderer in a ship.

**p. 236** "A sonnet is a moment's monument": Rossetti, sonnet introducing *The House of Life*.

**p. 240** "If yet I have not all thy love": To show the formal intellectual structure possible to poetry, let me paraphrase the argument of this poem in a prose brief. It would run:

---

I. I gave all the love I possibly could give to buy your love.

. . . . .

YET all your love may have been more precious than all my love.

. . . . .

THEREFORE I may not have bought all your love.

---

II. Again, perhaps you did give me all your love, at that time.

. . . . .

BUT new love, created since then, would not be included in the original bargain.

. . . . .

AND YET such new love should be my property, just as anything grown on a piece of land belongs to the owner of that land.

---

III. BUT (even granted that the gift of love was entire, and that the bargain included subsequent additions), I do not want all your love, FOR:
   All your love would prove a lack of love, SINCE:
      Your love, if genuine, will increase, BECAUSE:
         My genuine love increases every day, so

that "all" my love can never be given away
at any one time.
Love, unlike commercial products, increases by being spent.

. . . . .

THEREFORE, instead of barter and exchange,
we will join our hearts.

. . . . .

Such unity, which cannot be partial, makes love
infinite and complete.

---

p. 242    "one must look close to see the design in the argument":
A good example is Donne's "Lovers' Infiniteness," in
which Donne builds his effect by veering in tone near
the end from the sustained imagery of law and property
to the suggested Christian imagery ("thou with losing
savest it") and the Greek philosophical imagery of the
eternal and infinite One, an idea developed fully in
others among his poems, such as "The Ecstasy."

p. 242    "First, when Maggie was my care": This poem by Burns
is usually known by its refrain: *Whistle o'er the lave
o't!* "Lave" is *leavings, remnant, rest;* "spier" is *ask;* "na
by" is *not a bit.*

p. 247    "a feeble shadow of the original conceptions of the
poet": Shelley, *A Defence of Poetry.*

p. 248    "were closely wed": Keats, *Sleep and Poetry.*

p. 249    "All are but parts": Pope, *An Essay on Man,* I, 267.

pp. 250–51    Byron wrote *Don Juan* and *Childe Harold;*
Wordsworth *The Excursion;* Coleridge *Christabel* and
*Kubla Khan;* Keats *Hyperion;* Shelley *Prometheus Unbound;* Tennyson *Maud;* and Browning *The Ring and
the Book.*

p. 251    "a more than usual state of emotion": Coleridge,
*Biographia Literaria,* ch. xiv.

p. 251    "Something is wrong with the poetic spirit": The principal poems upon which this paragraph is based are Coleridge's *Christabel* and *Kubla Khan*, Byron's *Beppo* and *Don Juan*, Wordsworth's *Prelude*, Tennyson's *Idylls of the King*, and Morris' *Earthly Paradise*.

p. 252    "the sense of musical organization": It is not without point here that one of Yeats's latest works was entitled *Words for Music Perhaps* and that Eliot's and Auden's most recent volumes have been *Four Quartets* and *For the Time Being, a Christmas Oratorio.*

p. 254    "Dead, then?": Shakespeare, *Antony and Cleopatra*, IV, xiv, 34.

p. 254    "There's beggary": *Antony and Cleopatra*, I, i, 15.

p. 255    "the mind is its own place": Milton, *Paradise Lost*, I, 254.

p. 256    "Cleopatra's underlying constancy to Antony and her surface variability": As an example, note in Act I, scene iii, how consistently and masterfully Shakespeare develops these two formalizing conceptions.

p. 256    "the compassion she moved to herself": Dryden, Preface to *All for Love.*

p. 257    "Sometime we see a cloud": *Antony and Cleopatra*, IV, xiv, 2–13.

p. 258    "I am again for Cydnus": *Antony and Cleopatra*, V, ii, 228–29.

p. 258    "Stay for me": *Antony and Cleopatra*, IV, xiv, 50–54.

p. 259    "O goodness infinite": Milton, *Paradise Lost*, XII, 469–73.

p. 260    "the bare convex of this World's outermost Orb": Prose argument prefixed to *Paradise Lost*, Book III.

# BOOK LIST

THIS LIST is made for use and not for ornament. It is therefore kept short, and brief descriptions of the items are given, so that a reader with limited time or funds may select further books with an intelligent economy. If this list is not long enough, it will become so when it is supplemented by the bibliographies in many of the volumes given below.

Also, to help readers to know in advance what may lie ahead of them, I have used an asterisk (*) to indicate books which they might find easier reading than this present volume, and a dagger (†) for those of greater difficulty. Titles without either notation seem to me about on the level with *The Nature of Poetry*. These classifications, of course, are not measures of value: I have included no books that I would not consider worth the reader's time.

In the main I have chosen books in which the approaches are somewhat similar or sympathetic to that of this present volume. A few, however, have been included because they develop coherent individual positions. I have felt it unnecessary to list the poets themselves or the various modern anthologies. One or two good anthologies, plus single volumes of the collected poems of those authors mentioned in the text and the notes, would form a library of poetry which might amply occupy a lifetime of serious reading.

Abercrombie, Lascelles: *The Theory of Poetry; Romanticism; Poetry: Its Music and Meaning.** Sympathetic, eclectic, and traditional. The third of these volumes is a short and persuasive introduction to poetry.

Alden, R. M.: *English Verse.* The best survey of types of English versification, with generous illustrations for each, chronologically arranged.

Arnold, Matthew: "The Study of Poetry" in *Essays in Criticism,* 2nd Series. A classical statement.

Babbitt, Irving: *The New Laocoön.* A survey and distinguishing of the arts by rigorous, systematic standards, from the point of view of a Neo-Humanist.

Blackmur, Richard P.: *The Double Agent;†* *The Expense of Greatness.†* Subtle, searching, and difficult criticism, principally of individual modern authors.

Bowra, C. M.: *The Heritage of Symbolism.†* A lucid introduction to some of the most difficult and important modern European poets.

Brémond, Henri: *Prayer and Poetry.* One of the few studies on the important question of the relation of poetry and belief.

Brooks, Cleanth: *Modern Poetry and the Tradition.* Clear and illuminating; written with a predilection for Metaphysical poetry.

————, and Warren, Robert Penn: *Understanding Poetry.** In design, an anthology with separate, progressive critical discussions and running commentaries. An excellent practical introduction to poetry.

Bullough, Geoffrey: *The Trend of Modern Poetry.* Sympathetic, intelligent, and detached.

Coleridge, Samuel Taylor: *Biographia Literaria.†* Rich ore, which demands strenuous mining.

Croce, Benedetto: *The Defense of Poetry.* A brief lecture which shows how the principles of his famous *Aesthetic†* fare when applied to a specific art.

Drew, Elizabeth: *Discovering Poetry.** A first-rate introduction, written with intelligence, balance, and sensitivity.

————, and Sweeney, J. L.: *Directions in Modern Poetry.* A dependable guide, with good proportions of sympathy and common sense.

Eastman, Max: *The Enjoyment of Poetry.*\* An easy approach, which should frighten away not even the most skittish or timid amateur.

Eliot, T. S.: *Selected Essays; The Use of Poetry and the Use of Criticism.*† Profound and influential ideas on literature, often stated obliquely or elliptically.

Empson, William: *Seven Types of Ambiguity.* A revelation of the complexities of poetic language.

Garrod, H. W.: *Poetry and Life; The Profession of Poetry.* Urbane, opinionated, witty judgments, resting on a broad culture.

Greene, Theodore M.: *The Arts and the Art of Criticism.* A good systematic orientation of poetry in its relation to other forms of literature and to other arts.

Hopkins, Gerard Manley: *Letters* (2 volumes).† Fascinating remarks on poetry by a poet.

Housman, A. E.: *The Name and Nature of Poetry.* A provocative lecture which everyone should know.

James, D. G.: *Skepticism and Poetry.*† An impartial, luminous, and adult consideration of the nature of poetry and of poetic belief.

Johnson, Samuel: *Lives of the English Poets* (particularly the lives of Cowley, Dryden, and Pope). The best examples of neoclassical opinions on poetry.

Keats, John: *Letters.* Keats's passing remarks succeed in getting closer to the heart of poetry than many entire volumes.

Ker, W. P.: *Form and Style in Poetry; The Art of Poetry.* Profitable studies by a comprehensive and trustworthy academic critic.

Lewis, Cecil Day: *A Hope for Poetry.* A defense of the recent English group of Auden, Day Lewis, and Spender.

Lowes, J. L.: *Convention and Revolt in Poetry.* A competent handling of this important subject. *The Road to Xanadu.* An absorbing study of the actual sources of poetry, limited to Coleridge's *Kubla Khan* and *Ancient Mariner.*

MacNeice, Louis: *Modern Poetry; William Butler Yeats.* Informal personal discussions by a contemporary poet.

Neff, Emery: *A Revolution in European Poetry 1660–1900.* A historical study especially valuable for its wide range.

Osgood, Charles Grosvenor: *Poetry as a Means of Grace.* Profound remarks beautifully and simply expressed, on such figures as Dante, Spenser, Milton, and Samuel Johnson.

Poe, Edgar Allan: *The Poetic Principle; The Rationale of Verse; The Philosophy of Composition.* Three essays containing striking ideas on the genesis and technique of poetry.

Pottle, Frederick: *The Idiom of Poetry.* A series of lectures defending traditional ideas concerning poetry but giving serious consideration to the latest critical thought.

Prescott, Frederick C.: *The Poetic Mind.* A consideration of the nature of the poetic mind and of the origins of poems, based on psychology and psychoanalysis, and extremely sympathetic to the theories of the Romantic poets.

Ransom, John Crowe: *The World's Body;* † *The New Criticism.*† Books of essays that advance a coherent and formal theory of poetry, which has already proved a working basis for other critics and readers.

Read, Herbert: *Phases of English Poetry; Form in Modern Poetry; Collected Essays in Literary Criticism.* Volumes with a personal, philosophical, and esthetic focusing.

Rhys, Ernest (editor): *A Preface to Poetry.* A handy collection of famous English critical essays and pronouncements, chronologically arranged.

Richards, I. A.: *Principles of Literary Criticism; Practical Criticism;* \* *Science and Poetry; Interpretation in Teaching.*† Among the most influential modern books on poetry, these volumes show Richards' original and pragmatic approach, his interest in psychology, and his close study of words in their different meanings and uses.

Rylands, John: *Words and Poetry.* A close and interesting study of the suggestiveness of words as used in poetry.

Saintsbury, George: *History of English Prosody*. An exhaustive, pioneering, chronological study.

Santayana, George: *Poetry and Religion*. A series of essays distinguishing and relating its two subjects.

Smith, Logan Pearsall: *On Reading Shakespeare*.* A good introduction to the reading of any poetry, which successfully communicates its good taste and enthusiasm.

Spurgeon, Caroline: *Shakespeare's Imagery*. A study of a poet's instinctive use of images peculiarly vivid to his own experience and habits of thinking.

Squire, J. C.: *Essays on Poetry*.* The views of a traditionalist.

Stauffer, Donald A. (editor): *The Intent of the Critic*.† Four essays by Edmund Wilson, Norman Foerster, John Crowe Ransom, and W. H. Auden, presenting various approaches to literature and particularly to poetry.

Sutherland, James: *The Medium of Poetry*. A consideration of the effect of the artificial demands of a poet's medium in changing and developing his thought and images.

Tate, Allen: *Reactionary Essays;* † *Reason in Madness*.† Provocative and strenuous judgments, as part of a search for a philosophical foundation for poetry.

——— (editor): *The Language of Poetry*.† Four essays by Philip Wheelwright, I. A. Richards, Cleanth Brooks, and Wallace Stevens, considering the common subject in limited and broad aspects.

Wilder, Amos N.: *The Spiritual Aspects of the New Poetry*. The relation of modern poetry to the Christian tradition.

Wilson, Edmund: *Axel's Castle*. Pioneering discoveries concerning modern literature, simply and clearly presented.

Yeats, William Butler: *Collected Essays; Autobiography*. Thoughtful and searching remarks on poetry, often casually introduced.

# INDEX

This index lists only literary figures referred to in the text either by name or by quotation from one of their works so well known that the author is not mentioned. It includes from the Notes the few additional names not in the text. The small number of short anonymous poems or literary works, and the schools of poets, are listed under their first lines or their usual designations.

Aeschylus, Note to 183
Aesop, 132
Allingham, William, 58, 60-61, 66, 128
Aquinas, 110
Ariosto, 262
Aristotle, 95, 96, 98, 100, 127, 161, 182, 187, 194, 202
Arnold, Matthew, 39, 57, 69-72, 100, 131, Note to 156, 180, 181, 182, 185, 187, 229, 231-36, Note to 236, 237, 241, 250, 251
Auden, W H., 62, 75, 78, 154, Note to 252, 253

Bacon, Francis, 97-98, 100, 190
Balzac, Honoré de, 171
Bentley, Richard, 185
Bible, The, 108, 156, 189, 217, 248
Blair, Robert, Note to 130
Blake, William, 53-55, 108, 112, 185, 248
Boccaccio, 45, 100
Bradley, A. C., 103-4, 183
Brémond, Henri, 105
Bridges, Robert, 40, 56, 136-38, 203, 212, 229
Brontë, Emily, 189
Browne, Thomas, 189, 202, 204
Browning, Elizabeth Barrett, 85, Note to 114

Browning, Robert, 43, 72-73, 76, 128, 176, 178-79, 214, 225, 251
Burke, Edmund, 155
Burns, Robert, 32-34, 115, 160, 163-66, 242-43
Byron, Lord, 14, 166, 204, 236, 250, 251

Calderón, 100
Carroll, Lewis, 108, 109
Cavaliers, The, 240
Cervantes, 168
Chapman, George, 36, 37, 38, 43
Chaucer, Geoffrey, 12, 46-48, 49, 50, 61, Note to 62, 87, 97, 100, 126, 196, 209, 236, 262
Chesterton, G. K., 77, 179
Coleridge, Samuel Taylor, 35, 36, 55, 56, 64, 99, 118, 193, 214, 224-25, 231, 250, 251
Cowper, William, 61, 206, 219
Crane, Hart, 229
Croce, Benedetto, 100

Daniel, Arnaut, 187
Dante, 16, 67, 77, 100, 109, 111, 115, 153, 155-57, 158, 159, 167, 177, 180, 181, 187, 252
de la Mare, Walter, 105, 214-17, 229, 238-39, 247, 249

De Quincey, Thomas, 202
Dickens, Charles, 202
Dobrée, Bonamy, 49
Donne, John, 11, 16, 73-74, 76, 80,
85-87, 88, 115, 135, 139-40, 151-53,
155, 213, 219-21, 240-42, 247, 249,
Note to 219, 220, 240, 242
Dryden, John, 32, 42, 43, 45-50, 51,
52, 55, 58, 99, 130, 134, 151, 185,
198, 199, 236, 248, 249, 250, 253-56

Eliot, T. S., 12, 78-80, 109, 116, 131,
154, 174, 175, 177, 182, 188, 201, 212,
229, 252, 253
Euclid, 155
Euripides, 110

Flaubert, Gustave, 102
France, Anatole, 102
"Frankie and Johnnie," 89
Frost, Robert, 56

Gawain Poet, The, 61
Goethe, 262
Gray, Thomas, 16, 33, 51, 162, 199
Guest, Edgar, 11

Hardy, Thomas, 14, 183
Hemans, Felicia, 50-51
Henley, William Ernest, 62, 204
Herbert, George, 135, 248
Herrick, Robert, 56, 78, 160, 162-63
Homer, 11, 37, 38, 43, 62, 69, 94, 95,
96, 110, 111, 171, 187, 204, 262
Hopkins, Gerard Manley, 40-42, 74-
75, 76, 155, 214, 247
Horace, 45, 96, 98, 160, 162, 194
Housman, A. E., 22-24, 53, 56, 65,
66, 103, 104-5, 106-8, 140-47, 150,
156-59, 217-19
Huxley, Aldous, 149

Johnson, Samuel, 36, 52-53, 99, 120,
185
Jonson, Ben, 99, 184
Joyce, James, 202
Juvenal, 45

Kant, Immanuel, 100
Keats, John, 11, 35, 36-38, 42, 43, 66,
67, 84, 85, 88, 100, 122, 123, 132-33,

135, 165, 176, 177, 190, 213-14,
221-23, 246-47, 248, 249, 250
Kipling, Rudyard, 214, 225, 230
Kyd, Thomas, 187

La Fontaine, Jean de, 155
Lamb, Charles, 229-30, 262
Lamb, Mary, 262
Landor, Walter Savage, 56
Lawrence, D. H., 204, 205, 229, 231
Lear, Edward, 108, 109
Lessing, G. E., 100
Longinus, 115
Lowell, Amy, 204
Lowes, John Livingston, 118, 203
Lucan, 110
Lucretius, 45, 89
Lydgate, John, Note to 62
Lyly, John, 204

MacLeish, Archibald, 121-25
Mallarmé, Stéphane, 108
Marlowe, Christopher, Note to 67,
106, 196-97
Martial, 11
Marvell, Andrew, Note to 153
Masefield, John, 225-26
Meredith, George, 214, 225, 226
Metaphysicals, The, 131, 240, 253
Milton, John, 14, 32, 35, 39, 43, 46,
48-49, 50, 51, 52, 55, 56, 65, 71, 73,
81-83, 87, 88, 89, 97, 99, 100, 106,
110, 111, 112, 114, 115, 126, 155, 177,
184-87, 194, 204, 206-9, 211, 229,
230, 249, 253, 259-62
Mirror for Magistrates, A, Note to
62
Molière, 177
Moore, Edward, 193
Moore, George, 103, 105
Moore, Thomas, 214
Morris, William, 166, 252
Musset, Alfred de, 66

Nerval, Gérard de, 187
"New Metaphysicals," The, 154
Newton, Isaac, 113

Ovid, 45, Note to 62

Parnassians, The, 117

Pater, Walter, 102-3, 189
*Pervigilium Veneris*, 187
Petrarch, 96, 100
Pindar, 250
Plato, 22, 68, 97, 126, 187
Plutarch, 78
Poe, Edgar Allan, 134
Pope, Alexander, 34, 42, 43, 51, 56, 99, 128-30, 131, 160-62, 185, 198, 199, 230, 237, 248, 249, 250
*Pre-Raphaelites, The*, 117
Proust, Marcel, 60
Pythagoras, 73

Racine, Jean, 105
Ransom, John Crowe, 14
Richards, I. A., 140, 158, 159, 160, 177
Richardson, Samuel, 193
Riley, James Whitcomb, 134
Rossetti, Dante Gabriel, 68-69, 123, 236-37

Schwartz, Delmore, 78
Scott, Walter, 115, 166
Scotus, Duns, 110
Shakepeare, William, 14, 34, 35, 44, 45, 46, Note to 49, 50, 51, 57, 78, 80-81, 83-84, 85, 88, 89, 91-92, 100, 106, 111, 114, 115, 118, 128, 147-49, 155, 162, 163, 167, 168, 171, 172, 176, 181-84, 187, 189, 193, 204, 209, 210-11, 249, 251, 252, 253-59, 262
Shelley, Percy Bysshe, 42, 51, 66, 99, 100, 111-12, 115, 119, 133, 185, 189, 231, 236, 247, 251
Sidney, Philip, 50, 95, 96, 97, 98, 127-28, 189, 194, 204
Skelton, John, 115
Sophocles, 127
Southey, Robert, 134
Spenser, Edmund, 22, 32, 33, 63, 87-88, 95, 96, 97, 99, 102, 106, 110, 155, 166, 177, 188, 197, 209, 230, 252, 262-63

Stein, Gertrude, 108, 202
Stevenson, Robert Louis, 202
Swift, Jonathan, 189
Swinburne, Algernon, Charles, 38-40, 41, 149, 150, 187, 199-201, 214, 230
*Symbolists, The*, 131, 168, 169

Tasso, 110
Tate, Allen, 155
Tennyson, Alfred, 35-36, 66, 94-95, 123, 134, 165, 185, 187, 190, 192, 224, 251, 252
Thackeray, William Makepeace, 172
Theocritus, 62, 162
"There lived a wife at Usher's well," 214
Thompson, Francis, 185
Thomson, James, 31-32, 33, 34, 62, Note to 130
Thucydides, 190
Trollope, Anthony, 252

Upanishads, 187

Vergil, 45, 187
Verlaine, Paul, 134
Villon, François, 41, 149

Waller, Edmund, 198, 199
"Western wind, when will thou blow," 63
Whitman, Walt, 62, 113, 204, 205
Winckelmann, J. J., 100
Wordsworth, Dorothy, 35
Wordsworth, William, 35, 39, 43, 50, 55, 56, 57, 58, 63-65, 67, 78, 89, 99, 110, 115, 118, 130-31, 191-94, Note to 204, 219, 231, 250, 251, 252

Xenophon, 127, 189

Yeats, William Butler, 115, 131, 154, 157, 168-75, 182, 229, 243-46, 247, 249, 252, Note to 252, 253